THE REVENUE COMMITTEES

This book is printed on 100 percent recycled paper

The Ralph Nader Congress Project

The Judiciary Committees: A Study of the House and Senate Judiciary Committees

The Commerce Committees: A Study of the House and Senate Commerce Committees

The Environment Committees: A Study of the House and Senate Interior, Agriculture, and Science Committees

The Money Committees: A Study of the House and Senate Banking and Currency Committees

The Revenue Committees: A Study of the House Ways and Means and Senate Finance Committees and the House and Senate Appropriations Committees

Ruling Congress: A Study of How the House and Senate Rules Govern the Legislative Process

A Study of the House Ways and Means and Senate Finance Committees and the House and Senate Appropriations Committees

Richard Spohn AND
Charles McCollum, DIRECTORS

The Ralph Nader Congress Project

Grossman Publishers

A DIVISION OF THE VIKING PRESS
NEW YORK   1975

THE
REVENUE
COMMITTEES

THE REVENUE COMMITTEES—Ralph Nader Congress Project
Copyright © 1975 by Ralph Nader
All rights reserved
First published in 1975 by Grossman Publishers
625 Madison Avenue, New York, N.Y. 10022
Published simultaneously in Canada by
The Macmillan Company of Canada Limited
Printed in U.S.A.

Library of Congress Cataloging in Publication Data
Ralph Nader Congress Project.

    The revenue committees: a study of the House
Ways and Means and Senate Finance Committees
and House and Senate Appropriations Committees.

    Includes bibliographical references and index.

    1. United States. Congress. House. Committee
on Ways and Means. 2. United States. Congress.
Senate. Committee on Finance. 3. United States.
Congress. House. Committee on Appropriations.
4. United States. Congress. Senate. Committee on
Appropriations. I. Spohn, Richard. II. McCollum,
Charles. III. Title.
HJ257.2.R34 1975   328.73'07'65   75-16420
ISBN 0-670-59622-1

Contributors

Part I. The House Ways and Means and
Senate Finance Committees

Richard Spohn, Project Director

Robert Brandon

Judy Berkman
B.A., Wellesley (1970); student at Boston University Law School

David Case
B.A., University of Massachusetts, Amherst (1972)

Jerry Eyster
B.A., Yale (1972); student at Stanford University Business School

Chester T. Lane, Jr.

Arthur Magida, Editor

Bruce G. Rosenthal

Joseph Schmidt
B.A., Harvard College; Peace Corps, 1970–72; student at Harvard Law School

Part II. The Appropriations Committees of the House and Senate

Charles McCollum, Author

Bruce G. Rosenthal

Contents

Introduction

The changes that swept over the House of Representatives at the beginning of the Ninety-fourth Congress had their roots in a reform movement begun six years earlier by House reformers and their organizational forum, the Democratic Study Group. Advances in cutting down congressional secrecy, the seniority system, and the autocratic rule and obstructionism it fostered were part of a long, gradual reform process. And by any fair measure the new House reforms affected most significantly that body's most powerful institution—the House Ways and Means Committee—and its most powerful figure—Chairman Wilbur D. Mills.

The power and importance of the Ways and Means Committee itself and the misuse of that power by its chairman have left their mark on our nation's tax laws. Our tax system will remain profoundly distorted for years to come as a result of the methods of legislating described in this book. Ironically, it was a realization of these undemocratic practices that stimulated the House reform movement. This introduction will discuss the reforms that have been enacted, and what those reforms may mean for the future of our tax laws.

As the reader will discover, secrecy has been a major factor in the making of our unfair tax laws. The beginning of the decline of secrecy in the tax-writing Ways and Means Committee came at the opening of the Ninety-third Congress. At that time the House of Representatives adopted a rule requiring that all committee meetings be open to the public unless a majority of the committee members first voted, on the record, to meet in secret session. At least the members advocating secrecy would be on the public record.

Despite public and congressional sentiment for reform, the Ways and Means Committee voted to keep its bill-writing sessions closed on several occasions at the beginning of the Ninety-third Congress. Committee members had justified secrecy as a means of preventing lobbyists from "breathing down our necks." They also suggested that "the public would be confused by the alternatives the committee considers."

While the committee was maintaining the shield of secrecy, which it has used for years in protecting special interest favors, pressure for open meetings was building. New revelations about campaign contributions from the same special interest groups that influenced the committee's bill-writing sessions made the committee's excuses for secrecy more transparent. On June 18, 1973, the committee room was packed with members of the press and the public wishing to observe the drafting of the foreign trade bill. The advocates of a closed session argued that Nixon administration officials would be testifying on the "sensitive matter" of trade negotiations. After some heated debate, this new argument triumphed as the committee members voted 15 to 10 to remove the press and public from the room and write the bill behind closed doors. In fact, the trade bill markup was closed not just during discussion of the administration's trade negotiation posture but for the entire three months the committee devoted to the lengthy piece of legislation.

But that October the secrecy advocates ran out of excuses. In the absence of Chairman Wilbur Mills (D., Ark.), hospitalized with a back ailment, the committee agreed for the first time to meet in public to draft a pension reform bill. Since that time the

Ways and Means Committee has held open markup session for all its legislation.

Two major tax bills were drafted in open session in 1974. These bills, the energy tax bill of 1974 and the tax reform bill of 1974, were delayed and never passed the Congress but did provide important lessons about open committee meetings. Some special interest groups abandoned the Ways and Means Committee and concentrated on the still secret sessions of the Finance Committee, the Ways and Means counterpart in the Senate, to obtain legislation to benefit their causes.

Other special interest groups found that members were less willing to champion special tax breaks in open session. In some cases, those who did were subject to immediate adverse public exposure and quickly abandoned their efforts. This was the case with Herman Schneebeli (Pa.), ranking Republican on the Ways and Means Committee, who offered an amendment to anonymously help bail out the Piper Aircraft family of Pennsylvania from a bad business deal. He immediately received strong criticism in the press back home and quietly dropped the amendment. But other members continued voting for special interest legislation to help large campaign contributors. Two such members, Republicans Joel Broyhill (Va.) and Donald Brotzman (Colo.), were defeated in their 1974 reelection bids, with their committee special interest voting records as a major issue.

Despite the open sessions, Ways and Means Committee members have found another way to help favored campaign contributors. The committee often meets in a small room in the Capitol building when the House is in session. The room has only about a dozen seats for the press and the public, an obvious circumvention of the "open meeting" rule. There, many special interest amendments were added without record votes to last year's "tax reform" bill late in the day, after the press had left to meet their story deadlines. And regardless of the open session, the Committee's transcripts have never been made public. One reporter asked the tax committee chief of staff, Dr. Lawrence Woodworth, why it seemed that the public interest fared better when the committee met in the large committee room than in the small room in the Capitol. He replied, motioning to the small room, "Have you ever thought that these meetings are a lot like closed sessions?"

The Ways and Means Committee in the Ninety-fourth Congress has again planned to use a small room in the Capitol for "convenience" and not to make transcripts automatically available for inspection by the press and public. In the meantime, the Senate has adopted an open committee meeting rule similar to that of the House. It remains to be seen how successful the special interests will be in the Ninety-fourth Congress.

One thing is certain. Special interest groups will keep trying and committee members will continue to respond until their age-old alliance becomes more of a liability than an asset. That will happen only when the influence of campaign contributions is curbed and legislative sessions are completely open to the press and the public. Under such conditions, elections can work a more democratic will.

By far the most dramatic change in the congressional tax-writing process is the end of the long and enigmatic rule of Wilbur Mills as the chairman of the Ways and Means Committee. There is certainly an element of personal tragedy in his well-known antics with a striptease dancer, his subsequent hospitalization, and his sudden fall from power. But the real tragedy of Wilbur Mills's career is that in his seventeen-year tenure as one of the most powerful men in Congress, heading its most powerful committee, he did so little to accomplish major reforms in our tax system—a system that he himself termed grossly unfair when he first came to power.

Mills's presence as the key figure in tax legislation officially ended on December 10, 1974, when he informed House Speaker Carl Albert that he would not seek reelection as Ways and Means chairman. But his power had actually been eroding for several years. The chairman's invincibility on the House floor was first challenged in the Ninety-second Congress on member's bills.

For years, member's bills, which are special interest bills supported by particular members of the Ways and Means Committee for favored industries or particular unnamed taxpayers, had been routinely reported by the committee and passed by the House without argument or dissent. But in 1972 a number of House reformers, supported by the Public Citizens' Tax Reform Research Group, objected to over $400 million in special tax breaks contained in some twenty member's bills. Mills had brought them to the House floor on the consent calendar, a procedure used to pass bills of a "noncontroversial nature" without debate. After they were blocked initially, a number of these bills were later offered on the floor but were defeated by majority vote, forcing Mills to withdraw the remainder. He brought them up again toward the end of the session but met the same opposition. This special interest legislation was stopped, the first defeat in memory for Mills. Not only did he lose, but he lost trying to pass many special tax breaks for unnamed beneficiaries.

In the same year, Mills stepped out of his traditional role of legislator and entered presidential politics, briefly running for the nomination in 1972. This move added to the erosion of his stature and power in the House. His flirtation with higher ambition undercut the aura of a powerful and statesmanlike legislator that his fellow House members had ascribed to him. The presidential campaign also brought with it huge legal and illegal campaign contributions from many of the special interests that benefited most from the unfair tax system and special tax legislation for which Mr. Mills and his committee were responsible.

There were revelations of illegal contributions from oil companies, milk producers, and others by the Senate Watergate Committee and the special prosecutor, and a report by the Public Citizens' Tax Reform Research Group connecting Mills's campaign contributions with favored tax treatment for those contributors. These combined to raise serious questions about Mills's integrity and about his concern for his constituents in Arkansas. The public accounts brought Mills his first serious election challenge in many years, from a young Republican woman who said she would make his campaign contributions and special interest representation the major issue in the campaign.

Since much of Mills's power was perceived as resting on an aura of statesmanlike invincibility, these various challenges eroded that aura and therefore his power. With his perceived power declining, the next step was inevitable. It was a challenge from within his own committee against his autocratic rule. That challenge came in the spring of 1974 over the issue of repealing the controversial oil depletion allowance.

For years Mills had brought committee legislation to the floor under a "closed rule." The closed rule barred any floor amendments and therefore excluded the other 410 members of the House, as well as the liberal minority on the committee, from any say in tax legislation other than a yes or no vote on the whole tax package. Congressman William Green's (D., Pa.) proposal to completely repeal the depletion allowance was rejected by Mills in favor of a three-to-five-year gradual phase-out. Mills, serving notice that he would again seek a closed rule, also refused to allow Green's amendment to be voted on by the full House.

Green took his fight to the Democratic caucus under a new procedure that had been adopted at the beginning of the Ninety-third Congress with Mills's approval. An overwhelming majority supported Green's efforts and directed Mills and the Rules Committee Democrats to report the bill for floor action, allowing a vote on the Green amendment. Instead of following the caucus instruction, Mills refused to bring the bill to the floor for seven months, trying to avoid the whole issue. It was this action that insured continued oil company windfall profits and embarrassed congressional Democrats.

The November 1974 elections, however, made it clear the newly elected Democrats were concerned and were ready to reform the Ways and Means Committee and punish its defiant chairman. In an effort to ward off reforms and punishment, Mills and the Ways and Means Committee, who should have acted seven months earlier, reported out a new, tougher oil bill just before the newly elected Congress members convened but too late for its passage by the Ninety-third Congress.

Mills's defiance of the Democratic caucus on the oil depletion allowance, a defiance shared by half the Democrats on the Rules Committee, added to the impetus to limit his power. One thing became clear. The more Mills was challenged the more he was forced to adopt dilatory or heavy-handed tactics. His change in tactics further cut into the appearance of statesmanship that was the pillar of his power. Each challenge chipped away at the leader's façade—a façade that kept him in power all those years.

Aside from the failure to end the oil companies' windfall profits, challenges also stemmed from the committee's inability to deliver on promised tax relief and tax reform legislation generally. The committee's huge jurisdiction but small size and lack of subcommittees made it a major target of the House reorganization plan developed during the Ninety-third Congress by the Bolling Select Committee on Committees. The Bolling reorganization plan would have severely curtailed Ways and Means jurisdiction. It, however, was defeated in October and replaced with an alternative plan with less impact on the Ways and Means Committee. But once the reorganization plan was defeated, caucus reformers —who were bitterly divided on its other aspects—were able to unite in reducing the power of the Ways and Means Committee. When the newly elected Democratic caucus met in December 1974, the stage was set to make dramatic changes in the traditional power relationships in the House.

The first such change was aimed at the Ways and Means Committee's major source of power among House Democrats. On a 146–122 vote, the caucus removed from Ways and Means members the authority to appoint House members to other committees. The Ways and Means Democrats, as the Committee on Committees, have long been responsible for committee assignments and have, therefore, commanded the voting loyalty of younger members of Congress who wanted to be assured of good committee assignments. With many of the seventy-five freshman Democrats providing the deciding margin, the caucus transferred the committee assignment function to the Democratic Steering and Policy Committee, a group much more representative of House Democrats than the traditionally conservative Ways and Means Democrats.

Once the caucus had struck at the "king" and won, the other needed reforms followed easily. To begin with, the membership on the Ways and Means Committee was increased from twenty-five to thirty-seven, further diffusing its power. Also, the committee reorganization plan passed earlier in the year had mandated that every legislative committee set up at least four subcommittees. (The committee subsequently settled on six subcommittees, with tax legislation remaining in the full committee.) These two moves eliminated Chairman Mills's internal control of the committee, control which for many years was virtually absolute.

Wilbur Mills had abolished subcommittees shortly after becoming chairman in 1957 and had since exercised almost total authority over all substantive issues and proposed legislation. The size of the committee concentrated his power and made it easier to retain his grip on the committee members. Now, with thirty-seven members and six subcommittees, the power and authority of the new committee chairman, Al Ullman (D., Oreg.), will be more diffuse.

Expansion of the committee, coupled with election-year retirements and defeats, has significantly changed the committee's ideological makeup. Two of the more conservative and less intellectual committee Republicans, Harold Collier (Ill.) and Charles Chamberlain (Mich.), have retired and two other Republicans, Joel Broyhill (Va.) and Donald Brotzman (Colo.), were defeated. On the Democratic side, liberal Martha Griffiths (Mich.) retired and Hugh Carey (N.Y.) left to run successfully for the governorship of New York.

Ten of the twelve new Democrats on the committee are decidedly more pro tax reform than the older committee membership. And three of the new Republicans are vast improvements over the members they have replaced. While the enlargement of the tax-writing committee makes it more reform minded, there probably will not be an absolute majority in favor of major tax reform legislation. The new committee should, however, develop substantial minorities who, with new modified closed rule procedures, will be able to press tax reform issues on the House floor. Apparently that is where tax reform will succeed or fail in the next several years.

Of course the committee's new chairman, Al Ullman, will be central to how the committee will operate in the future. He is generally considered as conservative as Mills on many tax reform issues, but has handled the committee in a more open and democratic way. It is not clear which way he will move on tax reform legislation in the future. But given the recent upheavals against unresponsive committee chairmen, his views will probably reflect those of the majority of Democrats on the committee more often than not.

There are some other problems which should not be overlooked in analyzing the effectiveness of the new Congress in reforming the tax laws. First, there is no guarantee that all the new reform-oriented members will agree on any particular legislative package. If they do not, they could easily lose to a coalition of antireform members who have often voted together in the past.

The winds of change that blew strongly over the House have only gently rustled the Senate structure. The kinds of reforms that have diminished Mills's and the Ways and Means Committee's power to stop reform legislation in the House have not been enacted in the Senate.

Perhaps the largest single obstacle that remains substantially unchanged by recent reforms is the Senate Finance Committee. Any legislation that does make it through Ways and Means and is passed by the House will then have to go through the Senate, where Russell Long (D., La.) and his Finance Committee can rewrite the legislation to suit their own antireform and special interest orientation.

It remains to be seen whether the Senate Finance Committee will consistently hold its meetings in public or not. Senator Long did open the bill-drafting session for the 1975 Tax Cut Act, but the results were not encouraging. During the markup the committee chairman and other nonreformers succeeded in approving a series of special interest tax breaks while blocking consideration of many significant tax reforms. Finance is still a small and autocratically run institution that has not shown itself interested in tax reform—including bills that come over from the House. Tax reformers on the committee are greatly outnumbered and subcommittees have little staff and are not very active. Tax reform efforts in the Senate, therefore, have been confined to activity on the Senate floor, where a 40 percent minority can still block major reform bills by use by the filibuster. Of course, any meaningful tax reforms need the backing of the tax-writing committees to succeed.

While there is much that remains to be done, the procedural reforms that have been made in the House and to a limited extent in the Senate reflect a growing public dissatisfaction over the lack of tax reform. One point is clear. Removing the influence of monied special interests from politics and sanitizing the legislative process with the sunlight of public scrutiny will hasten the day when citizen groups will be able to demand and receive a fairer tax system.

Far less attention to the administration of the tax laws is given by the committees than to their other functions. Committee oversight of the Treasury Department is poor and infrequent. This failure relates to more than the question of fair treatment of taxpayers; there are the little-examined areas of tax expenditure enforcement (investment tax credit and accelerated depreciation ranges, for example), and the auditing of large corporations. Neither committee has ever undertaken an investigation of these vast activities, nor has a hearing been held to receive testimony. Indeed, the tide has been in the other direction, with Treasury specialists swarming over the committees with their advice, lobbying, and drafting services, and even sitting in on executive sessions closed to the legislators' own staff as well as the public. It is a situation of a one-way check without a two-way balance.

If the congressional tax-writing committees are emerging into the public spotlight, the Appropriations committees remain in the land of the obscure. Operating under heavy hearing schedules and decisional deadlines, the committees involve themselves with intricate details about millions and billions of dollars that bore or overpower the media's interest and resources. It is in the murky maw of these committees' suites that deals are made, temptations are tendered, and taxpayers so repeatedly taken. Consider the fact that the average worker in this country spends about a fifth of a year earning the money to provide these Appropriations committees with their dollars, yet their operations are as remote from the worker's attention as the island of Tasmania. Even the staff scandals that close observers know are persisting in certain sections of the committees' operations—payoffs, gifts, facilities, improper job offers as deferred bribes, and procured women—remain the private chuckles of lobbyists working the vineyards. The tradition among the seasoned staff is—mum's the word.

Such susceptibility, until recently wholly shielded by the most impenetrable of congressional secrecy cloaks, makes these committees and subcommittees child's play for executive branch and corporate persuaders, notwithstanding the hoary demeanor of firm-lipped and veteran chairmen. The White House is more the Appropriations committees' shaper than the Congress, both at the beginning, with the submission of the annual budget to Congress, and at the end, in determining when and even if money duly appropriated is spent for the assigned purpose. In the past generation the presidency has increasingly seized the initiative from a passive Congress right to the blatant display of impoundment defiance during the later Nixon years. Litigation to declare impoundments illegal proliferated in the years 1972–74 and in a number of cases the plaintiffs were members of Congress. The Nixon administration lost most of these cases but remained intransigent because the courts did not impose personal sanctions on the responsible officials. Each time the court ordered the impounded funds to be released in accordance with the law, the Nixon forces' strategy was to go on to the next impoundment undeterred, knowing they had innumerable bites of the apple.

For years close observers of the Congress and many members themselves criticized the closed-door policy of Appropriations committee hearings and markup sessions in both houses. They decried the power of the committee and subcommittee chairmen and the imperial role of House-Senate conferences as far as the rest of the legislators were concerned. The House committee's practice of retaining FBI agents on the staff as investigators raised the question of conflicting allegiances and a breach of the principle of separation of powers between the two branches of government. And the absence of sufficient staff, computer capability, and other facilities spread the sense of futility on Capitol Hill in dealing with the Department of Defense and the rest of the executive branch.

Recently there have been some changes. Most of the hearings in both House and Senate Appropriations committees are open. A small but growing trend toward opening markup sessions is discernible. The Democratic caucus can now elect the Appropriations subcommittee chairmen in the House—a power subcommittee chairman Jamie Whitten (D., Miss.) felt in January 1975 when, anticipating a move to unseat him, he strategically dropped his subcommittee's jurisdiction over environment.

The major change in Congress may come from the Congressional Budget and Impoundment Control Act of 1974, which established a Budget Committee in each House, and a Congressional Budget Office (CBO) of analysts. Hailed by most of Congress as landmark legislation, the law is designed to impress a coherent budgetary process on piecemeal and runaway appropriations that have disturbed both liberal and conservative legislators. The CBO's purpose is to reduce the dependence of the legislature on the White House and its Office of Management and Budget and present clear choices and priorities to the lawmakers within an overall budget limit. Because the new law is on a two-year phase-in schedule, it is too early to say whether there will be good changes or bad overlaps with the existing Appropriations committees. The Budget committees will have to develop their working relationship with these Appropriations committees, yet keep enough stress on them to rationalize the budgetary process as a unified policy program. Other than floor votes on conflicting policies, the Budget committees have little power over Appropriations beyond persuasive public discussion.

The impoundment section of the new act was treated in astonishingly curled-lip fashion by Roy Ash, head of the White House's Budget Office, who said it has not hampered the president's ability to impound. The act says that the president's deferral of spending within a fiscal year can be stopped if either the Senate *or* the House passes a resolution of disapproval. If the president tries to rescind expenditures of funds, he can succeed in doing so only if Congress passes a bill authorizing the rescission within forty-five working days of the proposed rescission. All deferrals and rescissions are required to be reported to the Congress. It remains to be seen whether Ash's observation will prove durable. For the flexibility of slippery budgetary definitions and the lethargy or subservience of Congress before a determined White House can transform even specific laws into fluff.

The political genius who can make the taxing and spending activities of Congress interesting to the taxpayers, who make all this possible, deserves an entire hall of fame. One of the great paradoxes of government is how people in society can care so much about obtaining an adequate income and do so little to those who take a third of it away. Perhaps this is in part due to another political genius who several decades ago dreamed up the tax withholding technique to take the "bite out of the bite." It would be permissible even to settle for a parity principle, under which taxpayers would pledge to spend as much time each year monitoring the congressional taxing and spending drives as they do preparing their own tax returns. That would be more than a good start: it would hasten the day that the Founding Fathers thought came in 1776—the day when there will be taxation with representation. That might help to usher in an even more unlikely time of government spending with accountability.

Ralph Nader

I

THE HOUSE WAYS AND MEANS AND SENATE FINANCE COMMITTEES

I am not about to turn over the responsibilities of this division [Ways and Means] to a lot of feather-headed reformers over there [motioning toward the Capitol building] who wouldn't do anything about the tax bill or tax reform.

    —Congressman James Burke, member of Ways and Means, during tax reform proceedings of March 9, 1973

1

Filling the Coffers:
The Revenue Committees

I wanted Ways and Means simply because it is the most important.

— *Representative Omar Burleson (D., Tex.)*

Unlike most of us, members of Congress have a strange, and many would say a morbid, attraction to taxes—next to conscription, the most vilified and cursed of all government programs. The tenants of Washington's Capitol Hill flock to the committees that write tax legislation quite as readily as taxpayers would like to march on the Internal Revenue Building and dismantle it brick by brick.

Taxes are at the root of the economy. By sitting on a revenue committee, a member of Congress can help decide whether the economics of Keynes or McKinley will prevail; whether oil depletion allowances or other concessions to industry will persist; whether there will be equitable distribution of income or whether the gap between the wealthiest and the poorest in the world's richest country will remain.

Though Congress may be a nest of contradictions and paradoxes, one truth seems to permeate its entire committee system: the more powerful a committee, the more conservative its members. And since the revenue committees are among the most powerful in Congress, they are filled with some of the more conservative men and women on the Hill. Ways and Means can boast Wilbur Mills, its immensely powerful chairman from Arkansas, and ranking Republican Herman Schneebeli; Finance has chairman Russell B. Long (D., La.) and ranking members Wallace Bennett, Carl Curtis, Paul Fannin, and Clifford Hansen. The Joint Economic Committee—the least powerful of the revenue committees—has the highest proportion of legislators who question the economic status quo. The senators on it include chairman William Proxmire (D., Wis.), Abraham Ribicoff (D., Conn.), Hubert Humphrey (D., Minn.), and Jacob Javits (R., N. Y.)

POWER AND TAXES: THE HOUSE WAYS AND MEANS COMMITTEE

Ways and Means is the most difficult committee in the House to join. The House Democratic caucus chooses its party's members on the Ways and Means Committee. Although every Democrat in the House sits on the caucus, and ideally the elections should be entirely independent of considerations other than seniority and geographical representation, it is actually the Democratic *leadership* that selects the Democratic candidates for the committee. As political scientist Randall Ripley noted in 1967, "Only three times in recent years have candidates other than those supported by the Speaker won."[1] Republicans on Ways and Means —a ten-member minority—are selected by their party's Committee on Committees (COC). This consists of one representative from each state which has Republican representatives (usually the senior member of the delegation) and is chaired by the Republican floor leader. Since all members of the COC are allowed one vote for each Republican member of Congress from their state, the more populous states retain their generous representation on Ways and Means. Like the Democratic caucus, the Republican COC meets in secret.

Since Ways and Means is the most powerful committee in the

TABLE 1.
Ways and Means Members at End of 92nd Congress
Length of Committee and House Service

	First Elected to House	Terms in House	First Elected to Committee	Terms on Committee
Democrats				
Mills	1938	17	1943	15
Ullman	1956	8	1961	6
Burke	1958	7	1961	6
Griffiths	1954	9	1963	5
Rostenkowski	1958	7	1965	4
Landrum	1952	10	1965	4
Vanik	1954	9	1965	4
Fulton	1962	5	1965	4
Burleson	1946	13	1969	2
Corman	1960	6	1969	2
Green	1963	5	1969	2
Gibbons	1962	5	1969	2
Carey	1960	6	1971	1
Waggonner	1960	6	1971	1
Karth	1958	7	1972	1
Republicans				
Byrnes	1944	14	1947	13
Betts	1950	11	1959	7
Schneebeli	1960	6	1961	6
Collier	1956	8	1963	5
Broyhill	1952	10	1964	4
Conable	1964	4	1967	3
Chamberlain	1956	8	1969	2
Pettis	1966	3	1970	1½
Duncan	1964	4	1971	1
Brotzman	1962*	5	1971	1

* Out of office 1965–66.

House, it takes years to work one's way up into its ranks.* The twenty-five members of the committee at the end of the Ninety-second Congress had served an average of 7.72 terms in the House. The three ranking Democrats—Mills, Burleson (Tex.), and Landrum (Ga.)—for example, had served seventeen, thirteen, and ten terms respectively. And the three ranking Republicans—Byrnes (Wis.), Betts (Ohio), and Broyhill (Va.)—had served fourteen, eleven, and ten terms respectively.* (See Table 1.) Seats on Ways and Means are usually reserved for those representatives who have been severely tested and have proved their loyalty to their party. They have been pitted against opponents in numerous elections, and their electoral strength has given them the confidence to take stands independent of their constituents' interests. They can thus be considerably insulated from ordinary voters' pressure while sitting on the committee. An index of the members' power and electoral assurance is their recent election situation—whether or not they ran unopposed or virtually so. (See Table 2). In 1972 nearly a third of the committee sought reelection and 40 percent of the members from the majority party ran unopposed. Of the sixteen members whose seats were contested, only three—Carey, Broyhill, and Chamberlain—received less than 60 percent of the vote, and the average winning margin was a startling 65.3 percent, a landslide figure by almost any standard.†

* Once on the committee, members stay there. The average member of the committee in the 92nd Congress had been there for 4.1 terms. Mills had served on it for seventeen terms, eight of them as chairman.

† The two Republicans selected to succeed retiring John Byrnes and Jackson Betts for the 93rd Congress—William Archer and Donald Clancy—have seats as safe as those of their predecessors. Archer comes from the solidly Republican seventh district in Texas. The Republican congressional candidate from the seventh ran unopposed in 1968. When Archer first ran for Congress in 1970, he won by a smashing 65 percent. He stretched this commanding lead to 83 percent in 1972. And 72 percent of the voters in Donald Clancy's second district, in Ohio, first elected him in 1966. He was then reelected during the next six years with pluralities of 67 percent, 56 percent and 63 percent. See *Congressional Quarterly Weekly Reports*, Vol. XXVI, No. 45 (November 11, 1966), p. 2799; Vol. XXVI, No. 46 (November 15, 1968), pp. 3165–66; Vol. XXVIII, No. 46 (November 6, 1970), pp. 2776–77; Vol. XXX, No. 46 (November 11, 1972), pp. 2998, 3000.

TABLE 2.
% Popular Vote for Ways and Means Members
1972 Election

	% of Vote		% of Vote
Democrats		Carey	51.8
Mills	unopposed	(15th, N.Y.)	
(2nd, Ark.)		Waggonner	unopposed
Ullman	unopposed	(4th, La.)	
(2nd, Ore.)		Karth	72.4
Burke	unopposed	(4th, Minn.)	
(11th, Mass.)		Republicans	
Griffiths	70.8	Schneebeli	72.5
(17th, Mich.)		(17th, Pa.)	
Rostenkowski	73.1	Collier	61.2
(8th, Ill.)		(6th, Ill.)	
Landrum	unopposed	Broyhill*	56.6
(9th, Ga.)		(10th, Va.)	
Vanik	64.7	Conable	67.4
(22nd, Ohio)		(35th, N.Y.)	
Fulton	62.9	Chamberlain	50.6
(5th, Tenn.)		(6th, Mich.)	
Burleson	unopposed	Pettis	75.1
(17th, Tex.)		(33rd, Calif.)	
Corman	67.6	Duncan	unopposed
(22nd, Calif.)		(2nd, Tenn.)	
Green	63.7	Brotzman*	66.5
(3rd, Pa.)		(2nd, Colo.)	
Gibbons	67.3		
(7th, Fla.)			

* Broyhill and Brotzman lost their seats in the 1974 elections.
SOURCE: *Congressional Quarterly Weekly Report*, Vol. XXX, No. 46, (November 11, 1972), pp. 2993–3000.

Republican Barber Conable, who persuaded 64.7 percent of the voters in New York's thirty-fifth district to return him to Congress in 1972 for his fifth term, frankly admitted in 1971 that one of the major Republican criteria for Ways and Means assignments was a representative's appeal at the polls:

> There is a tradition in the Republican Party that someone doesn't get on Ways and Means unless he is from a fairly safe district. I wouldn't have gone on [Ways and Means] unless I had moved my plurality from 53 percent to 68 percent.[2]

In addition to strength at the polls, the Democrats require a balanced geographical distribution of their Ways and Means Committee. (See Table 3.) Since 1911 it has been customary for the Ways and Means Committee to function as the Democratic committee on committees. For purposes of committee assignment, House Democrats are divided according to geographic region, or "zone." Each Ways and Means Democrat represents the Democrats of his or her zone in the bargaining to fill the House committee vacancies. Such an arrangement makes Ways and Means Democrats, and particularly powerful chairman Wilbur Mills, people to be crossed only at the expense of a much desired com-

TABLE 3.
Ways and Means Committee Geographical Distribution
92nd Congress

Deep South	Border States	West	Midwest	Northeast
Democrats				
Mills (Ark.)	Fulton (Tenn.)	Ullman (Ore.)	Griffiths (Mich.)	Burke (Mass.)
Landrum (Ga.)		Corman (Calif.)	Rostenkowski (Ill.)	Green (Pa.)
Burleson (Tex.)			Vanik (Ohio)	Carey (N.Y.)
Gibbons (Fla.)			Karth (Minn.)	
Waggonner (La.)				
Republicans				
N	Duncan (Tenn.)	Pettis (Calif.)	Byrnes* (Wis.)	Schneebeli (Pa.)
O	Broyhill (Va.)	Brotzman (Colo.)	Betts* (Ohio)	Conable (N.Y.)
N			Collier (Ill.)	
E			Chamberlain (Mich.)	

* Retired end of 92nd Congress. New Republicans: Donald Clancy of Ohio, William Archer of Texas.

mittee assignment and, in some cases, a successful congressional career.

The Republicans have no southerners on the Ways and Means Committee, but because of the Democratic zone divisions, one-third of the Democratic members are from below the Mason-Dixon line. One northern Democrat sighed that the "South demands equal treatment for each member from the North added to the committee." He preferred that the committee more accurately reflect the *people* represented by the House Democrats. (The committee's 20 percent representation from the Deep South is not really disproportionate since slightly less than a quarter of the country's population lives there.)

The Chosen Few

One indication of how popular Ways and Means is, as compared to other House committees, is the rate of transfers to and from the committee. Of nineteen standing committees in the House, Ways and Means was the only one from which no one transferred between 1949 and 1968. During these same nineteen years there were forty-seven transfers *to* Ways and Means, a figure second only to that of the Appropriations Committee (which is more than twice the size of Ways and Means).[3]

About two-thirds of Ways and Means members indicated that the committee's prestige, power, and importance attracted them, and only one respondent listed tax reform and specific policy objectives as reasons for having joined the committee. The representatives' positions on particular legislative areas did, however, determine whether or not they would be given assignments to the committee.

Illinois Republican Harold Collier joined the committee in 1963. He denies charges that he was appointed to the committee because he opposed Medicare. Rather, one of Illinois' traditional seats on the committee was vacant and he had more seniority than the only other Illinois representative who wanted it. He explained that the practice of reserving seats on the committee for Illinois was based on his party's desire to have the large "revenue producing" states solidly represented on the committee that determines how the revenue will be apportioned.

The selection of the committee's present Democratic representative from Illinois, Dan Rostenkowski, illustrates how extracongressional forces can influence its makeup. The death of Tom O'Brien in 1964 had left Chicago without representation on the committee. Since Mayor Richard Daley is a major political force in Chicago, he could virtually dictate who O'Brien's successor would be, and he preferred Rostenkowski, known as "his" man in the House. (One reporter has said that when Rostenkowski "makes a political statement, he speaks for Daley." Another observes that "Rostenkowski does what the mayor wants done."[4]) To preserve a façade of democracy, Daley first polled the Illinois delegation for its preference between Rostenkowski and a token challenger, Roman Pucinski. Predictably, there was no opposition to Rostenkowski, who was immediately appointed.

Several forces propelled New York's Republican Barber Conable toward Ways and Means. At the beginning of his second term, in 1967, he wanted to transfer from the Science and Astronautics Committee to Appropriations. The head of the New York delegation advised him to consider moving to Ways and Means. He was also encouraged to join Ways and Means by Republican leaders Melvin Laird (Wis.) and Gerald Ford (Mich.), as well as the Republican Committee on Committees. When Conable told the rest of the New York delegation that the Republican hierarchy stood behind him, his three challengers, including Charles Goodell, withdrew their candidacies. Even though the seat was his if he wanted it, he was still interviewed by some of the committee members and a few of his party's House leaders about his views on such strategic issues as tax-exempt municipal bonds and the oil depletion allowance.

Another Republican, Jerry Pettis, had a stiff fight to join Ways and Means. He later confessed that his three-month campaign to get his name on the Ways and Means roster was more grueling than his fight to get reelected to Congress. Four members of the

California delegation were interested in the committee position after Californian James Utt retired in 1970. One of Pettis' campaign tactics was to advise his opposition not to join, since they could help California more with their present committee appointments, where they had seniority. (Pettis was then beginning his third term.) As Pettis gradually nurtured a majority on the Republican Committee on Committees, Ford told him, "When you get the votes, I'll call a meeting." Pettis soon got the votes, his opposition soon got the message and withdrew from the race, and Pettis got his seat. Though Pettis, like Conable, was tapped by the Republican leaders to join Ways and Means, Pettis' selection did not preclude a hard and long campaign. Pettis attributes much of his success to his support from his "freshman class" of fifty-six representatives. Also crucial was the support from the Republican members of the New York delegation.

Although some members have to fight within their delegation to get onto Ways and Means because their state has a traditional seat there, others are almost hand-picked by the leadership because of their stands on certain crucial issues. Al Ullman of Oregon, now the second-ranking Democrat, thinks his knowledge of economics helped land him on the committee. Martha Griffiths (D., Mich.) maintains that her advocacy of free trade helped her. Charles Vanik believes that he was put on the committee to help pass the Medicare bill, which the Committee reported out to the House floor by one vote. Vanik's stance on Medicare countered some of his otherwise unpopular stands such as his opposition to the oil depletion allowance, which he attacked in his maiden speech in the House.*

At least one member of the committee, Hugh Carey (D., N.Y.), had a specific incentive to get onto Ways and Means. While serving on the Interior and the Education and Labor committees, he had noticed the difficulty of getting more than 30

---

* Vanik once attacked the oil depletion allowance so unrelentingly that Speaker Sam Rayburn, a perennial champion of the allowance, turned his chair so that his back was toward the chamber for the rest of Vanik's speech.

percent of the funds necessary for existing programs. Since taxes produce funds, by joining Ways and Means he could do more for his district—a section of Brooklyn, New York—by dealing directly with taxes, welfare, and social security.

Committee Imperialism

Such local and personal motives are rare for anyone who finally rises to the apex of House committees. For most, Ways and Means is neither the way to consolidate power at home nor a means of aiding their constituents. Instead, it is the way to consolidate power in Washington, the tool to intimidate others on the Hill, and the lever to mainipulate power throughout the country. It may be a battle to finally land on Ways and Means—but once there the victor can lean back and enjoy some of the sweetest booty in American politics. For the Ways and Means Committee is the most prestigious—and ambitious—committee in the House. Some have described it as a switchboard for the House, through which much of the important legislation must pass. A nineteenth-century political scientist, De Alva S. Alexander, saw the committee as "an Atlas bearing on its shoulders all the business of the House." Today it is more like some overweight monster that can never be satisfied, or a Sisyphus whose work is never done.

The Ways and Means Committee's work load is heavy, its subject matter arcane. But regardless of how obscure the committee's business is, it is at the very heart of the House's work and the federal government's affairs. Chaired by Wilbur Mills since 1957, it now controls the outcome of much of the key legislation sent to the House by the president. And in spite of the power it already has, the committee is continually broadening its jurisdiction. It has staked out authority over every area that involves revenue raising. Although appropriations are nominally excluded from its bailiwick, it is also usurping jurisdiction in this field, including health care and revenue sharing. Since the committee is explicitly responsible for taxes, which are levied on just about every conceivable item and service, the committee can exert power over almost any area imaginable. It considers bills to control narcotics and firearms, and even to conserve wildlife through taxes on archery equipment. Its turf includes foreign trade and tariffs; the national debt ceiling; and social security programs, including unemployment compensation, welfare, Medicare, and old age, survivors', and disability insurance. It recently claimed jurisdiction for national health insurance and education trust funds.

Although one Ways and Means staff member whispered "Who knows?" when asked how the committee got jurisdiction over national health insurance, several committee members noted that the committee had handled social security bills since they were first introduced in 1935. By the 1960s, this area had been extended to include welfare and Medicare bills.

As an authorization and appropriations measure, revenue sharing has an even more tenuous link with Ways and Means' traditional role as the House's revenue committee. But Title II of the original revenue-sharing bill, the State and Local Assistance Act of 1972, amended the Internal Revenue Code to allow the federal government to collect the states' individual income taxes. According to the House parliamentarian's legal assistant, Charles Johnson, this one provision was sufficient to put revenue sharing under the jurisdiction of Ways and Means.

The Nixon administration probably would have preferred that revenue sharing be dealt with by another committee. The committee's version of the President's general revenue-sharing proposal (H.R. 14370) was opposed by four of the committee's Democrats and three of its Republicans, including Byrnes of Wisconsin, the ranking minority member. They contended not only that the program would increase states' and municipalities' dependence on Washington, but that the formula for allotting funds was too arbitrary and "based on [the false] assumption that all states and localities face a common fiscal crisis."[5] But the keystone of the dissenters' report was their charge of improper jurisdiction: revenue sharing, they said, did not even belong in Ways and Means. The proper committee was Appropriations, the "only

Committee of the House that looks at federal expenditures on anything approaching a comprehensive basis." They warned:

> When the mechanisms that we already have are proving inadequate to meaningful expenditure control, the Ways and Means Committee—which should be keenly aware of the need for fiscal responsibility—establishes an extremely bad precedent in bypassing the Appropriations Committee.[6]

When the bill finally got to the floor of the House, one of the most vocal of the committee's dissenters, Sam Gibbons (D., Fla.), who had filed his own dissenting report as well as signing the committee minority's report, asked that the bill not be given the closed rule (barring floor amendments) that is usually granted for tax bills released by the committee.[7]

Both the committee's ranking Republican, John Byrnes, and the Democratic chairman of the Appropriations Committee, George Mahon (Tex.), agreed with Gibbons. Mahon, especially, bristled with irritation:

> Mr. Speaker, it is utterly incredible that one committee of the House, comprised of 25 members—and with the support of only 17 members of that committee, less than 5 percent of the Members of this House—should attempt to seize the authorizing authority of the legislative committees and ruthlessly—yes, ruthlessly—grab the appropriating jurisdiction of all 435 Members of the House, and at the same time be asking for a closed rule, in effect telling the 435 Members of the House, "You are not to be trusted. You cannot offer one single amendment to the bill, even though you are an elected Member of this Congress.[8]

Congressman Carey of Ways and Means defended the closed rule with the questionable argument that House members had abdicated their right to amend the bill since they had not submitted any amendments in advance. And he made an unconvincing call to precedent in attempting to justify the committee's jurisdiction:

During the conduct of the great Revolutionary War, the Committee on Ways and Means was empowered to vote for expenditures from day to day and to make appropriations from day to day and to carry on the conduct of the greatest Revolution in the history of mankind. . . . I remind my colleagues, there is a need for a new revolution—the most dynamic in the history of this country. This bill will be a plus for the country and the peaceful revolution.[9]

Under the bill's sharing formula, Carey's state, New York, was expected to receive more funds and more money per capita than the rest of the Union. This may have motivated him to keep the bill out of the hands of the full House.

After all the debate was over, the House finally voted—223 to 185*—to expedite the "peaceful revolution" that Carey had hailed on the House floor and President Nixon had forecast in his January 1971 State of the Union address. The closed rule remained. The next day the entire bill was approved, 274 to 122. Thirty billion dollars was committed to revenue sharing over five years and a new jurisdiction for Ways and Means was formally recognized by the House.†

One extension to the committee's continually augmented bailiwick came in August 1972, when Mills and Carey introduced a bill to authorize aid to public and nonpublic education (H.R. 16141). The bill would provide a trust fund for state elementary and secondary education and allow tax credits for tuition paid to private schools. Mills simultaneously introduced another bill (H.R. 13495), with James Burke (D., Mass.), to deal only with the tuition tax credits.‡

The aid to education provisions of the Mills-Carey bill would

---

* Of those supporting the bill in committee, all but Vanik voted on the floor to retain the committee's closed rule.

† In the 93rd Congress the full House voted to remove revenue sharing from the Ways and Means Committee's jurisdiction through passage of a new reorganization bill.

‡ H.R. 13495 was reintroduced in the committee at the beginning of the 93rd Congress as H.R. 49.

let the Ways and Means Committee expand its jurisdiction further, and the tax credit provisions of both the Mills-Burke bill and the Mills-Carey bill—though nominally within the traditional purview of the committee—were challenged by committee member Barber Conable as inappropriate for a committee that specialized in taxation and not education:

> This committee is not deeply involved in the problems of education here legislatively in Congress, so we may not have the overview that other Members of Congress would have of the education problem.[10]

Conable asked Elliot Richardson, who as Secretary of Health, Education and Welfare was testifying on the bill before the committee, whether he could

> anticipate [that] through this tax approach [of using funds from the Public Education Trust Fund to equalize educational opportunities throughout a state's educational system] this committee is likely to wind up playing a major role in education.
>
> I am interested and concerned about this because I don't know whether we have the expertise to do it.[11]

Other committee members have frequently urged that the jurisdiction of Ways and Means be kept within limits. Former Representative Jackson Betts advocated limiting the committee's jurisdiction to tax, trade, and social security legislation. John Byrnes said that it may be time to review the way bills are assigned to committees, since the last modification of the assignment system was during the 1957–58 session. Representative Joseph Karth (D., Minn.) recommended that legislation be assigned to committees "not so strictly along the lines of jurisdiction as at present, but on the basis of objectivity and work load."

Though Gibbons had protested Ways and Means' assumption of authority over revenue sharing, he still claimed that appropriations power ideally belonged with the same committee that wrote the tax laws. But Ways and Means had been relieved of its appropriations power in 1865, and Gibbons admitted that because of the present structure in the House, "we can't take over appropriations now since we have so many other things to do."

Another Ways and Means member, Al Ullman, evidently agreed with Gibbons that the jurisdictional boundaries between appropriations and revenue should be reviewed, clarified, and streamlined. Ullman's Title III of a 1972 bill to increase the public debt limit temporarily established a "Joint Committee to Review Operation of Budget Ceiling and to Recommend Procedures for Improving Congressional Control Over Budgetary Outlay and Receipt Totals." The House agreed and passed the Ullman amendment specifically. When it first met at the beginning of the Ninety-third Congress, the Joint Economic Committee had thirty members—twenty-eight from the House and Senate appropriations committees, the Ways and Means Committee, and the Senate Finance Committee, plus two members at large from each house. The committee has yet to have any effect on the vague demarcation in the committee system between federal taxing and spending or on the position of Ways and Means in relation to the House Appropriations Committee.

In a few cases—such as narcotics, airports and airlines regulation, the highway trust fund, and pension reform—the Ways and Means Committee has worked with other committees. But it has also ignored some of the legislation for which it has traditionally been responsible. While it was dealing in 1972 with welfare reform, revenue sharing, and national health insurance, for instance, it ignored a trade protectionist bill sponsored by Burke, James Corman's tax reform act,* and a bill sponsored by Mills and Senator Mike Mansfield (D., Mont.) to review fifty-four tax preferences over three years. (See Table 4 for the type of legislation that was finally enacted after being handled by the committee during the Ninety-second Congress.)

* H.R. 13857, dated March 16, 1972, purported to "gear the income tax more closely to an individual's ability to pay . . . broaden the income tax base of individuals and corporations, and . . . otherwise reform the income and estate tax provisions." See Legislative Calendar (final edition), Committee on Ways and Means, October 18, 1972, p. 377.

TABLE 4.
Ways and Means Bills That Became Law in 92nd Congress

Amendments to Internal Revenue Code	Trade and Other Tax Matters	Social Security
H.R. 1467. To Amend Sec. 152 (b)(3) of the Internal Revenue Code of 1954 for the purpose of including nationals of the United States within the definition of the term "dependent" in connection with deductions for personal exemptions. Approved 10/27/72	H.R. 1680. To extend for an additional temporary period the existing suspension of duties on certain classifications of yarn or silk. Approved 11/18/71	H.R. 1.* The Social Security Amendments of 1971. Approved 10/30/72
H.R. 9900.* To amend Sec. 112 of the Internal Revenue Code of 1954 to exclude from gross income the entire amount of the compensation of members of the Armed Forces of the United States and of civilian employees who are prisoners of war, missing in action or in a detained status during the Vietnam conflict. Approved 4/26/72	H.R. 3786. To provide for the free entry of a four-octave carillon for the use of Marquette University, Milwaukee, Wisconsin. Approved 10/27/72	H.R. 6065.* To amend Sec. 903 (c)(2) of the Social Security Act. Approved 12/29/71
	H.R. 4590.* Relating to the dutiable status of aluminum hydroxide, and oxide, calcined bauxite, and bauxite ore. Approved 11/5/71	H.R. 8313.* To amend the Social Security Act in order to continue for two years the temporary assistance program for U.S. citizens returned from abroad. Approved 7/1/71
H.R. 11091. To provide additional funds for certain wildlife restoration projects and for other purposes. Approved 10/25/72	H.R. 4678. To provide for the free entry of a carillon for the use of the University of California at Santa Barbara. Approved 10/27/72	H.R. 9410.* To amend Title V of the Social Security Act to extend for five years (until June 30, 1977) the period within which certain special project grants may be made thereunder. Approved 7/10/72
H.R. 11185.* To amend the In-	H.R. 5432.* To provide an extension of the interest equalization tax, and for other purposes. Approved 4/1/71	H.R. 10604. To amend Title II of the Social Security Act to permit the payment of the lump-sum death payment to pay the burial and memorial services expenses

ternal Revenue Code of 1954 with regard to the exempt status of veterans' organizations. Approved 3/29/72

H.R. 14628. To amend the Internal Revenue Code of 1954 with respect to the tax laws applicable to Guam and for other purposes. Approved 10/31/72

H.R. 7767.* To continue until the close of June 30, 1973, the existing suspension of duties on metal scrap. Approved 7/2/71

H.R. 8293.* To continue until the close of Sept. 30, 1973, the International Coffee Agreement Act of 1968. Approved 3/24/72

H.R. 8312. To continue for two additional years the duty-free status of certain gifts for members of the Armed Forces serving in combat zones. Approved 12/22/71

H.R. 10947. (1971 Revenue Act) To provide a job development investment credit, to reduce individual income taxes, to reduce certain excise taxes, and for other purposes. Approved 12/10/71

and related expenses for an insured individual whose body is unavailable for burial. Approved 12/28/71

H.R. 15587. To provide for a six-month extension of the emergency unemployment compensation program. Approved 6/30/72

* Written by a Ways and Means member.

Public Debt	Renegotiation Board	Treasury Department	Revenue Sharing
H.R. 4690.* To increase the public debt limit as set forth in Sec. 21 of Second Liberty Bond Act, and for other purposes. Approved 3/17/71	H.R. 8311.* To amend the Renegotiation Act of 1951, to extend the act for two years, modify the interest rate on excessive profits and on refunds, and to provide that the Court of Claims shall have jurisdiction of renegotiation cases. Approved 7/1/71	H.R. 13334.* To establish certain positions in the Treasury Department to fix the compensation for those positions and for other purposes. Approved 5/18/72	H.R. 14370.* (State and Local Fiscal Assistance Act) To provide payments to localities for high-priority expenditures, to encourage the states to supplement their resources, and to authorize federal collection of state individual income taxes. Approved 10/20/72
H.R. 12910.* To provide a temporary increase in the public debt limit. Approved 3/15/72			
H.R. 15390.* † To provide for a four-month extension of the present temporary level in the public debt limitation. Approved 7/1/72			
H.R. 16810.* To provide for a temporary increase in the public debt limit and to place a limitation on expenditures and net lending for the fiscal year ending June 30, 1973. Approved 10/27/72			

† Bill as amended by Senate included 20 percent social security benefit increase effective 9/72.

SOURCE: Legislative Calendar (final edition), Committee on Ways and Means, October 18, 1972, pp. 16–22.

Mills's extension of his committee's jurisdiction clearly indicates that he is not concerned about whether the committee is spreading itself too thin. And any move to curtail the committee's jurisdictional imperialism could be seen as a move against Mills.* To preserve both Mills's dignity and the committee's effectiveness, Ways and Means could start subdividing its work through a system of subcommittees. Despite the constantly increasing variety and quantity of bills considered by the committee, it is still the *only* committee that does not have any subcommittees.†

The Senate Finance Committee, with identical jurisdiction, has recently began to develop subcommittees. On February 26, 1973, Chairman Russell Long (D., La.) announced that he was establishing "six important subcommittees to expedite the flow of legislation on behalf of the Committee on Finance." Long's move will probably have no effect on Ways and Means. Ways and Means chief counsel John M. Martin, Jr., has said that any committee decision to establish subcommittees will be based solely "on what they [the committee members] think our own requirements would be."

A few committee members have favored subcommittees, but quietly and almost obliquely. They are not interested in alienating Mills, thereby losing whatever committee influence they may possess. At least one committee member, Charles Vanik, has said, "Too much sits on Mills—in his back pockets." James Corman has traced Mills's power to his control over the committee staff, which is small and relatively inaccessible to committee members, and he has suggested that this power be diffused through subcommittees. This arrangement, Corman says, would "divide power, [and create] more participation and increased staff." A larger staff would make it easier for committee members to con-

---

* Such a move was attempted by a House Select Committee on Committees headed by Richard Bolling (D., Mo.). The Bolling committee resolution, which would have severely curtailed Ways and Means's jurisdiction, lost out to a weaker substitute measure backed by Mills and most House committee chairmen.
† At least four subcommittees will be required in the 94th Congress as a result of the House committee reorganization bill.

sult with the staff lawyers, economists, and researchers. Distributing the chairman's power would also hinder Mills's present ability to scuttle bills through benign (or even malevolent) neglect.

Representative Harold Collier (R., Ill.) has suggested that subcommittees would help streamline the full committee: they "would relieve us of detail," which is one of the committee's biggest problems since it is "one of the most pressed committees in terms of time and legislation." Hugh Carey agreed that subcommittees would expedite hearings, which add to the volumes of data that committee members and staff must digest.

But most committee members oppose establishing subcommittees. "Our business is too intertwined," Jerry Pettis contended. Several members feared that belonging to one subcommittee would insulate them from the others, so that an information gap would develop between the twenty-five Ways and Means members. According to Dr. Laurence Woodworth, chief of staff for the Joint Committee on Internal Revenue Taxation, many who oppose Ways and Means subcommittees believe that such additional structures would waste the committee's time, not conserve it. Because of the complexity of the legislation handled, and the varied interests of most members, this argument runs, the full committee would have to examine the subcommittees' work; a bill's course through the committee would take twice as long. But third-ranking Democrat James Burke challenges this argument. He thinks the subcommittees would need a minimum of supervision by the full committee and says he would establish them if he were chairman.

Without subcommittees, all the Ways and Means Committee members are now able to participate in every issue before the committee. But they do so at the expense of a loss of power and pertinent information, because they are constantly at the mercy of the chairman's discretion, no matter who the chairman may be. His authority over the hearings held, over the bills considered, and over a committee member's access to committee staff means that he controls each member's knowledge of and participation in the committee's affairs. Each session, each day that the committee struggles without subcommittees, the chairman's power is enhanced and institutionalized. It is no wonder that one of Mills's first official acts as chairman in 1957 was to abolish all subcommittees of the Ways and Means Committee.

A Strategic Committee, a Minuscule Staff

Like the members of every committee in Congress, Ways and Means members depend on the research and knowledge of their staff. The staff assembles technical data, provides the members with booklets on possible and pending legislation, writes the committee reports that accompany bills to the floor, helps members write their own bills, aids them in preparing their floor remarks on committee matters, and handles questions from the other 410 members of the House.

For a major committee, Ways and Means has a very small staff.* In June 1972 it consisted of only twenty-seven people, including professionals, clerks and secretaries. The twenty-one standing House committees had an average of forty-two staff members.[12] The Ways and Means staff is dwarfed by the staffs of such other House committees as Administration, Appropriations, Education and Labor, Government Operations, Public Works, Banking and Currency, Internal Security, Post Office and Civil Service, Interstate and Foreign Commerce, Judiciary, Foreign Affairs, and Armed Services.

The committee's understaffing is often embarrassingly apparent. In late 1971 ranking Republican John Byrnes asked the committee's minority staff to write a critique on a pending revenue-sharing bill. But the minority staff lacked the time and the manpower to do a comprehensive job, so the minority counsel, Richard Wilbur, asked third-year law students in several tax classes at Harvard Law School to research the constitutionality of revenue sharing for Byrnes.

---

* For tax issues, Ways and Means committee members turn instead to the larger and more competent Joint Committee on Internal Revenue Taxation staff, also largely under Mills's control.

Chairman Mills and his chief counsel have instructed the majority staff to be absolutely nonpartisan, to help equally every member of the committee. Minority staff member Arthur L. Singleton has noted that this edict has been closely observed, and Republican committee member Harold E. Collier is pleased that "Mills's staff is most cooperative" and "not as tightly drawn" along party lines as are most other committee staffs. This attitude may improve the efficiency of a grossly understaffed committee, but it also coopts the minority to the point of not even getting their full allotment of staff, and when the minority party in Congress is not the party in the White House, congressional independence suffers.

As cooperative and efficient as the entire staff may be, there are still complaints about its size. Democrat Richard Fulton of Tennessee contends that it

> would be to our advantage to have a larger staff, to have more experts so that in executive sessions we would not need departmental heads to give opinions which have to be biased; or if we did call them in [with a larger staff] we'd have sufficient Ways and Means staff to repudiate them.

On August 29, 1972, the committee did try to improve its resources by requesting the House to authorize four additions to the Ways and Means staff. But by August 1973 the request still had not been approved at the first stage, by the Committee on House Administration. During the summer of 1972 some of the committee's tax reformers thought they would pool their resources to hire a tax expert on their own. But eight months later nothing had happened with this plan either.

Since the mid-1950s the committee's professional staff has expanded from merely a majority and a minority counsel to an eleven-member team, with eight serving the majority and three the minority. The chief counsel and staff director is John M. Martin Jr., now more an administrator than a technical legislative advisor. Martin practiced and taught law before joining the staff in 1956, but Congressman Pettis has said that he is no more of an expert than the members of the committee. Martin's specific jobs include staff recruitment, running public hearings, scheduling witnesses, and helping committee members prepare their presentation of committee matters on the House floor. Doubling as chief counsel for the Democratic committee on committees, Martin also maintains detailed data on the composition of the House committees and background information on Democratic members of the House relevant to their committee selection.

The assistant chief counsel, John Patrick Baker, performs basically the same jobs as Martin. Before joining the Ways and Means staff in 1963, Baker practiced law in Arkansas, worked in the Justice Department's Tax Division, and was a legislative assistant to Senator John McClellan (D., Ark.).

Harold T. Lamar joined the majority staff in 1967 as a specialist on tariffs and trade. An economist, he previously worked in the Commerce Department on import policy, with the Corps of Engineers on international transportation, and with the Library of Congress' Legislative Reference Service on international trade.

Three of the majority staff—James W. Kelley, William D. Fullerton, and Charles E. Hawkins—work on social security issues. Kelley, who joined the staff in 1967, concentrates on unemployment and old age insurance; Fullerton, who came to Ways and Means in 1970 from the Legislative Reference Service and the Social Security Administration, focuses on health; and public welfare is handled by Hawkins, who worked on Missouri's welfare programs for fifteen years and for twenty years on public assistance at the Department of Health, Education and Welfare and its predecessor, the Federal Security Agency.

The committee's two tax experts are Robert B. Hill and William T. Kane. Before coming to the committee in 1968, Hill had practiced and taught law in Arkansas and worked for the Internal Revenue Service. Kane joined the staff a year after Hill. He had also worked for the IRS—in the chief counsel's office and and the income tax division—and in the Justice Department's tax division.

The three members of the minority staff have been with the

committee for an average of only four years. The minority's counsel, Richard C. Wilbur, left the Internal Revenue Service in 1965 to join Ways and Means.* Arthur Singleton, who focuses on trade, debts, trust funds, revenue sharing, and unemployment compensation, has been with the committee since 1970, after working as a journalist, a teacher, and a public relations employee of United States Steel Company. Since John Meagher came to the minority staff in June 1972, he has worked on health, social security and taxes. He was previously a legislative assistant to Representative Alexander Pirnie (R., N.Y.), worked in HEW's Congressional Liaison Office, and was on a White House task force.

Thus eight of the staff formerly worked in some wing of the executive branch—the Internal Revenue Service, HEW, the Social Security Administration, even on a White House task force. This executive branch experience can both help and hinder the efficiency and the responsiveness of the committee's work. It can help because most of the staff is intimately familiar with the personalities and intricacies of the bureaucracies with which Ways and Means must work. And it can hinder because the staff can let its possibly latent biases toward the executive branch—or at least toward certain persons within it—shadow its congressional work. But since representatives from the executive try to be most influential with the committee in its closed executive sessions, only people attending those meetings know for certain the relationship between the staff and the executive's lobbyists—and they're not talking.

Under the 1970 Legislative Reorganization Act, all committee members must be allowed to participate in selecting staff. But most of the staff is still appointed by the chairman and ranking minority member, on the recommendation of either the chief counsel or the minority counsel, depending on whether the appointment is for the majority or minority staff. Although chief counsel Martin maintained that he approaches every committee

---

* Wilbur was approved as a judge of the U.S. Tax Court in 1974.

member about potential staff appointments, so they would be "acceptable to all elements and both sides of the committee," committee member Hugh Carey charged that members are traditionally not consulted on hiring new staff—for Ways and Means or any other committee.

The common assumption among Washingtonians is that Wilbur Mills dictates who will join his staff. For example, William Fullerton told us that when he introduces himself as a Ways and Means staff member, he is usually asked not where he is from, but what part of Arkansas he is from.

THE SENATE FINANCE COMMITTEE

The Family Assistance Plan passed the mossback House on April 16, 1970, by a vote of 243 to 155 . . . . Then FAP ran into the Senate Finance Committee, a carnival of egos and whims in which puffy senators bounce off each other randomly like big balloons in a crowded room. Unlike the quiet and businesslike, if secretive, Ways and Means Committee, the Finance Committee is a stage for symbolic politics and for grandstanding in public. Or so it operated in the case of family assistance.

—*Taylor Branch, "Patrick Moynihan's Ship of Fools,"* Washington Monthly, *January 1973, pp. 13–14*

The 1970 Legislative Reorganization Act ranked the Senate Finance Committee, along with the Senate committees on foreign relations, appropriations, and armed services, as a supercommittee. The act prohibited a senator from serving on more than one supercommittee. The Senate Finance Committee has jurisdiction not only over all areas covered by Ways and Means, but also over such diverse areas as sugar quotas and renegotiating defense procurements. The committee is so saddled with work that when a reporter asked Chairman Russell Long (D., La.) when his committee would release the revenue-sharing bill, he sighed, "We're doing the best we can. That's all a mule can do."

During the past few years the output of this workhorse of the Senate has not received much acclaim, especially from Senate tax reformers. The committee is tightly controlled by a profoundly conservative group of Republicans and Democrats led by Long. Because of its susceptibility to special interests, the committee has been called "the citadel of conservatism" and "the happy hunting ground" for tax pressure groups. Former Senator Joseph Clark (D., Pa.), who worked for congressional reform, was especially disturbed at the fantasy-like world the Committee had created for itself; he charged that it "lives in a vacuum removed from the disturbing fiscal theories of the modern world."

The membership of the Finance Committee is mostly rural as well as conservative. This is true of both Republicans and Democrats. During the Ninety-second Congress the committee's members came from states that represented 23.3 percent of the country. Five came from southern or border states; three from the Rocky Mountain states; and two from the Southwest. Only one came from the Northeast. Of the ten most populated states, only one was represented; there were no committee members from California, Texas, Pennsylvania, New York, or Illinois.

Both Ways and Means and the Finance Committee are to the political right of their respective houses, but the Finance Committee is even more conservative than Ways and Means and is almost twice as conservative as the rest of the Senate. In 1971 the average rating for Finance members by the liberal Americans for Democratic Action was 21.5 percent, while the average for the entire Senate was 41 percent. (See Table 5.) That same year the median ADA rating was 22 percent for Ways and Means members and 30 percent for the entire House. Conversely, the conservative Americans for Constitutional Action gave Finance members an average rating of 67.5 percent and the Senate as a whole only 39 percent. The ACA average rating for Ways and Means members was 54 percent, compared to 43 percent for the full House.

For years, appointments to the Finance Committee have been made by the Senate leadership, which awards positions only to loyal colleagues. Tax reformers like former senators Albert Gore

(D., Tenn.) and Paul Douglas (D., Ill.) had difficulty being seated on it. In the 1950s, Majority Leader Lyndon Johnson even appointed himself to the committee to keep Douglas out. Douglas, among others, charged that one of the criteria for committee membership was a secret pledge to defend the oil depletion allowance. Once on the committee, he said, campaign contributions from oil interests would help buttress the pledge. The distinguished economist waited for eight years while he watched five members of his 1948 senatorial freshman class make the committee. He became a member only after a columnist wrote about LBJ's maneuverings to keep the Illinois senator at bay. Even then, his performance on the committee—with his crusades for tax reform and his battles against the oil depletion allowance—was a lonely one. Once Gore fought his way to the committee, Douglas had at least one ally in his skirmishes with the conservatives. But Douglas was beaten by Percy in the mid-1960s and Gore lost in 1970. Tax reformers still look wistfully at those years when the dynamic duo sat on the committee.

The Finance Committee is largely controlled by Russell Long, the darling of the gas and oil industry and the protector of tax loopholes and depletion allowances. Long is also responsible for the inequitable spread of political viewpoints on the committee. For years he barred relatively liberal senators from membership —fellow Democrats like Walter Mondale (Minn.) and Thomas Eagleton (Mo.). When Gore's defeat opened up a seat on the Committee in 1971, Long lowered the barrier to give Gaylord Nelson (D., Wis.) the seat, but only to prevent more liberal, outspoken senators from gaining positions. Nelson had not even seriously thought about joining the committee until Long invited him, but the two were old friends.*

Because of its basically conservative makeup, the committee rarely has to struggle with opposing viewpoints. Former Assistant Treasury Secretary Stanley Surrey says that "no one stands up on the committee now and gets outraged." And no one does precisely

---

* Nelson has proved to be a tough tax reformer on most issues.

TABLE 5.
92nd Congress Finance Committee's Ratings

Member	ADA*	COPE†	NAB‡	ACA§
Russell Long (D., La.)	19	25	50	61
Clinton Anderson (D., N.M.)				
Herman Talmadge (D., Ga.)	22	70	73	70
Vance Hartke (D., Ind.)	81	82	33	13
J. W. Fulbright (D., Ark.)	66	75	18	14
Abraham Ribicoff (D., Conn.)	93	75	25	5
Fred Harris (D., Okla.)	63	78	22.2	17
Harry Byrd, Jr. (D., Va.)	15	0	75	87
Gaylord Nelson (D., Wis.)	96	83	10	5
Wallace Bennett (R., Utah)	0	25	83	70
Carl Curtis (R., Neb.)	4	10	100	100
Len Jordan (R., Idaho)				
Jack Miller (R., Iowa)	11	25	80	84
Paul Fannin (R., Ariz.)	0	25	75	95
Clifford Hansen (R., Wyo.)	4	8	100	96
Robert Griffin (R., Mich.)	33	8	78	65
Averages	36.21	42.07	58.72	55.85

* Americans for Democratic Action (1971)
† AFL-CIO Committee on Political Education (1971)
‡ National Association for Businessmen (1969–70)
§ Americans for Constitutional Action (1971)

because the group is quite satisfied with the present concessions to the oil and mineral interests and the loopholes in most tax laws.

But the increased tempo of the drive to reform the tax and welfare systems could impel more tax reformers onto Finance. Once there, they might produce some kind of balance to the fiscal status quo of Russell Long and his fellow conservatives, who currently rule the committee autocratically, as the following personality capsules show.

The Committee's Sixteen: Personalities and Issues*

At only fifty-four, Russell B. Long has been at the helm of Finance for seven years. In these years he has lost Senate favor in a bitter fight for a strict campaign financing law; defended, unsuccessfully,

* Expanded to seventeen members in the 93rd Congress.

former Senator Thomas Dodd (D., Conn.)* when he was charged with misuse of campaign funds; served as whip from 1965 to 1969; and begun to modernize his committee. Long is a bright man, with a quick mind and an uncanny memory, but many in Washington consider him undisciplined. In conversation his thoughts seem to come faster than his speech and he continually backtracks to put his ideas into words. His staff admits that he is unpredictable. A friend and close professional associate of the senator told us that he has "a very fast brain, but without enough internal checks on it." One former Treasury official, who had often seen Long operate in his committee's executive sessions, admired Long's intellectual grasp of complex revenue taxation but lamented that he has "an attention span of from five to twelve seconds." One aide stressed how important it is to screen out people wanting to see the senator; it would be "dangerous" to let him see too many visitors.

As if to confirm both his critics and Emerson's adage that "a foolish consistency is the hobgoblin of little minds, adored by little statesmen and philosophers and divines," Long seems to hop from one side of an issue to another, from one idea to another that contradicts the first. He is either one of the most agile politicians in Washington or one of the most confused. He has used chicanery to undermine the original Medicare bill but has simultaneously tried to increase benefits for the aged. He has attacked those exploiting the welfare system but frustrated all efforts to correct it. He has jeopardized his Senate career by advocating a controversial campaign financing bill and defended his colleague Dodd against charges of misusing campaign funds.

Long's southern-style populism has let him wage war against high taxes, secure a zero percent raise for social security benefits in June 1972, and be a frequent ally of trust-busters in antitrust battles. Former Senator Douglas told us that Long shared the "antimonopoly sentiments of his father," Huey Long, Louisiana's

* At the recommendation of the Senate Ethics Committee, Senator Dodd was formally censured by the Senate in 1966. He did not run for reelection and died in 1972.

demagogic populist governor and senator of an earlier time. For example, Long joined Gore and Estes Kefauver (D., Tenn.) in opposition to establishing COMSAT, the government-subsidized private communications satellite corporation.

As genuine as his trust-busting inclinations may be, Long is a true son of Louisiana when it comes to the oil and gas industry, which, he says, gives the state government 44 percent of its total revenues and 70 percent of its education funds. He has vigorously defended government favors to the oil and gas industry, including the depletion allowance. His own wealth is built on his father's oil investments, and he has assisted the oil interests in allocating campaign contributions to deserving senators.

The committee member with the next seniority in the Ninety-second Congress was Clinton Anderson, a New Mexico Democrat. Anderson began his career as the reporter who broke the story of the Teapot Dome scandal in the Harding administration. He ended it with retirement after the Ninety-second Congress as a seventy-eight-year-old senator who had chaired the Joint Committee on Atomic Energy and the Committee on Science and Astronautics. By the time of his retirement he had accumulated a fortune from insurance, oil, farming, and broadcasting. During the debate on the 1969 Tax Reform Act, Anderson favored cutting the oil companies' tax privileges for foreign royalties and "intangible" drilling and development costs. Although these ideas made Anderson one of the more venturesome members of the Finance Committee, he still refused to touch the percentage depletion. This position simply identified him with the major oil companies, rather than with the small independent oil firms that benefit more from the "intangibles" deduction.

After Senator Anderson's retirement, Herman Talmadge (D., Ga.) became the committee's second-ranking Democrat. He is a loyal member of the Finance Committee. On the floor or as a regular member of the House-Senate conference, Talmadge will always defend a committee bill, contending that its sponsors have analyzed the problems concerned better than the conference or the Senate as a whole could.

Talmadge rails against some of the executive agencies as "truculent" and "recalcitrant" bureaucracies. One of his worst tangles was with the Labor Department over its slowness in enforcing an amendment (a tax credit for employers) which he fought to add to what he proudly calls the "radical" 1971 Work Incentive Program.*

Senator Vance Hartke (D., Ind.) has a reputation for an ego that sometimes gets in the way of his work. Before announcing his candidacy for the 1972 Democratic presidential nomination, Hartke told his staff that there was only one man qualified to be president. After waiting a few seconds for Hartke's choice, they asked, "Who?" "Why me, of course," he snorted. He rarely attends the Finance Committee's hearings and executive sessions, but when he is there his tone and actions seem grating and abrasive to other members. Hartke landed on the committee when his mentor, Majority Leader Lyndon Johnson, rewarded him for his loyalty in a crucial showdown over the cloture rule. He has consistently used his Finance seat to cooperate with special interests: to protect the oil and steel industry from imports and to oppose cutting the oil depletion allowances; to get an investment credit for a large aluminum company (see Chapter Four); and to obtain a special tax break on contributions to professionals' pension plans.

It is generally believed that the Senate leadership and the Arkansas oil and gas industry urged J. William Fulbright (D., Ark.) to join the Finance Committee to block liberal William Proxmire, who the committee feared would be a determined crusader. Because of his greater interest in the chairmanship of the Foreign Relations Committee, Fulbright has rarely attended Finance meetings. He has, however, usually attended hearings or sessions concerned with foreign trade bills or welfare reform. He has faithfully protected Arkansas' oil, aluminum, and clay industries, and favors increasing the depletion allowance for aluminum.

Abraham Ribicoff (D., Conn.) is probably the most experienced

---

* A manpower training program designed to reduce welfare dependence.

member of the committee. He has been in the Connecticut legislature, served two terms as governor, and was Secretary of Health, Education and Welfare under President Kennedy. "Of course," he says, "I was put on the committee to help pass Medicare," but since then he has mostly worked for basic reforms in the welfare system. When President Nixon announced a program for welfare reform in August 1969, Ribicoff commended him for making "a sound and constructive first step in our fight to improve the lives of all our citizens."[13] But after further study Ribicoff became dissatisfied with the President's program. Even though the program emphasized "workfare rather than welfare" and job training for welfare recipients, Ribicoff noted, there was no provision to create jobs for those trying to escape from the welfare rolls. Ribicoff also criticized the amount of assistance proposed and the provision for eliminating the food stamp program. The senator made several suggestions for improving the administration's bill. Under his plan, guaranteed annual income would be set at $3,000 and rise above the poverty line in five years. It would benefit about 30 million people. The Nixon plan would have a guaranteed income of $2,400 with no increases and would aid 19.3 million people.

Ribicoff has voted to lower mineral depletion allowances and to increase personal exemptions on income tax. On the other hand, he has voted against tax reform proposals which would raise the minimum tax on the loophole incomes of the wealthy. Ribicoff's liberal name is notably absent from Senate tax reform bills, such as S.3378, sponsored by Senator Gaylord Nelson (D., Wis.) and other liberals. During the Ninety-second Congress Ribicoff introduced six tax bills, two of which proposed allowing parents to take tax credit for a percentage of their children's private school tuition, and another increasing the tax credit for retirement income for both single and married people. Many feel Ribicoff has surrendered his voice on tax reform to gain influence in committee on the welfare issue.

One member of the committee, Fred Harris (D., Okla.), left

Congress at the end of 1972, frustrated and angry. Harris started the New Populist Institute in Washington to organize support for tax reform. After his experience on the committee, Harris—who supported George McGovern's 1972 presidential campaign after an aborted campaign of his own—doubts that an effective tax reform can be led from Congress, especially without presidential support.

As late as 1969 Harris told his Oklahoma constituents that he would "do what I can to hold the line" on depletion allowances. On the Senate floor, he voted against one move to cut the allowance and for another to return it to 27.5 percent. But Harris' politics changed while he traveled around the country as the Democratic Party's national chairman between 1968 and 1970. When his populism led him to oppose depletion allowances and other concessions to private industry, powerful interests in Oklahoma called his transformation "terribly unpatriotic."

Harris is relieved to be off the Finance Committee. Exhausted by the conservative bloc, Harris said that for a tax reformer to attend the committee's executive sessions involved "a hell of a lot of wasted time." He called Long's ideas and those of ranking Republican Wallace Bennett on welfare and workfare "medieval notions" shared by a "reactionary" committee. The "quality of legislation has plummeted in the committee," he charged, until it is now "an abomination."

Harry F. Byrd, Jr., joined the committee, which his father had ruled for years, in January 1969. Heir to the powerful Byrd Democratic machine in Virginia, Harry Byrd came to the Senate in 1965 after experimental careers as a newspaper editor, apple grower, bank director, and state legislator. Now an Independent, Byrd calls himself a fiscal conservative; this quality often leads him to contentiously question government witnesses about the arithmetic in their reports of government expenses.

To learn about a bill's defects, Byrd habitually first goes to its minority report. Although he admits that this is "not a very good way to legislate," he likes Bismarck's philosophy that knowing how sausages or laws are made would cause one to reject both. "In the end," he says, "there's so much going on around here you have to take a little bit on faith."

Wisconsin's Gaylord Nelson landed on the committee when Long asked him to replace Gore in 1970. Nelson told us in the summer of 1972, "Finance is a hell of an important committee. I decided to get on so I could have some input there." But a former Treasury official has said that "it hasn't dawned on [Nelson] that he has a huge responsibility on the committee . . . he doesn't have the feeling of a Gore or a Douglas."

One of Nelson's aides remarked that the Senate's tax reformers are "a miserable bunch of leaderless misfits." Nelson has not moved to fill that vacuum. He is cautious and calls himself a novice on tax reform. As a popular governor of Wisconsin from 1948 through 1958, he instituted environmental and tax reforms before they became *causes celebres*—but it took him "ten years to learn about Wisconsin taxes and federal taxes are much more esoteric." *Business Week* stated in August 1972 that after Senators Paul Douglas, Albert Gore, and Fred Harris left the committee at the end of the Ninety-second Congress, Nelson would be one of the few remaining tax reformers. But at the outset Nelson did not see himself in this position, though he expected a drive for tax reform to materialize.

Backed by good staff work, Nelson has since become more involved. In 1971 he staged a floor fight against several business tax loopholes, and in 1972 he proposed a tax reform bill, which he described as having "a lot of problems." In the Ninety-third Congress Nelson has offered a number of tax reform measures that indicate that he has become one of the more knowledgeable and hardworking tax reformers on the Finance Committee and in the Senate.

The Republicans have not thrown their best forces onto the Finance Committee. One committee staff member has quipped that the committee's Republicans are "like auks. They just sit there and vote through their glands—bald and pudgy, no sense of humor." One labor lobbyist sniffed that Michigan's Robert Griffin "is the first Republican to get onto that committee in the memory of man who hasn't been an absolute troglodyte." (However, Griffin left the committee in 1973.) According to a *National Journal* article of April 10, 1971, the troglodytes are on the committee because of what one tax reformer called "the Republicans' . . . policy of putting their most conservative men on [it]. Just look who is there."

A former president of the National Association of Manufacturers, Senator Bennett is the committee's ranking Republican.* He always supports government aid to business, such as its guarantee in 1971 of $250 million in loans to the financially ailing Lockheed Aircraft Corporation. As a member of the Senate Banking and Currency Committee, Bennett has introduced a bank holding company relief bill, S. 311 (numbered S. 407 in the Ninety-third Congress) which Senator Wright Patman (D., Tex.) charged would grant "unwarranted tax relief" of millions of dollars.

Bennett is not anxious for his constituents to know about all his pro-business moves. For example, one of Bennett's 1971 newsletters told Utah voters that the personal exemption for federal income tax had been raised and the automobile excise tax lifted. But it failed to mention the senator's work for the Asset Depreciation Range, investment credit provisions, and the Domestic International Sales Corporation, all of which Bennett helped to get through Congress. Bennett told us that it was not his job to educate the public on what it was not interested in. Anyway, he said, smiling, "The cost factor in these programs is not that important." (He forgot to say that the "cost factor" was $7.8 billion, which would go to the corporate community annually over the next decade.)

Senator Carl T. Curtis of Nebraska, the second-ranking minority member in the Ninety-second Congress, is one of the more fiscally conservative members of the committee. His cumulative rating from the conservative Americans for Constitutional Action is an impressive 94 percent, while the liberal Americans for

---

* Bennett retired at the end of the 93rd Congress.

Democratic Action has given him a cumulative 3 percent rating. During the 1969–70 session he voted for 90 percent of the legislation favored by the U. S. Chamber of Commerce and for every bill endorsed by the National Association of Businessmen.

Curtis opposed deficit spending under Presidents Kennedy and Johnson and ignored his strong party loyalty to criticize President Nixon's budget proposal for fiscal 1973. After seeing the $25.5-billion deficit included in the latter, Curtis lamented, "I am one of the most unhappy men in Washington."

In the recorded votes of the Finance Committee for 1971, Curtis voted against increasing social security benefits by either 15 percent or 20 percent. In the committee, he supported President Nixon's welfare reform by voting against removing the Family Assistance Program from the bill, but he then opposed FAP on the Senate floor: "We do not solve the problems inherent in our welfare plan by enlarging the program and spreading it among more people."

Iowa's Jack Miller, who was defeated for reelection in 1972, was more familiar than most committee members with the details of tax legislation, having been tax lawyer with the Internal Revenue Service for a year, taught tax law for two years, and, while in the state legislature, practiced tax law for eleven years. As the committee's gadfly for details, he irritated his colleagues as he tenaciously waded through each bill's provisions.

Another fiscal conservative, Miller was a determined foe of deficit spending. He favored using the Internal Revenue Code to encourage business and proposed an "incentive" income tax to foster economic growth—individuals would be taxed less if their income was higher than the previous year's. Miller's 1970 amendment to this effect, which substantially weakened the 1969 income tax law, has cost the government $100 million annually and helped only wealthy taxpayers. In late 1972 Miller sponsored another weakening amendment, and the loophole became a central issue in his reelection campaign. As a result, Iowans ousted Miller in favor of challenger Dick Clark.

Len Jordan of Idaho, who retired at the end of the Ninety-second Congress, when he was seventy-four years old, was appointed to the Senate in August 1962 to fill the term of Henry C. Dworshak, who had just died. Jordan had previously been a governor and a state legislator. After leaving the governor's mansion Jordan had served on the International Joint Commission and then on the International Development Advisory Board. Jordan too had a consistently conservative voting record in the Senate. The Americans for Constitutional Action awarded him an 86 percent cumulative rating while the Americans for Democratic Action gave him an 8 percent cumulative rating. In the 1969–1970 session of Congress, Jordan voted for 60 percent of the bills favored by the U.S. Chamber of Commerce and 66.7 percent of those endorsed by the National Association of Businessmen.

Still another dedicated fiscal conservative is Paul Fannin of Arizona. One of the senator's aides told us that Fannin thinks the committee is not conservative enough. Fannin does not think that the major purpose of taxes is either to raise revenue or to encourage economic equality. Instead, they should stimulate and encourage business. He is a strong supporter of such business-oriented taxes as the Asset Depreciation Range, the Investment Credit, and the Domestic International Sales Corporation. He dismisses talk of tax reform as empty liberal rhetoric. What people really want, he feels, is to have their taxes cut, which is impossible with all those nasty liberal welfare programs eating their way through the government's treasury.

Clifford Hansen considers Finance an important place for a senator from Wyoming, a state rich in oil and gas, other minerals, and the largest coal reserves for strip mining in the country. And as a good Republican and a good spokesman for his state's business interests, Hansen wants all of these reserves tapped. The oil depletion allowance, he contends, should be returned to 27.5 percent and the resulting loss to the Treasury would not be unreasonable. One of his many close friends in the oil industry summed up its admiration for him: "He really cares; he's the only one who ever speaks out."

Hansen apparently has no compunctions about government dispensations for special interests, especially when those interests are his own. He grazes nearly 1,400 cattle on the public lands of Grand Teton National Park and National Forest under the protection and management of the National Park Service. In November 1972 the *New York Times* reported:

> Eleven thousand acres of Grand Teton National Park are now used by the Government to operate a fine cattle ranch for Senator Hansen. The fences were built by the Government. Miles of irrigation ditches have been dug. A mile-long water storage reservoir was constructed and grassland improvements were made on the park lands. Park employees irrigate the land and care for the cattle.[14]

The National Park Service has spent $300,000 over the past decade to raise Hansen's herd, which has caused serious environmental problems by "trampling seedlings and preventing establishment of young trees in clear cut areas." But Hansen, who also sits on the Interior Committee, recently introduced a bill to create preferences in grazing lease renewals. This bill, if enacted, would give him and his family over $1 million during a forty-year period.[15]

The Republican with the least seniority on the committee in the Ninety-second Congress was the Senate minority whip, Robert Griffin of Michigan. Griffin joined the committee in 1970 and left in 1973 to take a seat on Foreign Relations. Since his work as whip precluded attendance at some of the committee's executive sessions, he would have liked to send members of his staff to those he missed. This is not allowed under committee rules.

Though a Republican loyalist, Griffin has occasionally lapsed from his party's stands. During the Ninety-second Congress, for example, Griffin introduced a bill—which the administration opposed—to prevent the appropriation of any funds before all appropriation bills were passed. (This bill would give Congress a better view of the priorities involved.)

The Staff: Confusion in the Ranks

The Senate Finance Committee staff of six professionals and five secretaries and clerks seems to have been responsive and responsible—*not* to the public, the full Senate, nor even the entire Finance Committee, but to *one* man, Russell Long. The committee's former chief counsel, the late Tom Vail, boasted, "Hell, we represent the public interest, that's our job." Vail was referred to by everyone, from Long's legislative assistant to tax lobbyists and Treasury officials, as "Long's right-hand man." Though Vail contended that he and his staff were available to the entire committee, many members were reluctant to consult him. Senator Ribicoff explained, "I go there very seldom because they are hard-pressed, and it's a closely controlled operation. I think they reflect the chairman's views." Fred Harris agreed: "I assume their loyalty is to Senator Long." These suspicions were echoed throughout other senators' staffs. Paul McDaniel, who was an aide to Albert Gore, said that the staff members are "Long's people, and if they didn't agree with you, you didn't get help." Shirley Coffield, formerly Harris' legislative aide, commented: "If you want anything out of the staff, you only get the runaround. We're not the enemy, we're on the committee—we should get the information. I've never been so frustrated in all my life." On the other hand, Tom Owsley, Griffin's legislative aide, was pleased that "Long feeds the Republicans more often than the Democrats."

As an example of the staff's loyalty to Long, Ribicoff's legislative assistant, Geoffrey Peterson, charged that a staff member, Mike Stern, had deliberately sabotaged the estimates for Ribicoff's welfare reform proposal in 1971. Stern had asked HEW to use in its cost estimate of Long's welfare reform the number of individuals who would *actually* participate in his program. But he asked that Ribicoff's competing program be estimated on the basis of the total number of people who would be *potentially* eligible for the program, a distinction that was bound to create substantial extra costs for the Ribicoff plan. When Ribicoff then urged Vail to hire a private actuary to do the estimate, Vail chose Bob Myers, the former head of the Social Security Administration's actuary department. Peterson complained that Myers' "estimates are as loaded as HEW's. It's impossible to cost your program accurately in this town. Everyone's got a vested interest."

Shrugging aside such criticisms, Vail said that the important service his staff can offer is to work on issues "to the point where a senator can make a single decision on them." Vail was concerned, he said, that the Constitution, which states that the House, not the Senate, shall propose tax legislation, be upheld. Thus the staff leaned away from long-range planning and research, which, Vail explained, would give the committee the aura of a think tank and might lead to the drafting of legislation. Another staff member carefully explained why the staff has not assumed a more activist role:

> It's not part of our job to sit around dreaming up bills and then to go to the senator and tell him, "Here's something you ought to introduce." Sometimes we may find a *problem* in a bill, and then we might say, "You have a problem here and here's how you might take care of it." But whether the senator does or not is up to him. Sometimes, too, we'll take an idea which a senator has barely developed and help him make something of it. . . . But the idea always comes from the senator. Don't put us down as one of those staffs that manipulate their senators like a bunch of marionettes. We don't *act*; we react.

Many observers of Capitol Hill, though, think the committee's staff is much more calculating than it portrays itself. As one employee of HEW noted:

> The staff are very good at picking up the biases, the prejudices and slants of the committee. They take note of little remarks and points of view expressed in executive session. I think that's why they're allowed to prowl around there in the first place and then they write up something they know will be popular with the senators.

The staff and the committee members get their ideas from many places, but the most persistent and determined is the corps of idea peddlers called "lobbyists." Vail, who had both undergraduate and law degrees from George Washington University, was an effective buffer between lobbyists and the committee's members. "A lobbyist," he said, "will try to see a senator before us [the staff] only once. No," he added, "actually twice; the first time and the last time." He sees "every lobbyist who walks through my door. If a proposal is blatantly wrong, we steer it into the trash barrel; if it is blatantly right, we probably won't see it because it won't be an issue."

Vail's chief lieutenants are still with the committee. Mike Stern, who handled social security and welfare legislation, became chief counsel after Vail's death during the Ninety-third Congress. Stern is a New Yorker who came to the Finance staff in 1968 from HEW at Vail's invitation. He earns his $29,000 each year (now more) by handling the committee's protracted disagreements with HEW, a battle which has been long and heated and has recently focused on Medicare and Long's welfare—or "slavefare"—reform. Stern says he tries to stay aloof from the committee's partisan battles: "I suppose if the senators wanted to put us in a tough spot, they could. But they want a professional staff and they respect our position. We have never had any problems with that."

Jay Constantine, the committee's health care specialist, once worked with Blue Cross. Before joining the Finance staff in 1966, he worked on the Senate's Special Committee on the Aging, where he helped draft early Medicare legislation. Aside from his work, Constantine is probably best known for his invasion of privacy suit against the American Home Products Corporation, a drug manufacturer. When the firm discovered that Constantine had drafted a bill that would slash the cost of prescription drugs used in government programs, it had his personal life investigated. Constantine donated the $10,000 the court awarded him to the Washington, D. C., Children's Hospital.

Thirty-five-year-old Robert A. Best is the Finance Committee's chief economist and international expert. After a bachelor's decree from Villanova University and a master's degree in economics from Catholic University, in Washington, D. C., Best served with the Treasury Department from 1962 to 1964 as an international economist. He then joined the International Economic Policy Association as a senior economist, and came to the committee staff in 1967. While with the IEPA, Best wrote *The U.S. Balance of Payments—An Appraisal of U.S. Economic Strategy*. He has not written any books since joining the committee staff: Vail insisted that staff members should not take public positions on issues that might need legislative attention.

The youngest member of the staff is Dr. James Mongan, who graduated from Stanford Medical School in 1970. Mongan, who assists Constantine with health legislation, says his main job is to see the dozens of doctor lobbyists who swarm to the committee's offices. He is the only staff member who actively seeks advice from health law centers and public interest lobbies in the health field.

The most recent staff recruit is Robert Willian, who joined it in 1971 after twenty years as a tax specialist with the Internal Revenue Service. Willian is mostly concerned with the committee's correspondence and general inquiries about taxes. He insists that the committee's staff is neutral: "If you have strong feelings about something, you should be a lawyer or go into politics. A staff should implement other people's ideas."

The Finance Committee's staff has ability and knowledge, but it lacks independence. Throughout Washington it is known as "Long's staff," not as the committee's staff. Until it stops paraphrasing Russell Long's fiscal conservatism, until it starts serving the entire committee and not just the chairman, it will remain a vehicle for pro-business, antiwelfare, pro-loophole politics.

Personal Staff

Most Finance Committee members have an aide on their personal staff who keeps track of what the committee is doing. Senator Ribicoff has two, one for tax and one for welfare. Senator Curtis does without such a staff person, as did former Senator Miller. Personal staff members reflect the interests of the senator they work for, of course. Nelson's people are concerned with his reform package, Harris' with his aborted tax blockbuster, Ribicoff's with his perennial struggle for welfare reform, Hartke's with trade, Hansen's with oil and minerals, Byrd's with checking the addition of those columns. Given the overwhelming size and complexity of the committees' jurisdictions, the exclusion of personal staff from executive sessions is incongruous both with the technical problems dealt with and with the presence of Treasury personnel in the room. The committee's practice of exclusion is said to stem from a 1920 scandal when a senator from Connecticut allowed one of his "staff" to attend an executive session dealing with a particularly sensitive foreign trade bill. It later turned out that the man was really a lobbyist for the National Association of Manufacturers. Outraged, the committee banished personal staff from executive sessions for all time.

There are three major arguments for excluding personal staff from these sessions. First, the committee members want it to be a senators' committee, not a staff committee; they point to other committees that permit aides who end up as surrogate senators for principals who don't show. It is said that the best way for senators to learn the committee materials well enough to vote on them is to be present and do the learning themselves. Second, to let the aides in is to risk information leaking out. Telling what the committee is planning could have disastrous effects on the stock market or subject senators to intensified special interest pressures. The third excuse is that the executive chambers have room for only the senators, the committee staff, and executive agency representatives. The aides would "clutter up" both the room and the decision-making process, according to Long. Jay Constantine jokes, "Hell, we cram them in here two to a seat sometimes."

Tom Vail, for one, was not bothered by the aides' absence. He argued that a member could always place his aide outside the door and step out of executive session for a consultation, if necessary. But former Senator Gore, forced to use this system with Paul McDaniel, found it thoroughly unacceptable. Former Senator Harris dismissed Vail's suggestion of posting an aide in the hallway as "a ridiculous way to do the public's business." He complained that it "very much cut my effectiveness" in dealing with "complicated systems in which the placing of a word or the wording of a phrase makes an enormous difference. In any bill there are jillions, really jillions, of these little things, and there's no opportunity to get help. That's what we have personal staff for, to help us." Harris, Nelson, Hartke, and Ribicoff have all upon occasion expressed a desire to change the policy, but the majority roundly defeats motions to allow personal staff into executive sessions. Senator Nelson candidly explained the significance of the exclusion:

> I've raised the question with Russell Long, and told him I was handicapped without my staff in there. There is a team of experts from Treasury, there are the committee staff experts, and the Joint Committee experts—all of 'em—and I just don't know what it all means. . . . I try to take notes on what is being discussed, and then get back to my staff and get them to discuss it with me . . . but there is too much of a time lag to help much. The committee staff is Long's staff, so he's got no problem.

Long has reportedly promised the Wisconsin senator to "make some room" for personal staff in these secret sessions. As partial fulfillment of the promise, Long has instituted briefing sessions for the aides *after* each day's executive session. The aides charge that their briefings are not much more detailed than what the press corps gets and no substitute for being at the executive sessions.

The conservative bloc, with full input from the Joint Committee on Internal Revenue Taxation and committee staff members, are not hampered by the current policy. Senators Curtis and Miller said they did not need aides to help them cope with such things as the Internal Revenue Code, welfare, social security, Medicare, revenue sharing, foreign trade, and the debt limit. One reason Senator Hansen considered the committee staff was fine was that they were in the executive sessions. As he sees it, if a member doesn't know what to do by the time he gets into executive session, his aide couldn't help him. And Byrd's office did not think the absence of personal staff was a problem, since Byrd "stays on top himself" and has good relations with the staff. But a majority of the personal staff members—Republicans and

Democrats—agreed that being excluded from executive sessions substantially hindered their effectiveness in helping senators meet their committee responsibilities.

If personal staff people were able to play a responsible role in the committee, the Finance members might be able to attract highly competent aides and develop their skills to a level commensurate with the enormous responsibilities of Finance membership. As it is now, exclusion is just another facet of the seemingly willful slow up of the committee's functioning.

Dominated by a conservative coalition, the minority of legislative activists on the committee are deprived of technical help. Faced with "bandits" on all sides—the Treasury, special interest groups, the House committee, partisan committee staff, and unsympathetic peers on the committee—these members are given only secrecy for protection. This is not to slight the JCIRT staff, one of the finest in the Congress. It is merely to marvel at the systematic way individual senators are discouraged from getting a good grip on pending legislation. It is almost inconceivable that any rational decision-making body would force its members to station help out in the hall, where these eminent statesmen must go for counsel.

THE JOINT COMMITTEE ON INTERNAL REVENUE TAXATION

To supplement the work of both the Ways and Means and the Finance committees, the Joint Committee on Internal Revenue Taxation was established by the Revenue Act of 1926 as "a combination watchdog and law-simplifying organization." Its ten members include the chairmen of the Ways and Means and finance committees and the two highest ranking members from each party on each committee. The Ways and Means chairman is JCIRT chairman for the first session of a Congress; the Finance chairman is chairman for the second session.

JCIRT's chief of staff, Dr. Laurence N. Woodworth, has explained that "the principal functions of the Committee are to examine internal revenue refunds of over $100,000 to determine whether or not it believes that they should be appropriately made. In addition," Woodworth said,

> the Joint Committee meets to review administrative problems arising under the internal revenue laws. These may involve a review of administrative procedures in the Internal Revenue Service or, perhaps, the review of some proposed ruling or regulation brought to its attention by the [Internal Revenue] Service with respect to which a particular problem exists. In addition, the Joint Committee, from time to time, of its own volition raises questions . . . [about] an administrative procedure or proposed or final ruling or regulation. The Joint Committee, on occasion, has made recommendations with respect to legislation, but has not done so on any regular, or frequent, basis.[16]

"Our job," Woodworth concluded, "is to see that members of Congress get the facts on both sides so they can make their own decisions." The JCIRT also does intensive legislative work, including staff reports on all tax measures.

Former Representative John Byrnes, the ranking Republican on Ways and Means from 1963 to 1972 and a JCIRT member from 1961 to 1972, agrees with Woodworth that JCIRT could be invaluable but is not impressed with what it actually does. Since JCIRT's staff "follows the legislation from the House to the Senate and to conference . . . each does not have to act in a vacuum." But he stated that its ultimate aim—"to have a professional staff to serve both House and Senate"—has produced "more of a fiction than a committee," more of a dream than a reality.

The pivotal figure in this potentially pivotal committee is Laurence Woodworth himself. Many in Congress are so unfamiliar with this round-faced, bespectacled, pencil-mustached revenue expert that they call him "Woodward" or "Woodruff." But the Brookings Institution's Joseph Pechman, himself a nationally prominent tax economist, has called Woodworth "the most important man in taxation in this country." Woodworth majored in economics at Ohio Northern University and earned a master's degree in government management at the University of Denver in 1942. He worked briefly for the Civic Research Institute in Kansas City, Missouri, and the Tax Foundation in New York City. In 1960, while simultaneously working for the committee and being mayor of Cheverly, Maryland, Woodworth finished his doctoral dissertation for New York University.

Woodworth is a dedicated public servant. At \$39,999.96 a year, he is one of the highest paid staff members on Capitol Hill, but he could easily make more for a private firm or corporation.[17] In 1972 Woodworth became the first congressional employee to win the National Civil Service League's Career Service Award after the league named him one of ten outstanding government employees.

Members of Congress who do know Woodworth would certainly agree that he is an outstanding government employee. One staff member wrote that "Wilbur Mills and Russell Long rely heavily on Woodworth. . . . The chairmen's floor speeches on taxes are usually written by Woodworth; the chairmen will tell him what they want to say, but the tone and the language are his."[18]

At open hearings* Woodworth usually sits unobtrusively behind the committee chairman. In a quiet, barely audible voice he is almost continuously consulting with members, staff, and witnesses. He gives technical advice to both Republicans and Democrats, never appears as a witness, and is rarely quoted in

---

* The JCIRT itself held its most recent public hearing in 1953, although a number of secret meetings have been held since. These usually occur during a House-Senate conference between Ways and Means and Senate Finance, since JCIRT simply consists of the senior members of each of these committees. For instance, the decision to empower JCIRT staff investigation of alleged political use of the Internal Revenue Service by the White House came during a June 1973 conference on House and Senate versions of the debt-ceiling bill. In effect, Mills looked around the conference room, determined that a quorum of JCIRT was present, and called a meeting. Mills and Long then agreed to empower Dr. Woodworth to conduct a full investigation and report to the committee.

the news media. But in executive sessions of the Ways and Means or Finance committees and at House-Senate conferences Woodworth is an audible—as well as a visible—personality. Sometimes accompanied by a representative from the Treasury Department, Woodworth vigorously explains the legislation being considered. Many of the bills are so complicated that he must explain them several times. But to Woodworth it's all worthwhile "if I can come away from those meetings knowing that the committee has made its own decision in the light of this knowledge."[19]

The committees rely on Woodworth's staff almost as much as on him. The JCIRT staff works in secrecy to prepare confidential staff analyses of tax bills (committee "prints"). Woodworth keeps these prints locked up until just before distribution at executive sessions of the Ways and Means Committee. He refuses to issue further copies to other members of Congress, or even to tax committee members who were not on the committees when the reports were prepared. At these executive sessions staff members take notes on committees' decisions so that they can later translate them into legislation. After, say, the Ways and Means Committee has made its basic decisions and generally outlined a bill's provisions,

> the staffs begin the drafting of a tentative committee bill. This drafting occurs in the House Legislative Counsel's office and the technical drafting is under the direction of one or more attorneys from . . . [the JCIRT]. The Joint Committee staff and the Treasury staff representatives also participate in this drafting and are usually responsible for seeing to it that the basic committee decisions are carried out.

The staff enjoys wide discretion, since

> in some cases, this necessitates filling in areas where no specific decision previously had been made. This is true because it frequently is only upon conversion of the general ideas into specific statutory language that the gaps in policy are noted.[20]

The final responsibility for the draft rests with Woodworth, an unelected official. His notes, memory, and judgment determine what is decided by the committee. When a dispute arises as to what a committee has decided, there is a stenographic record to refer to for Ways and Means and a set of minutes for Finance. The committees review the finished draft, often not questioning technical sections on which the Treasury and Joint Committee staffs have agreed. As Byrnes appraised the situation, "If Treasury says something should be done and JCIRT staff agrees, nine times out of ten it will be." JCIRT legislative counsel. Nicholas Tomasulo indicates that the members' ready acceptance of advice from these two sources is not limited to technical matters: "There is no line in heaven between what's technical and what's substantial."

Once a tax law is passed, the influence of the chief of staff continues. He and his staff monitor the writing of regulations that make the law enforceable, and at times Woodworth becomes involved in Internal Revenue Service rulings that interpret tax law.

When Woodworth succeeded Colin Stam as JCIRT's chief of staff, he immediately moved to insure that the staff was nonpartisan and that all the members of both Ways and Means and Senate Finance had access to it. His success has earned him the high respect of many in Washington. Joe Pechman says, "Larry [Woodworth] is working in the public interest. Colin [Stam] didn't." According to one former Republican staff assistant, "When I tell Woodworth and those guys something, I expect confidence and I get it."[21] Senator Harry Byrd, Jr., relies on the Woodworth staff for its objectivity and accuracy: "The Treasury has been damn inaccurate," he added.

There is little chain of command but a lot of mutual respect on the staff. The entire staff is directed by and reports to Woodworth, who reviews everything it does. One staff economist, Albert Buckberg, commented that "the economists on the staff are usually used as if they were interchangeable. Woodworth tries to keep us all apprised of what's going on." Another JCIRT staff member, Arthur S. Fefferman, was happy that "we work on almost everything—speech writing, report writing—and are even called upon to speak on technical features of the law."

Woodworth has painstakingly recruited this kind of interdisciplinary staff.* "Economic analysis alone is not enough," he says. "Legal analysis alone is not enough. Tax requires a combination of economic and legal analysis." Woodworth's staff is so respected that Republican Representative Byrnes said that if he had become chairman he would have kept every member. The chairman of JCIRT approves appointments to the staff on Woodworth's recommendation. The director says he tries "to find the best qualified person. I don't inquire and don't really want to know a person's party affiliation. I don't really care. I want differing points of view." Staff attorney Herbert Chabot remembered that during his interview with Woodworth for a job with the committee, Woodworth looked through his folder and said, "I hope there isn't anything in here indicating party preference." Instead, Woodworth values dedication and experience. He requires people who are willing when necessary to work twelve hours a day, as he does every day. At the end of 1972 Woodworth had twenty-three professionals on his staff. (See Table 6.) Thirteen had worked for other government agencies such as the IRS, the Treasury, the Justice Department, or the Bureau of the Budget (now the Office of Management and Budget). Two—a lawyer and an economist—came to the staff directly from private practice.

But as good as the JCIRT's staff may be, it is still not good enough. The quality of its work is among the best on Capitol Hill; the expertise and objectivity of its members are widely admired. But it is too small to handle the work sent its way. Ways and Means member Hugh Carey complained that "you have to queue up to get access to the staff on a problem you want to work on." Woodworth maintains that his staff does

* Since Woodworth has been JCIRT's chief of staff, the size of the committee's legal staff has doubled. In 1972 JCIRT's budget was $745,891.70, more than the average allocation for the average House or Senate committee. See *Congressional Record*, August 1, 1972, pp. H.7299-7300.

TABLE 6.
Background of the JCIRT Staff

	Attorneys	*Economists*	*Statisticians*	*Accountants*
From federal govern- ment service	8	3	2	0
IRS	4	0	2	
Treasury	0	2	0	
Tax Court	1	0	0	
BOB (now OMB)	0	1	0	
Justice	3	0	0	
From private practice	4*	0	0	0
From teaching	1	0	1	1
From school	1	1	0	0
From state governments				
Total	14	4	3	1

* One staff member served with the House Legislative Counsel's Office before going into private practice.

"virtually all the work congressmen request of me." Carey agrees, but adds that it may be weeks or months before the Joint Committee's staff completes the work requested.

Some of Woodworth's professional peers have encouraged him to enlarge his staff further. To supplement his present staff, Woodworth often works closely with the Treasury Department. The 1954 revision of the Internal Revenue Code, for example, was a JCIRT staff–Treasury Department project. Woodworth describes the working relationship between the JCIRT's staff and the Treasury Department as very cooperative:

> While the Treasury Department presents the broad policy issues, the implementation of these issues in the form of specific proposals frequently is worked on together by the Treasury and Joint Committee staffs prior to the presentation of it to the tax committees. In participating in this effort, the Joint Committee's staff does not participate in or accept responsibility for the basic policies involved, but rather attempts to aid in developing concrete proposals given the broad policy objectives.[22]

Especially in 1954, 1962, and 1964, informal subcommittees of members of the staffs of the JCIRT and the Treasury Department were formed to resolve problems on major tax bills. They were given their directions by the proposed legislation and then tried "to make the thing workable. If they [the committee members] want to do something," Woodworth said, "the subcommittee says this is the way to go."

The tax analysts from the Treasury Department and from the JCIRT try to settle their differences before going to the tax committees. But many familiar with both the Joint Committee and the Treasury Department observe that there has been less cooperation and joint work during the Nixon administration than there was under the Johnson administration. This friction can be harmful to the quality of the Joint Committee's staff work, not only because the staff is small but because it has to rely on the Treasury's computers for complicated tax estimates. The four JCIRT tax revenue estimators must plod along with desk calculators and borrowed computer time. A former chief revenue estimator for the Treasury Department, Thomas Leahey, called the computer "absolutely essential" for making revenue estimates. "When you go before Congress," Leahey said, "you can't have too many numbers floating around."

The numbers may continue to float and JCIRT continue to be at the mercy of the Treasury Department's good will until it acquires its own bank of computers. Till then, the Joint Committee must carefully tread a balance between peaceful coexistence with the Treasury Department and adherence to its own principle of neutrality. This is often a difficult tightrope for both JCIRT's staff and members. As former Assistant Treasury Secretary Stanley Surrey said,

the [JCIRT's] Chief of Staff is very often the opponent of the Treasury Department before the tax committees. As a result, the difficulties for the average congressman on the tax committees become even greater. The issues get more and more complex as the "experts" disagree, and the congressman can hardly follow the technical exchanges. He is quite often content to fall back on the comfortable thought that, since the congressional expert appears to disagree with the Treasury experts, there is adequate technical justification to voting either way. Hence, the congressman is free to be guided by his own sympathies and instincts.[23]

As respected as the JCIRT's staff is, the Treasury Department seems to have the edge on recommendations to the tax committees. For example, the JCIRT's staff report clashed with the administration's and the Treasury Department's claims about the efficacy of the proposed Domestic International Sales Corporation. The staff report maintained that DISC would not appreciably increase exports, would overcompensate exporters, could cause tax exemptions rather than tax deferrals, would generally benefit large integrated companies, and would mean $600 million in revenue losses for only a $300 million increase in exports.[24] The tax committees and Congress generally ignored the staff report and sided with the administration. One long-time observer of the relationship between the tax committees, the Joint Committee, and the Treasury Department said that "generally speaking, if Treasury opposes, they [the Joint Committee] will not put them [alternatives suggested by the JCIRT staff] through." Woodworth seems resigned to this. He expresses respect for the intelligence and independence of the members of the tax committees and the power of the Treasury Department, and argues that his job is simply to present his information to the committee's members as objectively and lucidly as possible: "I don't lobby," he says somewhat too modestly. "It's not my role."

2

Inside the Committees:
Rules, Hearings,
and Conferences

If ever there were committees that needed to be efficient, to have good and mutually informative relations with the public and the rest of Congress, to have members who vote independently and not at the command of their chairman, it is the revenue committees. For taxes, their jurisdiction, affect everyone and everyone complains about them. And since the House Ways and Means Committee also has jurisdiction of social welfare bills, its decisions affect not only the pocketbooks, but also the health, of the entire population. But instead of being attuned to the nation, to its need to be economically and physically healthy, the committees are secluded and secretive; they are indifferent to the public and uncooperative with the rest of Congress. This negligent privacy does not make for good government nor good laws, but it does make for powerful men.

HOW THE WAYS AND MEANS
COMMITTEE WORKS

Sources of Information

It takes more than members and a staff to make a committee. It takes meetings and hearings, executive sessions and conferences, rules and parliamentary maneuvering. Sitting on the committee means distilling information, protecting the committee's jurisdictional bailiwick, and, it is to be hoped, becoming an expert in the committee's area. If nothing else, a committee can be a continuing symposium on its field. Its ideal purpose is to extract information from various sources both within and without the government and to weave it into a more refined and technical form, legislation.

Ways and Means Committee member Representative Jerry Pettis has compared the process of gathering information on Ways and Means matters to "gettting a drink from a fire hydrant." The committee has plenty of information to work with; the problem is sorting and interpreting it. There is some question, though, about how comprehensive and balanced all this material is, since information from the executive branch and special interest groups vastly outweighs that from private citizens and citizen groups.

The primary source of data for the committee staff is governmental bodies. Formal committee contact with official spokesmen in executive departments is inevitable on any major bill, but the staff also relies on executive contacts to provide information not contained in official statements. The staff often finds the agencies reluctant to give out information that might undermine the executive branch's policy positions. The staff's chief counsel, John Martin, says that sometimes he can only "get information with a crowbar." But sometimes, he says, "you can use the resources of the people downtown [in the executive agencies] and use them in the way you want to. The whole government is at your disposal," he said, if one knows how to "make them produce."

Harold Lamar, the Ways and Means staff's trade expert, said he gets trade statistics from the Commerce Department and some information from the Library of Congress' Congressional Research Service, but relies most on the specialized staff of the Tariff Commission, an independent government agency that studies tariff questions. Staff member William Fullerton jocularly said he relies on "spies," which he clarified as "the Library of Congress to some extent, lobbyists not much, and departments, though not always through formal contacts." Staff members' experience in the executive branch is important, he feels: "I got the [HEW] Secretary's background book on health insurance before he did. I know the Department better than they do, and can find out what's really going on." Lamar also feels at home with executive department officials, since he is dealing, as he says, "largely with the same people as before," when he worked in the Commerce Department.

Yet the staff professes that its operations are independent from the executive branch. As background for hearings on the 1970 trade bill, for example, it prepared a study of thousands of products for the committee. The executive agencies assigned personnel to research the data and "do the computation, but *we* put it together in the way we wanted it," says Martin. The staff appears to feel that informal contacts in the executive departments make them less reliant on official government spokesmen. Fullerton says he is on the lookout for the "tendency of people at the top of the departments and agencies to proselytize. Keeping the department [HEW] honest I view as one of my main functions. And they know it." To balance HEW's presentations, Fullerton has developed his own contacts in the department to get behind the official veneer, to assure that department spokesmen don't "overrun the committee" by dazzling its members with information they cannot challenge.

One way to outflank and doublecheck the departments is to get as much information as possible from nonexecutive sources. The Library of Congress is one alternative, but at least one committee member, Joseph Karth, feels that relying on this source indicates a critical staff shortage. "It's crazy as hell," he says, "when committee members have to go to the Library of Congress to get information on committee matters."

The inevitable lobbying groups crowding the door of Ways and Means are another source of information. Fullerton says lobbyists talk to him "all the time," and Charles Hawkins says he "sees a good many people during the year." Lamar sees about "two people a day from an embassy, trade association, or a company."

In their dealings with the staff, lobbyists do not rely on constituent leverage as they often do with committee members, so their role is more purely "informational." Lobbyist Jack Beidler of the United Auto Workers said he goes to the staff not to convey his "broad concept, because they will follow the chairman. I inform them what we are after and hope for some input."

Some committee staffers find lobbyists valuable, others do not. Minority counsel Richard Wilbur feels they can be a "useful information source. They have a perspective and you have to analyze what they say." But, he adds, "they know the problems and have the facts. It cuts down on the amount of time, like stipulations at a trial on which all agree—downtown and industry."

Hawkins is more skeptical about lobbyists. "Testimony is usually what you'd expect," he says. "If it's not, if it's surprising, it makes you question how good your sources are." And in Fullerton's view, lobbyists "are not all that good. Lots of them are stupid, lazy, and do a bad job." He says he tries to keep lobbyists honest in their relations with the staff: "Lobbyists come in here and we tell them we told so-and-so you lied to them and not to try to do it again." Fullerton told how the staff once prepared a report to get data to the members before the public hearings "so the lobbyists couldn't lie much." But, he says, "the witnesses used it as a resource book in preparing their speeches," and as a result their testimony was even less informative than usual.

Since lobbyists are sometimes uninformative, frequently inaccurate, and always biased, staff reliance on them has obvious drawbacks. And contacts with people in the executive branch, even "informal" ones, are slanted as well. Significantly lacking in the staff's summary of its research activities was any major effort to solicit information from experts outside these two spheres or from representatives of the general public.

A logical way to supplement inadequate committee staff resources, and to keep individual members better informed and more active, would be for a member's personal staff to participate more in committee matters. But personal staff members are excluded from executive sessions of Ways and Means as rigorously as from Senate Finance. Committee Republican John Duncan says that when Beidler of the UAW points out the effect of this exclusion on the committee:

> If you were a member and wanted to offer a substitute proposal or major amendment, you would have to go through a long process of being thoroughly educated because you couldn't take an expert to the meetings. . . Those who disagree with the chairman are at a big disadvantage. The departmental and staff experts throw facts and arguments on the table. You need your own experts to be equal. One can't expect members to be expert. I've worked on welfare matters for four years, but I wouldn't be able to debate with experts.

Various excuses for excluding the staff have been offered. A common one is that the room the committee uses (in the Capitol next to the House chamber) is too small, but a hearing room in the Longworth House Office Building, where the committee also frequently meets, is enormous. Another reason, offered by committee member Fulton (D., Tenn.), is that the closed executive session "wouldn't be much of an executive session" with so many people present. Fulton undercut that reasoning, however, by adding, "There's no such thing as an executive session anyway. All too often what we agree to in the morning is in the afternoon papers." This means simply that personal aides have a chance, along with everyone else, to learn from the newspapers what the committee has just decided. But what the committee has decided might have been vastly different if some alert personal aides had been assigned to study alternatives or amendments and then been allowed to work with individual members in presenting them at executive sessions.

Chief counsel Martin cautions that allowing personal staff into executive sessions might let members rely too much on them: it would create an excuse for members not to attend the sessions and could lead to increased proxy voting. On the other hand, members who are better informed might be more anxious to attend executive sessions, since they would have greater confidence and increased incentive for offering suggestions and voting independently. The committee could always forbid personal staff members to attend without their bosses, to insure that proxy voting would not occur. In any case, it is unrealistic to expect any member to be an expert on all the matters before the committee. The present staff, no matter how conscientious or well managed, cannot prepare workable alternative proposals for each member.

The Hearings: Who Hears What?

One of the best methods for Ways and Means members to keep informed of the issues before their committee is to attend committee hearings. But very, very few committee members even bother to make this nominal gesture. Thomas Stanton and Robert Brandon of the Public Citizens' Tax Reform Research Group told the two committee members present on March 9, 1973, that absenteeism at the committee's expert panel discussions the previous month had averaged 52.8 percent. Some members had missed more than three-fourths of the sessions and a majority of the committee had attended less than half the hearings. (See Table 7.)

The sessions that so many members had missed were not routine ones. On the contrary, they had been what Stanton and Brandon called a "rare opportunity for members to have their questions answered by nationally recognized experts" whom the committee had invited "to highlight important tax issues." The low attendance was symptomatic of either lack of concern or too great a work load, or both.

Representative Burke was defensive about committee absentee-

TABLE 7.

Members Missing More than Half the Sessions	% Time Absent from Expert Panel Discussions, February 1973
Rostenkowski	80.4
Fulton	78.3
Green	77.1
Carey	73.4
Burleson	67.0
Chamberlain	66.0
Waggonner	60.5
Broyhill	60.1
Conable	59.7
Collier	56.5
Landrum	56.1
Griffiths	55.1
Ullman	54.7
Pettis	53.4

SOURCE: Thomas Stanton and Robert Brandon, Testimony before Committee on Ways and Means (March 9, 1973).

ism. "You would have to be a centipede with a hundred legs to cover all the ground that you are supposed to cover," he said in his lengthy answer to Stanton and Brandon.[1] But Burke did not explain why the panel discussions with tax experts had been so poorly attended. He was more concerned with explaining the poor attendance—only 8 percent of the committee—at the hearings he was now conducting. He noted that the newly created Joint Study Committee on Budget Control* had been holding hearings "all this week while the hearings of the Ways and Means Committee are going on."[2] But this would have accounted for the absence of only Representatives Burke, Ullman, Griffiths, Rostenkowski, and Broyhill. (Collier, also on this joint committee, was in the hospital, according to Burke.) Burke pointed out that Mills, Ullman, Schneebeli, Collier, and himself were on the Joint Committee on Internal Revenue Taxation, but he did not mention that the JCIRT was less a committee than a mechanism for hiring and directing a staff. A third duty that competed with

* Created by Public Law 92-599, October 27, 1972.

committee hearings for the members' time, he said, was floor
activity. Burke added that he was proud of his own floor attendance record and that he had been present for 99.7 percent of the
roll-call votes on the floor in his fifteen-year House career. This
information did not explain the committee's generally poor
attendance and more particularly the record of those on Stanton's
and Brandon's list.

The most interesting reason Burke gave for the low attendance
at hearings was pressure from constituents and special interest
groups:

> . . . during the past week . . . I must have had twenty
> different groups—veterans of foreign wars, savings bank
> groups, insurance groups, groups from some of the various
> organizations up there, coming in calling for us, and I
> would have to leave this Committee and go outside and
> meet them in the back room here.[3]

The implication here is that a personal meeting with a lobbyist
"in the back room" has a higher priority than a hearing, in which
witnesses are trying to influence legislation through public chan-
nels. One lobbyist who has been involved with the Ways and
Means Committee claims that "the staff of that committee is
almost every effective lobbying group in Washington, D. C." An
attentive ear to interests such as Burke mentions, especially organizations from "up there" (the home district, presumably) may
help the members acquire politically useful information, but
when hearings are missed, their official information gathering
function is obstructed.

A decisive factor in whether hearings are well attended is the
members' own sense of priorities. It is unfortunate that so many
members assigned a low priority to hearing the Public Citizens'
Tax Reform Research Group's testimony. Such public interest
groups are vastly underrepresented at the committee's hearings
compared with special interest groups. The committee's opportunity to get a representative sampling of information and
opinion is reduced by not hearing such arguments.

Chief counsel Martin, who arranges the hearings, states: "We have always taken the public hearing function to be very important. . . . In the great majority of cases . . . you get a diversity of opinion." Despite Martin's claims, witnesses who represent business and organizations with particular interests in pending legislation far outnumber those who speak for the general public. Hearings in the tax and trade areas of Ways and Means jurisdiction provide good examples. On September 8, 1971, the committee began seven days of hearings* on tax proposals contained in the President's New Economic Policy. Among the matters of great concern to business covered by the hearings were the ADR (Asset Depreciation Range) and DISC tax subsidies. Sixty-two percent of the witnesses were from the business bloc.† This is almost five times the percentage represented by private citizens and citizen groups such as the Tax Reform Research Group or Taxation with Representation. It outweighs by more than three to two the other four categories combined. (See Table 8 for a breakdown by category of the seventy-one witnesses.)

Witnesses differ greatly in the amount of information they present to the committee. The executive branch witnesses who normally appear on the first and last day of hearings on major bills submit voluminous written testimony for the record. Testimony from many special interest witnesses is also filled with impressive charts and statistics. (See Table 9 for a typical breakdown of 4,584 pages of oral and written testimony from over three hundred witnesses on tariff and trade proposals in 1970.) The "business bloc," in the Table 9 example, includes the large number of witnesses representing import concerns, which are listed separately to highlight their identity as a specific pressure

* This was quite a short period for airing the proposals since the resulting bill—the 1971 Revenue Act—provided about $7.8 billion in annual tax subsidies to business.[4]

† This figure is derived by adding category one in Table 8 (which includes both representatives of particular areas of business, such as steel and real estate, and those appearing for a particular company), and category three (organizations that represent general business interests, such as chambers of commerce and the National Federation of Independent Business).

group in trade matters. Categories one, two, and five add up to 71 percent. These business interests produced almost five times as much testimony as the twenty-three executive branch witnesses, and more than six times as much as private citizens, citizen groups, and labor unions combined. The information obtained from citizens and citizen groups alone was almost negligible.

The low representation of citizen groups at Ways and Means hearings and the small amount of testimony they contribute are partly explained by the relatively small number of such groups operating at the national level. But the congressional hearings system, as practiced, also militates against the effective participation of groups that are not lobbies or do not have resources to lobby effectively. At hearings on tax reform, in March 1973, Father William L. Matheus of St. Louis spelled out the disadvantages that ordinary citizens face in Congress when he protested the treatment that he and a group of St. Louis citizens were given by Ways and Means:

TABLE 8.
Witnesses Appearing at Ways and Means
Hearings on Tax Proposals in the President's
New Economic Policy, September 8, 9, 13–17, 1971

Category	Percentage of Total Number of Witnesses (71)
1. Industry Representatives	47.9
2. Elected Public Officials	15.5
3. Business Community Representatives	14.1
4. Private Citizens, Citizen Groups*	12.7
5. Executive Department Officials	8.4
a. Treasury (3 witnesses)	
b. Office of Management and Budget (3 witnesses)	
6. Labor Unions	1.4

* This category includes an occasional expert, such as economist Dr. Norman Ture, appearing on his own behalf.
SOURCE: Congressional Information Service, *Abstracts of Congressional Publications and Legislative Histories*, Annual ed., 1971, pp. 320–22.

TABLE 9.
Testimony of Witnesses Before Ways and Means Committee
Hearings on Tariff and Trade Proposals, May 11–June 25, 1970

Category	Approximate Percentage of Total Testimony (4,584 pages—23 days)
1. Industry Representatives	38
2. Importers	28
3. Executive Department Officials	15
a. Agriculture (1 witness)	
b. Commerce (7 witnesses)	
c. Labor (3 witnesses)	
d. State (2 witnesses)	
e. Treasury (6 witnesses)	
f. Office of the Special Representative for Trade Negotiations (4 witnesses)	
4. Labor Unions	10
5. Business Community Representatives	5
6. Elected Public Officials	3
7. Private Citizens, Citizen Groups	1

SOURCE: Hearings on Tariff and Trade Proposals Before the Committee on Ways and Means, 1970.

Mr. Chairman and members of the committee, let me clarify beforehand that I am testifying under protest in the manner in which six taxpaying citizens of St. Louis were treated after making their request to appear before the Ways and Means Committee. Miss Lucille Adams and Mrs. Mary Ann Fiske are members of the St. Louis Tax Reform Group, Mrs. Delta Eaton represents the Southside Welfare Rights Organization, Mr. Richard Teitelman is a young St. Louis law student representing himself and I represent myself. *At first we were all lumped together as a group with one spokesman to read a ten-minute statement.* After many contacts with our area representatives and senators, many phone calls, much postage expense, many letters back and forth from Washington and St. Louis, four of us came to Washington in a car pool traveling almost one thousand miles to participate in the hearings. Some had to take off of work; one individual, Mrs. Barbara Bates, was unable to get off of work at the last minute and of course could not come. *It was not until the middle of Mr. [George] Meany's testimony this morning that we were informed of the amount of time each of us would be given to testify.* This hampered us in preparing copies of our statements for the press and for the committee; therefore we had none to distribute this morning. We went from one ten-minute statement representing all five of us to two ten-minute statements plus two five-minute statements. *We feel such an experience as ours, whether deliberate or not, discourages participation in these hearings by the ordinary taxpayer* as well as talented local groups whose research and ideas I believe would contribute significant input as the Ways and Means Committee goes about implementing tax reform legislation. [Emphasis added.][5]

Is it possible that the committee was not sincerely interested in what these citizens had to offer? Only through great persistence were they even able to speak as individuals instead of a "lumped together" group.

Chief counsel Martin had not encouraged these citizens to appear before the committee at all. In a February 23 letter to what he called the "St. Louis Tax Reform Group" (sent to each of the six, not all of them members of the St. Louis Tax Reform Group), Martin suggested:

If you so desire . . . we can simply include your statement in the record of the hearings, which would make it unnecessary for you to go to the expense of coming to Washington to appear in person. In such case, you may be assured that your full statement will be printed in the text of the hearings and will be made available to the Members of the Committee as it proceeds to develop a bill on the subject of tax reform.[6]

Martin's promise that the statement of these citizens' statements "will be printed in the text of the hearings" is not very reassuring. Members may not listen too carefully to much of the oral testimony, but there is no guarantee they will even be *aware* of what is only printed in the record. And the text of a hearing may come out months after the proceedings, as committee member Sam Gibbons stressed during the 1971 New Economic Policy hearings:

> MR. GIBBONS. First of all, let me say how much I appreciate the material you have sent me in the past to read. I have found it very informative and very stimulating as far as my thinking is concerned. I hope you will continue to send me that.
>
> MR. THOMAS FIELD of Taxation with Representation. Thank you, Mr. Gibbons. We will.
>
> MR. GIBBONS. I am glad you are going to put these* in the record, because I think they will help us to understand our problem. Will you send a copy to my office? It will be months before we get this record. I want to read it before it gets in the record.[7]

By the time the record of hearings is published, it may be too late for statements to have any kind of meaningful effect on the members. The 1971 Revenue Act, for example, was formulated, drafted, reported by the committee, and passed by the House all within three weeks after the last day of hearings.

In all, these hearings are not an effective informational device, as they are now carried out. Several members of the committee and its staff disagree with the contention that "the public hearing function is very important." One staff member says that much of the testimony is not very informative. It "is written for the people who pay the lobbyist's salary." As Representative Corman sees it, "Hearings are mostly for publicity. You learn something if you listen long enough, but. . . ." A lobbyist spoke more bluntly: "Hearings in general are a charade and even more so before that committee."

Committee member Vanik refuses to waste his time at hearings when statements are being read verbatim. He says members

---

* Field presented a compendium of eighteen essays on the administration's tax proposals; all were written by tax experts, most of them university professors.

should be given a chance to read the statements before the hearings so witnesses need only summarize their testimony and then have time to field questions from well-prepared committee members. (The Joint Economic Committee operates this way, with a five-minute limit on the summary.) This, of course, points up the most obvious advantage of a personal appearance over a written statement: a question-and-answer session permits committee members to pursue specific points raised by the witness. But if the members are not familiar with a witness' testimony until it is read, they must, as Vanik said, do "instant thinking" at the hearings. On complex tax issues, in-depth, instant questioning is a formidable task. As an information-gathering mechanism, the hearing becomes a "charade" if committee members are not able to probe deeper into the points raised and clarify ambiguities in a witness' testimony than if they were alone in their offices with the written statement. Through discussions with witnesses, the alert committee member can not only get more information available from them, but can determine to some extent the degree of their conviction and their motives of self-interest.

Jealously Guarded Information

Real committee business takes place not in public hearings but in executive (i.e., secret) sessions. In 1972, 63 percent of Ways and Means meetings (including hearings) were held in secret.* The average for the twenty-three standing committees that year was 44 percent.[9] Traditionally, these crucial sessions of intense debate and compromise have been closed to all except staff and *executive branch* officials, unless they are specifically opened by committee vote. The committee's self-defined right to work unfettered by public scrutiny has been largely taken for granted by the members. On March 7, 1973, however, the House approved, by an overwhelming 370 to 27 vote, House Resolution 259, providing

* In 1970 and 1971 the percentage of closed meetings was about 50 percent higher for Ways and Means than for the average House committee.[8]

> that each meeting for the transaction of business, including the mark-up of legislation, of each standing committee or subcommittee thereof shall be open to the public except when the committee or subcommittee in open session with a quorum present, determines by rollcall vote that all or part of the remainder of the meeting shall be closed to the public.[10] *

Not surprisingly, the issue brought some Ways and Means members into the floor debate. As indicated by the vote, most of the committee members finally supported the resolution—only Burleson and Waggoner voted against it. But for many Ways and Means members there was a problem with the resolution's original stipulation that only "members of the committee and such congressional staff as they shall authorize" could attend meetings that the committee decided to close. Ways and Means relies heavily on administration experts in its executive sessions, and was not about to relinquish this relationship without a fight.

Representative Martha Griffiths revealed the extent to which the committee relies on the Treasury Department when she replied to a contention of Bob Eckhardt (D., Tex.) that committees could function effectively by recessing their executive drafting sessions just long enough to get administration advice, then returning to a fully closed session. The idea was "ridiculous," Representative Griffiths said:

> We spent three weeks in the committee on Ways and Means going over the revenue-sharing formulas. One formula after another was suggested and one time after another the Treasury Department operated its computers. Do you mean to tell me you are sitting here suggesting that we hold a session in which for five minutes it is executive and then the next ten minutes it is open, and then we want to ask another question? How are we going to do that?[11]

---

* The approved (amended) version of the resolution stated that the vote to close a meeting need not take place on the day of the meeting. But the vote has to refer to a specific day: a single vote cannot close a whole series of meetings on the same topic.

Eckhardt offered no real solution to the problem of running a closed markup session if executive department advice was in fact needed every few minutes. But he implied in his answer to Griffiths that Ways and Means relied too much on the executive when drafting bills:

> Every one of our committees, in particular the committee on which the able gentlewoman from Michigan (Mrs. GRIFFITHS) sits, is highly versed in the matters that they are working with. And surely after advice by the experts, in the presence of their staff who may remain after the experts leave, they would not be hampered but actually be aided by being permitted to deal with this matter without the experts and executives looking over their shoulders, I would think.[12]

Martha Griffiths, however, had less confidence in the capacity of her committee and its staff to do without the Treasury Department. Excluding the department, she said, would require erecting "another building as large as the Rayburn Building to house the [Ways and Means] staff."[13] Another Ways and Means member, Phil Landrum (D., Ga.), also objected to forcing the committee to have either totally open or totally closed meetings:

> You close a meeting to the public and then decide during the mark-up of a section of the social security bill that we need the expertise and the information that an actuary from the Social Security Administration can give us, and we bring him in; under this proviso in [H. Res. 259] there is no way to get by except to open it up to the public. And I would say to my distinguished friend, the gentleman from Texas [Eckhardt], that we should not have another social security bill in the next forty years on that committee.[14]

An amendment offered by Samuel Stratton (D., N.Y.) provided a remedy for this situation. Closed meetings could, by this amendment, include not only staff but "such departmental representatives" as the committee might authorize.[15] The amendment passed by a mere three votes—201 to 198. Four-fifths of the voting members of Ways and Means approved it.* Only Gibbons, Green, Karth, and Vanik voted to preserve the stricter definition of a closed meeting.[16] The defection of just two of the sixteen committee members who voted for the amendment would have meant the loss of this escape clause and a move toward redressing the imbalance of power between the executive and Congress.

Open Session: "Keeping Up the Calories"

Implicit in Griffiths' and Landrum's remarks on H. Res. 259 is the expectation that Ways and Means would continue to close its meetings. The "prevailing sentiment in the House"—which had earlier moved the Appropriations Committee to adopt open sessions on its own, according to Chairman George Mahon (D., Tex.)[17]—may have been one of reform, but the language of the resolution left the procedure for individual meetings up to committee discretion as before.

And most Ways and Means members still favor closed sessions. "You'd live to regret the day you shackled the process by having it open," warned banking Republican John Byrnes near the end of his congressional career in 1972. He favored the informal manner in which the committee made decisions. Opening the meetings, he feared, would destroy this process by inhibiting the members. Conable said that a lack of privacy in sessions where bills are discussed would impede reform. In 1969, for example, he was planning reforms in ways of taxing charitable contributions. His plans were not kept secret, and special interests pressured him to retract them. He said later that if he had known that there would be so much controversy "I might not have started at all." Perhaps Conable would have fared better with *more* publicity instead of less. If his plans were truly reformist and truly in the public interest, wider public knowledge of them might have helped him politically, even if some special interest lobbyists had been antagonized. But this story indicates that the

---

* Chairman Mills, along with Broyhill, Collier, Corman, and Rostenkowski, failed to vote on either the amendment or the resolution.

members' fear of controversy *can* inhibit attempts at reform until additional openness helps develop a constituency for broader reform.

Carey stopped short of advocating open sessions but admitted that the present restrictive policy diminished representation of the public interest in committee meetings. He thought the committee should do more to keep the outside world posted on committee activities, to keep bills from "losing calories": constant scrutiny by the public of Ways and Means bills as they were being prepared might prevent strong reforms from being emasculated through political compromise.

Some members of the committee, such as Vanik, Corman, and Gibbons, favored open meetings and might be expected to regularly vote against closing them. Corman said he resented having to leak information that should be made public. And during House debate on the issue Gibbons admitted:

> In my four years of experience I believe I would feel much better had the evidence which we took in markup sessions, with the doors closed, and the large amounts of staff that attend from the executive branch . . . had the public also had access to the knowledge that was given to me. . . . I think the public ought to know what the administration is advising us.[18]

But a majority of the Ways and Means Committee does not agree that the committee should be liberal with its powerful fund of information or that it should allow the public to scrutinize its innermost workings. And the spirit of reform expressed on the House floor in March 1973 cannot be realized in Ways and Means without the consent of its members.

In June 1973, in the first two tests of policy under the new rules, the committee voted 25-0 and 15-10 to keep legislative drafting sessions secret. While the Ways and Means Committee did, on a percentage basis, close less than half as many meetings in 1973 as in 1972, it still held three times more secret meetings than the average for all House committees. In fact, Ways and

Means held more closed sessions than all but two of the other twenty-three House committees.

At least the House resolution is an omen of reform—and of democracy—requiring the members to vote publicly on whether or not to keep a meeting open. Those opposing open meetings will be accountable not only to the rest of the House but also, ultimately, to their constituents.

FOLLOWING THE LEADER: VOTING ON WAYS AND MEANS

> *[Mills will] compromise, bargain, cajole, swap, bend, plead, amend, coax, and unite until as much of the controversy as possible is drained from the bill, and as many members of the committee as possible support it.*
> —*Stephen A. Merrill, in* Citizens Look at Congress, *p. 170*

A distinctive feature of the Ways and Means Committee is that its members (except for a few dissenters) vote alike and stand by Chairman Wilbur Mills. Mills uses several methods to make sure that he obtains a consensus. His patience with even the most long-winded committee members is almost infinite. He understands the constraints placed on members of Congress to vote in certain ways because of pressures from their constituency. He tries to avoid compromising a member with important local interests. Mills shrewdly combines these skills with a determined nonpartisanship: he will always consider introducing or supporting a bill or speaking in a member's district regardless of that member's party. At Ways and Means hearings Mills lets each member question a witness extensively, alternating between Democrats and Republicans. According to members, this fairness carries over to the executive sessions. The cordial atmosphere in the hearings, initiated by Mills, gives the chairman the latitude to compromise and create a consensus, especially with the Republican members of the committee.

During the Ninety-second Congress, Mills had such influence, especially with the Republican committee members, that the committee voted unanimously with him on 48 percent of the recorded votes. But he was able to recruit the support of the Republican members much more often than that of the Democrats. (See Table 10.) Fifty-four percent of the Democratic membership voted against him on at least 59 percent of the recorded votes, while 90 percent of the Republican members sided with him on at least 63 percent of the votes.

Several members relate the "consensus-building" on Ways and Means to the expertise and persuasiveness of Mills and the former senior Republican on the committee, John W. Byrnes. Their influence was so extensive that committee members who were not anxious to participate in making decisions often relied on them and did "not . . . study as hard" as they might have on other committees. Landrum praised Mills and Byrnes for their "very, very alert minds." He described Byrnes as "studious" on the essence of bills, while Mills "remembers all the commas and why they were put there. When either talks, a member listens and says to himself, 'that must be it,' unless he knows something else." So when Mills and Byrnes agreed on an issue their combined influence was overwhelming.

According to both the members and the recorded votes, Mills and Byrnes agreed quite often. They sat together at hearings and in executive sessions in what Vanik terms an "incestuous relationship." They would chat at the head of the committee table and reach an agreement that pleased both. Byrnes said that Mills "often" offered the compromise, but "sometimes he and I visit there at the desk and come to agreement. Then he throws it out [for discussion] and I support it." Recorded votes in Ways and Means executive sessions reveal absentee rates that may be indicative of attendance at all the committee's sessions. Although many members were not present when recorded votes were taken, those absent almost always voted by proxy.* Republicans had a greater

* If a House committee agrees to use proxy votes, under the Legislative Reorganization Act of 1970 they must be authorized in writing and be limited to a specific amendment, measure, matter, or motion.

TABLE 10.
Voting of Ways and Means Members:
Conformity with Chairman*
Number Times Voting with Mills

Social Security (14 votes)	Tax (8 votes)	Revenue Sharing (5 votes)	Total (27 votes)
(D) Griffiths 13	(D) Ullman 8	(R) Betts 5	(D) Griffiths 22
(D) Gibbons 10	(R) Byrnes 7	(R) Brotzman 5	(D) Rostenkowski 21
(D) Watts† 10	(R) Conable 7	(D) Burke 5	(D) Ullman 21
(R) Betts 9	(D) Rostenkowski 7	(D) Carey 5	(R) Betts 20
(R) Brotzman 9	(R) Betts 6	(R) Collier 5	(D) Landrum 20
(D) Burke 9	(R) Broyhill 6	(R) Conable 5	(R) Brotzman 19
(D) Carey 9	(D) Burleson 6	(D) Green 5	(D) Carey 19
(R) Chamberlain 9	(R) Duncan 6	(D) Griffiths 5	(R) Conable 19
(D) Corman 9	(D) Landrum 6	(D) Landrum 5	(D) Green 19
(D) Fulton 9	(R) Pettis 6	(R) Pettis 5	(R) Chamberlain 18
(D) Green 9	(R) Schneebeli 6	(D) Rostenkowski 5	(R) Byrnes 17
(D) Landrum 9	(D) Watts 6	(D) Ullman 5	(R) Collier 17
(D) Rostenkowski 9	(R) Brotzman 5	(R) Chamberlain 4	(R) Duncan 17
(R) Schneebeli 9	(D) Carey 5	(R) Duncan 4	(R) Pettis 17
(R) Byrnes 8	(R) Chamberlain 5	(D) Karth‡ 4	(R) Schneebeli 17
(D) Ullman 8	(R) Collier 5	(D) Fulton 3	(D) Burke 16
(D) Vanik 8	(D) Green 5	(R) Broyhill 2	(D) Fulton 16
(D) Waggonner 8	(D) Waggonner 5	(R) Burleson 2	(D) Gibbons 16
(R) Collier 7	(D) Fulton 4	(R) Byrnes 2	(R) Broyhill 14
(R) Conable 7	(D) Gibbons 4	(D) Corman 2	(D) Corman 14
(R) Duncan 7	(D) Griffiths 4	(D) Gibbons 2	(D) Waggonner 14
(R) Broyhill 6	(D) Corman 4	(D) Schneebeli 2	(D) Burleson 13
(R) Pettis 6	(D) Vanik 3	(D) Vanik 2	(D) Vanik 13
(D) Burleson 5	(D) Burke 2	(D) Waggonner 1	

* Based on the twenty-seven recorded committee votes in the 92nd Congress.
† Died September 24, 1971. Cast only thirteen social security and seven tax votes.
‡ Joined committee October 6, 1971.
SOURCE: Committee Reports, 92nd Congress.

percentage of proxy votes than Democrats. Only Byrnes did not vote by proxy. Betts, Conable, and Donald Brotzman (R., Col.) had the next lowest proxy percentages. John Duncan (R., Tenn.), Charles Chamberlain (R., Mich.), and Broyhill (R., Va.), used proxies for 10 to 20 percent of the votes. Herman Schneebeli, Collier, and Pettis all voted by proxy on over 25 percent of the votes.

Of the fifteen Democrats on the committee, four—Ullman, Vanik, Gibbons, and Karth—did not vote at all by proxy. William Green (D., Pa.) and the late John Watts (D., Ky.) had the highest number of proxy votes. Corman, Griffiths, and Richard Fulton (D., Tenn.) also frequently used proxies. Chairman Mills voted by proxy only twice—during his short campaign for the 1972 presidential nomination.

When the chairman adopts the ideas of other committee members and works out legislative complexities with Byrnes, Mills's name is stamped on the bills. This tactic creates an added aura of consensus (and adds to Mills's power) and also causes some resentment. Pettis' legislative aide referred to a bill for which Pettis argued extensively in committee. It would relieve spouses of tax liability on money the other spouse obtained without his or her knowledge. Mills made a few changes in the bill, adopted it as his own, and received credit for the legislation. Committee member Griffiths described the effects of Mills's tactic: "It's hard for a Ways and Means member to show what you can do because Mills gets all the credit—his name goes on the bills."

Another aspect of committee decision making is the steamroller process at the end of the markup sessions in which the final draft of a bill is written. The members are tired. They have already analyzed each section of one or two drafts of the long bill. And at markup sessions the members' own aides are not present to help with the rapid succession of important decisions that must be made.

Those who traditionally dissent from the committee's actions view the committee's processes as bargaining. Collier mentioned that on Ways and Means you have to be "responsible, and negotiate and compromise in committee, or arbitrate, to get the best you can with a majority support. If not, you would be deciding that no legislation would be better than compromise." He added that "flexibility with an eye on the goal could also be interpreted as back scratching."

The process is not always entirely in the hands of Ways and Means members. A frequent dissenter, Vanik has often gone outside the committee for support on reform amendments. His office claims that there are 140 members in the House who will support him on Ways and Means matters, and Vanik keeps them informed about what happens in committee sessions, cooperating with them as much as he can. For example, in 1971 he polled them on several tax bills before a final committtee vote, then he returned to the committee with that information. It "had an impact" on the final vote, according to an aide.

Under Mills's leadership, consensus "develops rather quickly," Pettis says, but one or two cantankerous members usually disagree with it. He cited Vanik as a frequent objector who says, "Now wait a minute—I don't buy that." Gibbons has been identified as another dissenter, but more of his votes conform to the committee majority than Vanik's and Corman's. Gibbons feels the futility of being a constant reformer: "'You can't beat on the wall all the time. If you isolate yourself, you can't raise the issues every time."

Despite these dissenters, Mills still wields extensive consensus-building power. The prestige and persuasive ability that he uses to achieve his legislative goals in committee also contribute to his success on the floor. Mills exercises excessive caution and scrupulosity in seeking high consensus votes and in reporting from committee only those measures that will pass the House. Mills has lost only two floor votes as chairman, a remarkable record. This extreme caution has retarded the committee's output, the House's opportunities to make its own decisions, and the reform of tax and welfare legislation.

MUZZLING THE HOUSE: THE CLOSED RULE

> *There is one question I must ask . . . that is why such hysterical insistence by the proponents of revenue sharing that the bill be considered under a closed rule.*
>
> *Are the provisions of the bill bad, so bad that they cannot be defended against amendments by a majority of the committee and its chairmen?*
>
> *Or is the chairman and the majority of the committee so ineffective that they cannot manage the bill under the normal procedures?*
>
> *Why are they so afraid to let the House work its will?*
>
> *—Representative John Byrnes on the House floor, June 21, 1972*

Mills uses a procedural anomaly called the closed rule to prevent Ways and Means bills from being amended on the House floor. The rule, used almost exclusively by the Ways and Means Committee, protects bills that have been drafted in the committee from unforeseen and potentially drastic changes. But barring non-committee members from amending Ways and Means bills has been attacked both by representatives wishing to change the committee's bills and by those who argue that the closed rule is inherently unfair and antidemocratic. Nevertheless, a majority of the committee—usually a large majority—stands behind Mills's requests for closed rules on committee legislation, and the House grants these requests.*

---

* This closed rule granted on June 21, 1972, for the committee's revenue-sharing bill is typical of the closed rules given the committee: "After general debate, which shall be confined to the bill and shall continue not to exceed eight hours, to be equally divided and controlled by the chairman and ranking minority member of the Committee on Ways and Means, the bill shall be considered as having been read for amendment. No amendment shall be in order to said bill except amendments offered by direction of the Committee on Ways and Means, and said amendments shall be in order, any rule of the House to the contrary notwithstanding. Amendments offered by direction of the Committee on Ways and Means may be offered to any section of the bill at the conclusion of general debate, but said

A closed rule must first be discussed in both the Ways and Means Committee and the House Committee on Rules. After Ways and Means adopts the final draft of a bill, the committee votes to report it to the floor and to seek a closed rule. If a member objects to the closed rule proposal, "it doesn't sit well with the chairman," according to Vanik's administrative assistant Mark Talisman. Vanik says that the vote is usually about 21 to 4. Gibbons and Vanik often form the core of the opposition to the closed rule, with Burke, Corman, and others occasionally joining them. On the revenue-sharing bill, for instance, the closed rule proposal passed 20 to 5 with the minority consisting of Vanik, Corman, Gibbons, Fulton, and Duncan.

After Ways and Means has approved a closed rule, Mills and the committee's ranking Republican testify at an open "hearing" before the House Rules Committee to explain the bill and justify their request. The Rules Committee then goes into executive session. The votes here are usually very close, often 8 to 7 in favor of bringing the closed rule to the floor for a final vote. A spokesman for the Rules Committee* introduces the rule on the floor, where it is debated under a one-hour time limitation that is generally strictly enforced.

Congressmen are not always willing to vote for the closed rule, since it heavily influences the fate of a bill. The debate on the closed rule is sometimes spirited; but once the rule is accepted, members count the battle against a bill virtually lost. During the 1972 revenue-sharing battle, Representative William Colmer (D., Miss.) told the House that bothering to comment on the bill

amendments shall not be subject to amendment. At the conclusion of the consideration of the bill for amendment, the Committee shall rise and report the bill to the House with such amendments as may have been adopted, and the previous question shall be considered as ordered on the bill and amendments thereto final passage without intervening motion except one motion to recommit."[19]

* Representative William Colmer, Rules Committee chairman until his retirement in January 1973, usually opposed closed rules except for tax bills, and would assign another member of his committee to offer closed rules to the House.

would be tantamount to "futility . . . since the real vote (on the closed rule) was taken yesterday. That pretty well decided the issue."[20] A floor statement by John Anderson (R., Ill.) in November 1970 is typical of House sentiment and helps explain why members not on Ways and Means generally abdicate their decision-making powers over the committee's bills:

> In Rules Committee on September 24, I voted for a closed rule on the 1970 trade bill. In doing so, I deferred to precedent, the conventional wisdom and the leadership of Chairman Mills.
>
> And there was good reason not to tamper with tradition on this matter. Since the end of World War II the United States and the Congress have compiled an enviable record of leadership and intelligent policy-making in the area of international trade. Much of the credit for this achievement, I believe, must be ascribed to our determination and the practice to deal with these sensitive and complicated issues in the calm, quiet atmosphere of committee deliberation rather than amidst the hurried bustle of this chamber.[21]

The terms "sensitive" and "complicated" that Anderson uses are often applied to tax legislation. Generally the proponents of closed rules for Ways and Means bills fear that "crippling amendments" —stemming either from special interest demands or too zealous a concern for the "public" interest—may upset the balance of a bill drawn up after careful deliberation and compromise. They argue that such amendments, even if they improve specific sections of a bill, may be damaging within the context of the entire piece of legislation.

But even on tax bills the traditional closed rule has sometimes drawn fire from House leaders. In 1969 Democratic whip Thomas O'Neill (D., Mass.) was dissatisfied with the privileged treatment granted to the Ways and Means Committee's draft of the 1969 Tax Reform Act, although he said that a closed rule was the only "practical" way for the committee to report the bill:

> The Ways and Means Committee must know and realize that it cannot continue to give the House ultimatums.

> Everything is up or down, yes or no. . . . It is unfair. The
> Ways and Means Committee is a powerful committee, but
> it should not rule the House on such important matters as
> taxation and social security.[22]

Rules Committee chairman William Colmer used a less repri-
manding tone when speaking about the 1971 Revenue Act, but he
clearly thought that closed rules were not procedurally fair:

> Some day I am very much in hope that this House will
> grow up to the point where it will assume its responsibility
> for discussing a bill of this nature, a revenue bill, under an
> open rule where all of the Members may have an oppor-
> tunity to offer amendments, and have their amendments
> considered by the House.[23]

Some House members are more direct in their criticism. Com-
menting on the closed rule on the public debt bill, February 9,
1972, Congresswoman Bella Abzug stated:

> I am generally opposed to such a rule on the ground that it
> is an insult to our intelligence as well as a violation of our
> constituents' right to have their representatives—even the
> ones not fortunate enough to be on the Ways and Means
> Committee—represent their interests in the process of for-
> mulating legislation.[24]

But a year later, near the end of the Ninety-second Congress,
O'Neill complained that Ways and Means still frequently came to
the Rules Committee to seek a special privilege on tax bills. Since
there is virtually no important piece of legislation for which Mills
does not request such a rule, less than 6 percent of the House
directly influenced the issues under Ways and Means jurisdiction,
the broadest jurisdiction of any committee in the House. (See
Table 11 for those Ways and Means bills enacted into law in the
Ninety-second Congress that passed under a closed or modified
closed rule.) This situation was exacerbated by the committee
members' high rate of absenteeism in markup sessions and their
dependence upon the executive branch's representatives at closed
committee meetings.

Bill	*Date Passed House*

Full Closed Rule†

H.R. 5432, "a bill to provide an extension of the interest equalization tax, and for other purposes." (Closed by H. Res. 277.) — March 10, 1971

H.R. 8311, "to amend the Renegotiation Act of 1951, to extend the act for for two years, modify the interest rate on excessive profits and on refunds, and to provide that the Court of Claims shall have jurisdiction of renegotiation cases." (Closed by H. Res. 466.) — June 8, 1971

H.R. 10947 (Revenue Act of 1971), "to provide a job development investment credit, to reduce individual income taxes, to reduce certain excise taxes, and for other purposes." (Closed by H. Res. 629.) — October 6, 1971

H.R. 12910, "to provide a temporary increase in the public debt limit." (Closed by H. Res. 809.) — February 9, 1972

H.R. 14370 (Revenue Sharing), "to provide payments to localities for high-priority expenditures, to encourage the States to supplement their revenue sources, and to authorize Federal collection of State individual income taxes." (Closed by H. Res. 996.) — June 22, 1972

H.R. 15390, "to provide for a four-month extension of the present temporary level in the public debt limitation." (Closed by H. Res. 1021.) — June 27, 1972

H.R. 15587, "to provide for a six-month extension of the emergency unemployment compensation program." (Closed by H. Res. 1028.) — June 28, 1972

Modified Closed Rule‡

H.R. 1 (The Social Security Amendments of 1971), modified rule would prohibit floor amendments except striking of Title IV, "Establishment of Opportunity for Families Program and Family Assistance Plan." Motion to strike Title IV defeated. — June 22, 1971

H.R. 4690, "to increase the public debt limit set forth in Sec. 21 of Second Liberty Bond Act, and for other purposes." Modified rule allowed floor amendment only for the purpose of striking Sec-

TABLE 11.

Bill	Date Passed House
tion 3. Amendment striking Section 3 rejected. H.R. 16810, "to provide for a temporary increase in the public debt limit and to place a limitation on expenditures and net lending for the fiscal year ending June 30, 1973. (By H. Res. 1149, "No amendment shall be in order to said bill except (1) amendments offered by direction of the Committee on Ways and Means to title I of the bill; (2) an amendment containing the text or a portion of the text of H. Cong. Res. 713 if offered as an amendment in the nature of a substitute to title II of the bill H.R. 16810; and (3) an amendment proposing to strike out title III of the bill.")	March 3, 1971 October 10, 1972

* This list includes all Ways and Means bills enacted into law in the 92nd Congress for which the closed rule resolution was *specifically noted in record*.

† A full closed rule prohibits any additions or deletions from the House floor.

‡ A modified closed rule permits only deletions from a bill. It strictly forbids any additions or other changes.

SOURCES: *Legislative Calendar* (final edition), Committee on Ways and Means, October 18, 1972; *Congressional Record*.

Skeletons and Christmas Trees

MR. MATSUNAGA [D., Hawaii]: The objection, then, that we may end up with a Christmas tree is not applicable to the rule that the gentleman offers in view of the fact that the gentleman's proposal would only permit the striking out of certain items; is that correct?

MR. GIBBONS: Yes, sir. There would be no Christmas tree. There might be a skeleton but no Christmas tree.[25]

This exchange during the floor fight over the 1970 trade bill illustrates the inherent problems of trying to find a way between the repression of the closed rule and the potential chaos of an open one. The issue was whether the House, denied the power to make a "Christmas tree" out of the bill by adorning it with amendments, should be able to reduce it to a "skeleton" by voting to delete provisions according to a modified closed rule.

Representative Gibbons proposed to amend the closed rule that Colmer's committee had passed by an 8 to 7 vote. Defending his amendment, Gibbons said:

> Mr. Speaker, the proposal I make is a very simple one: that is, after the bill is read, amendment to strike provisions of the bill would be in order. . . . It does not open up this bill so that other new material, new items can be added to it, but only motions to strike will be in order.[26]

Gibbons reassured his colleagues that there was a precedent for his proposal—the Rules Committee's modified rule for a trade bill in 1953. And John Anderson (who, as earlier noted, had "deferred to precedent" by supporting a closed rule in committee) favored the Gibbons proposal since it allowed the House to "improve and pare down this bill" and to "trim down the many ill-advised and dangerous portions."[27]

Among those who protested against allowing the House to "pare down" the bill was Representative Louis Wyman (R., N.H.):

> If we start the process suggested by the gentleman from Florida [Gibbons] of allowing deletions from the bill one by one, it is bound to mean the loss of the bill itself.
>
> Those gentlemen who are familiar with our parliamentary procedures know that there are not enough votes on separate amendments to take care of shoes alone; not enough votes to take care of textiles alone; but if we all stand together across industry lines to protect the jobs of the American working men and women, we can pass this legislation and it ought to be passed by this House.[28]

Wyman's reasoning was obviously based on his personal feeling that the bill was a good one. The argument was essentially anti-democratic; he was telling his colleagues that they had no right to oppose specific provisions simply because they had different ideas on how to treat "shoes" or "textiles."

And Burke, who desperately wanted to protect the textile and shoe industries of his district,* also spoke against allowing deletions according to Gibbons' amendment. Like fellow Bay Staters Silvio Conte and Margaret Heckler, both Republicans, Burke opposed the bill's price-inflating oil import quota provision. But he told his House colleagues that the Senate could delete that provision.[29] His argument, like Wyman's, was based on politics, not principle: Burke was against opening the rules so the House could delete provisions that he favored, but he urged the House to defer to the Senate for the one amendment that he wanted deleted.

Other members contended that Gibbons' amendment was *too* restrictive, since members could not extend the bill's protections to other industries. Representative Pucinski of Illinois told the House:

> We know that by April 1 of 1971, there is not going to be a single color television set made in America any place.†
> I represent a district that has a large electronics industry— at least, had it, but is not going to have it after April 1. There is nothing in the amendment offered by the gentleman that would give this Member an opportunity to improve this bill to bring some relief to that particular industry.‡

Gibbons' amendment was, of course, designed to restrain just this impulse to "improve" the bill by augmenting it.

In the end, the fate of Gibbons' modified rule was determined largely by the House's desire to keep the bill from being scuttled by procedure. H. R. Gross (R., Iowa) said the trade bill would be "bad legislation" even if amendments were allowed; he hoped that the leadership (presumably Mills) would "carry out the threat that has been expressed here on every hand that if the Gibbons amend-

---

* The eleventh district of Massachusetts, which was hard hit by unemployment.
† Because of foreign competition, according to Pucinski's theory, the electronics industry would have to cut back.
‡ Curiously enough, Pucinski voted for the closed rule after Gibbons's modified rule had been rejected.

ment is adopted that the bill will be junked for the rest of this session."[30] In other words, Gibbons' move to reform the conventional procedure was in danger of backfiring, since deviating from the Rules Committee's norm might mean no bill at all. Gross was supporting Gibbons' proposal not because he wanted a chance to offer or vote on amendments, but because a liberalized rule could completely scuttle the bill.

Absent from the debate until now was Wilbur Mills, who spoke only after Representative Alton Lennon (D., N.C.) requested a clarification of the Ways and Means Committee's intentions. Mills's announcement that the bill would be withdrawn if given anything but a closed rule was phrased not as a threat but as a humble statement of his committee's wishes:

> I have specific instructions from a majority of the Ways and Means Committee—the vote was seventeen to seven with one member voting "present" to order the bill reported, and even a greater majority with reference to the rule—to bring this bill to the floor of the House under a closed rule. The committee by votes specifically rejected the proposals by the gentleman from Ohio [Vanik] and the gentleman from California [Corman] who wanted a different type of rule. If a closed rule is not agreed to, I could not bring the bill to the floor of the House until I go back to the committee and get further instructions from the committee. And certainly, that would not occur today.[31]

Despite his self-effacing manner and conciliatory tone, Mills was putting psychological pressure on the House. Procedurally, the House could have kept the bill alive under Gibbons' modified rule and perhaps ended up with a very different product from what had come out of Ways and Means. But Mills's warning that the bill could not be returned to committee for new "instructions" and come back to the floor "today" (meaning not that year or even in the Congress) was effective. The modified rule was rejected 192 to 201 and the closed rule passed 203 to 187.[32] Mills immediately initiated debate on the bill; it was passed the next day, November 19, by a 215 to 165 vote.[33] *

Another modified rule—this one for the 1972 revenue-sharing bill—failed without even coming to a House vote, mostly because of Mills's prestige with the House Rules Committee. H. Allen Smith (R., Calif.), a member of the Rules Committee, questioned Ways and Means jurisdiction over sections of the revenue-sharing bill that didn't deal with raising revenue, so he devised a substitute to the closed rule that would allow amendments to the first 143 sections of the bill while insuring that its provisions relating to the Internal Revenue Code would remain intact. But as he explained to the House on June 21:

> The Rules Committee adopted House Resolution 996 [a closed rule] by a vote of eight to seven. Thus, they did not have the opportunity to vote on my original motion [the modified rule] which I intend to present, if recognized, and if the previous question [on H. Res. 996] is voted down.[34]

But by not pushing harder for his substitute resolution, Smith had missed his chance to have the House consider a more accommodating rule. And his strategy of courtly deference to the wishes of Chairman Mills was no match for Mills's all-or-nothing tactics.

Among those who protested these tactics on the floor was John Byrnes himself. Byrnes had been against the bill's provisions, against vesting revenue-sharing authority in Ways and Means, and against giving the bill a closed rule. He urged the House to adopt Smith's substitute and warned that Mills would be breaking faith with his own committee by withdrawing the bill if the House defeated the closed rule:

> A majority of the committee voted . . . "to order favorably the bill and instruct the chairman to use all parliamentary means to secure its early passage."

---

* The 1970 Trade Bill eventually failed after all; it passed the Senate but could not be pushed through the conference committee before the end of the 91st Congress.

True, it subsequently voted to ask the Rules Committee for a closed rule, but that was not a condition imposed on consideration. It was only an expression of desire.[35]

So the stage was set for a parliamentary battle between Mills and his own ranking minority member if the House was bold enough to vote itself a voice in shaping the bill. But once again it would not buck the chairman. The closed rule passed by 223 to 185.[36]

More Gags in the Future?

Members of the House are continually trying to reform the House's tradition of automatically giving closed rules to bills coming from the Ways and Means Committee. In 1970, Sam Gibbons, who has called the House's amending procedure "about as sloppy as the Florida legislature," proposed modifying the closed rule to allow sections of Ways and Means bills to be voted on as separate groups. Ways and Means could designate—at the approval of the Rules Committee—how the bills would be divided. Any "log-rolling" could then be apparent in the voting record.* Gibbons thinks this is the best proposal he has made in his entire political career.

The Florida representative has proposed other ways to modify the closed rule. Amendments could be submitted three days before their floor vote so that the House could study them. Evaluating the proposed amendments and the priority that each should receive could be done by Ways and Means. (This might be the equivalent of leaving a flock of sheep to be watched over by wolves. But provision could presumably be made for the Rules Committee to have a check on Ways and Means' power to scuttle proposed amendments.)

Morris Udall (D., Ariz.) is furious with the present closed rule system:

> I represent a half-million people, and I'm forbidden to have any say in the tax code. Any drunk can stagger out of the Senate cloakroom with a two-hundred-page amendment to the Internal Revenue Code and get a roll-call vote on it.[37]

* "Log-rolling" is trading votes on the floor to promote special interests.

He proposed a modified rule that would permit amendments if each is sponsored by at least twenty House members. Udall's proposed rule should discourage amendments favoring very parochial special interests, but if it included no stipulation that sponsors be from more than one or two states, the states with small delegations would be handicapped in the amending process.

It is very unlikely that reforms of the closed rule for Ways and Means bills will come from within the committee. But a change in the rules of the Democratic Caucus at the beginning of the Ninety-third Congress may indicate a slight step toward reform, since a full closed rule can now be blocked if there is sufficient pressure for a specific amendment. As summarized on the House floor March 15, 1973, the new rule gives the House four legislative days from the time a bill is reported on the floor before a closed rule can be "sought or granted." Fifty or more representatives who submit in writing their intention to support a particular amendment can require a meeting of the party caucus to decide the merits of the amendment, and whether the Democratic members of the Rules Committee "should be instructed to make the amendment in order."[38]

This 1973 rules change incorporates Udall's notion that substantial support for amendments increases the justification for opening the rules; and it represents a new direction for the House. According to the House Democratic Caucus head, Olin Teague, the rule is binding on all Democratic House members (including, of course, a majority of the Rules Committee), and all who violate it must answer to the caucus. (Actually, absolute enforcement of the rule is possible only to the extent that the members value party solidarity.)

The new rule has produced no legislative changes so far. No conclusions can be made about how Ways and Means bills will be affected, if at all, until a bill is introduced that generates pressure for amendments. The rule undoubtedly placates some House members who have felt excluded from certain legislation. At the same time, it cannot reasonably be tagged a "sell-out" by hard-line proponents of the closed rule. But it may provide the basis for a real showdown between Ways and Means and the House.

3

How the Committees
Avoid Oversight

The committees' responsibilities extend beyond shepherding a bill through the gantlet of committee hearings, closed rules, modified closed rules, amendments, conferences, conference reports, and final floor votes. A bill that has endured this test is now subject to oversight by the committees, which are authorized to maintain continual surveillance to be sure that the bill fulfills its original purpose, that it is being properly enforced, and that neither new enforcement provisions nor stronger laws are required. It is here that the committees' failure is most evident; the overseeing done by Ways and Means and Finance is among the worst in Congress.

Most members of Ways and Means deny that the committee should take the initiative in monitoring programs. Instead, they contend that the initiative should come from constituents with complaints. Oversight for them is more of a response to maladministration than to inefficiencies or inadequacies. For example, one member of the staff works almost exclusively on constituent mail relating to social security. When the same sort of complaint occurs repeatedly, the Social Security Administration is notified.

Several committee members admit that the lack of incisive monitoring of the committee's legislation is a serious deficiency. Ranking minority member Byrnes, who opposed creating a staff bureaucracy to check on the executive, suggested that the committee could concentrate on reviewing one area in its jurisdiction each year. Carey preferred a more activist role for the committee's oversight—more field travel and personal investigations by the committee members:

> Mills is averse to travel, but we could go and see the problems of hospitals and delivery of services. We did with the Common Market. It had a profound effect on the members' interest in trade activity. We should not consider welfare again without consulting with the administrators and those who receive the assistance. And I don't mean take pictures of us in Bedford-Stuyvesant.

The Finance Committee participates as little in the oversight process as Ways and Means does. Many Finance members contend that the committee should be concerned with legislation only until it has been passed by Congress. Oversight for this committee consists mostly of hearings on proposed nominations for top agency positions or reviewing constituents' complaints.

Some of Finance's members would like to reduce their oversight responsibility even further. They contend that oversight is the job of the executive agencies themselves: departments with tasks assigned by Congress should not only administer programs but be the arbiters of how well they are being performed. Vail theorized that "systematic oversight is helped by an administrator wanting to do a good job," but he neglected to add that administrators of programs are most often the ones charged with incompetence or pandering to the interests of private business. But Vail and the committee persist in their reluctance to conduct effective oversight. As Vail said, "We don't go out on a lot of lousy witchhunts."

Abdication of oversight over IRS by the Ways and Means and Finance committees has shifted this function elsewhere. The Joint Committee on Internal Revenue Taxation, composed of senior members of the tax committees, exercises sporadic oversight, for instance in the decision to follow up Watergate Committee revelations with a staff study of the political use of IRS to harass opponents and help friends of the White House. Unfortunately, JCIRT does not hold public hearings, and the committee staff does little to displease co-chairmen Mills and Long. Thus its oversight has in some cases turned into an opportunity for Mills and Long to exert their own political influence on behalf of their friends.

For years Senator Long pressured the Treasury Department (and IRS, one of the responsible arms of Treasury) to issue depletion regulations satisfactory to the cement industry.[1]

Chairman Mills, at the behest of shoe industry lobbyist James Riddell, intervened with IRS to have IRS suspend audits of shoe corporations. Riddell gave the Mills-for-President Campaign $2,700, and lent another $17,000—he was Mills's largest single benefactor in the campaign. IRS field auditor Edward Joyce told a Senate subcommittee that the revenue loss, and corresponding shoe industry benefit, would be about $100 million.

Because of the failure of Ways and Means and Senate Finance to hold systematic hearings on the important topic of IRS taxpayer assistance and compliance programs, other congressional committees have stepped into the breach. Under the late Senator Edward Long (D., Mo.) the Subcommittee on Administrative Practice and Procedure held a long series of hearings on invasion of privacy by IRS tax officials. More recently, Senate Appropriations Subcommittee Chairman Joseph Montoya (D., N.M.) has begun what he promises will be an annual series of oversight hearings on IRS.* The Montoya subcommittee held three days of hearings early in 1973, and held open the possibility of further hearings that year.

* Montoya hearings: Senate Appropriations Subcommittee for Treasury, Postal Service, and General Government. February and March 1973. "IRS, Taxpayer Assistance and Compliance Programs. Fiscal Year 1974."

Within a few months the new IRS commissioner, Donald Alexander, announced improvements in IRS procedures of informing taxpayers of their rights when they undergo audits. The public pressure generated by open hearings had accomplished within a short time a reform which JCIRT had been unable to make in years of secret IRS oversight.

Many agencies are aware of the committees' antipathy to oversight and have grown lax without prodding from Congress. The following case study on Medicare shows what the committees do when they conduct any oversight at all.

MEDICARE—DOCTORING AN AILING PROGRAM

The Medicare bill, as signed into law by President Lyndon Johnson in June 1965, broadly outlined the health plan's policies and programs.* The actual administration of Medicare, which would ultimately determine the success or failure of the program, was left undecided. The two major proposals for its administration were that Congress would leave all administrative duties and program development to the Bureau of Health Insurance (the branch of the Health, Education and Welfare Department that was charged with implementing Medicare); that Congress itself would assume the responsibility of overseeing the program.

As the authors of the Medicare bill, Ways and Means and Finance were responsible for the oversight of the program to insure that Medicare was administered according to congressional intent. But because these committees have been reluctant to assume this

* Medicare was designed in two parts: Part A provided hospitalization insurance for all Americans eligible for social security benefits through a compulsory payroll tax on employers and employees in industries covered by the Social Security Act. Part B was a voluntary medical insurance plan financed by monthly premiums paid by participating individuals sixty-five or over, and supplemented by federal matching payments from the general treasury. Medicaid was a separate program providing hospital and physician care to the medically needy and administered by the states. (Currently, only Alaska and Arizona do not participate.)

responsibility, Medicare has suffered and taxpayers have not gotten their money's worth. Senator Ribicoff's remark about oversight was typical of the committee's attitude: "I believe once a matter is concluded you have to push it out of mind." Most senators are too concerned with the issues immediately before them to take genuine interest in oversight, so it falls to the committee staff, if anyone, to keep tabs on existing programs. When the director of the Bureau of Health Insurance, Tom Tierney, was asked why Medicare seemed to receive more attention from the Finance Committee than any other program under its jurisdiction, Tierney replied simply, "Jay Constantine." Constantine is the energetic Finance staffer in charge of watching the health care programs created by the committee's legislation, as well as keeping the members informed of national health insurance schemes that may surface in Congress. Alvin David, the gravel-voiced deputy director of BHI, said that Constantine

> is driven to achieve and produce, he's ambitious, and I think he tries harder than most to show the senators on the committee how important he is to them. Sometimes I think he tends to overcompensate for problems he finds.

Since its first year Constantine has found plenty of problems with Medicare. Although Medicare was projected to cost $3.2 billion annually, hospital and medical costs skyrocketed after the program's enactment and pushed its costs to $1 billion more than anticipated during its first year and $7.1 billion by 1970.[2] During the late 1960s and early 1970s the consumer health index was increasing at twice the rate of general price rises. By 1970 hospital daily service charges had increased 71 percent. In short, health care costs, and especially hospital costs, had accelerated every year since Medicare was enacted.

Hospital staff wages and services charges were depressed when Medicare began, but with Uncle Sam paying the bill many hospital administrators have raised wages and recovered a larger share of their operating costs. Doctors around the country took unjustified advantage of the new federal program. They saw dozens of patients on "gang visits" to hospitals and then charged the government for individual visits. The American Medical Association did little to prevent this exploitation of Medicare. Even BHI Director Tierney now admits, "I think frankly a lot of people thought of Medicare as a gold mine." Then he warned, "Don't forget the vast majority of doctors did not abuse the program."

Constantine saw another reason for accelerating costs—the poor administration of the entire program. "The beginning of the program had been a sell-out," he feels. "Everyone was getting into the act, nursing homes were being treated as hospitals. HEW even had a veterinarian on its staff passing as a doctor!"

To monitor the administration of Medicare, Constantine has a large staff. He works on his legislative ideas with two administrators in HEW's welfare office, Jim Edwards and Tom Trout, toward whom members of the Finance Committee feel a certain animosity. "I wouldn't call it a feud," says Trout, "because we don't reciprocate in kind. But everyone knows the staff and committee often refer to HEW in sarcastic and derogatory terms." Despite the formal relationships between Trout and Edwards and Constantine, the two HEW liaisonmen are usually the last to know what is going on behind closed committee doors.

Constantine maintains a special relationship with a reliable friend in the BHI, Irwin Wolkstein, deputy director of BHI in charge of program policy. Wolkstein's official biography states:

> He regularly attends executive [closed] sessions of both the Committee on Ways and Means of the House of Representatives and the Committee on Finance of the Senate when they consider changes in the Medicare program.

This privilege is usually denied other HEW officials, including Trout and Edwards. Constantine finds Wolkstein more trustworthy than the Washington HEW office and often goes to the Baltimore office of BHI to discuss staff reports and proposals in the working stage.

The year before Medicare payments were to begin, these men had to write rules, contract with insurance intermediaries to provide coverage, and launch the program in conformance with Congress' intentions. By law, the rules governing the administration of the program had to be published by HEW at least thirty days before the date Medicare would be effective, July 12, 1966. To the irritation of the Finance staff, the rules were not released until the thirtieth day, "and when we finally looked at them," Vail recalls, "we just found too many giveaways and loopholes." Constantine immediately drafted a formal memorandum for the Finance Committee on the proposed regulations' shortcomings and the committee asked the General Accounting Office to prepare an independent report.

The first part of the GAO report praised HEW's regulations as sound and fair, but the second part—a more detailed analysis— seemed to condemn them. Vail told us that GAO admittedly refrained from criticizing the Medicare regulations for fear of destroying the entire program. But, Vail said, GAO officials now admit to him that they were mistakenly restrained in criticizing HEW.

In late 1966, at the staff's urging, Long called the first formal oversight hearings on Medicare. The ostensible purpose was to examine HEW's reimbursement formula for paying participating hospitals and doctors, but the hearings may have been intended to have wider ramifications.

In any event, they marked the beginning of much ill will. Alvin David, the Social Security Administration's commissioner for program evaluation and planning, was unhappy with the way the committee approached oversight. He charged that the members were after headlines rather than facts. "Before the hearings we were never told what the content of the questions they were going to ask would be. They carefully withhold that information so the Secretary of HEW will not be better prepared than they can help."

The hearings left Constantine and Vail with grievances of their own. HEW officials were reluctant to give up information that could be incriminating, and Constantine became frustrated by delays. Although David insists that all information requested from him was delivered as quickly as possible, another Medicare administrator admits, "I guess you could say we've been footdraggers in certain instances."

From 1966 to 1968, Constantine continued to watch the developing program and worked more with Wolkstein and the Baltimore officials on the administrative details so important to the program. Vail felt that "by 1968 we knew they [HEW officials] were running a grab bag operation over there." Vail thought that many of the HEW regulations were open-ended, vague, and without incentives to restrain costs. In recalling these formative years David points out:

> Medicare was a massive undertaking, and it was bound to have bugs. I don't think President Johnson was exaggerating much when he said it was the most complicated undertaking since the invasion of Normandy. The participation in the program was overwhelming, and after the first months we had a huge backlog of claims to be resolved.

Tierney also remembers "pipelines of bills." The decision was made to move ahead on the claims and worry about the bugs later. "The thrust of the administrative effort in the early months was 'for God's sake get the bills paid and the system running,'" said Tierney.

In 1969 Constantine was responsible for preparing a "blue book" for each senator to outline general areas to be covered by the hearings and legislative remedies that might be required. By July 1969 the staff had persuaded Senator Anderson to call for hearings on several obvious abuses, including the use of the Medicare program to finance operation of teaching hospitals by providing extraordinary allowances for supervisory personnel. As had become the practice, Constantine took the preliminary version of the blue book to Wolkstein and John Rettig, another official in the Department of Program Evaluation and Planning, for their comments.

Although Wolkstein accepts this practice and continues to work with his friend even on reports that are highly critical of Medicare's administration, Constantine's visits do put him on the spot. These tête-à têtes are undertaken by Constantine "just between us staff," leaving Wolkstein to walk the line between confidentiality and disclosing information to his superiors. But as Rettig describes the problem: "All we can do is tell him [Constantine] this isn't exactly right, or this would be more accurate, in a report that's going to murder us. He'll tell you not to tell your boss, but at some point you have to say, 'Wait a minute, let's take this down the hall.'"

Although Alvin David denies having seen the report, sources confirm that a copy of the "blue book" prepared for the July hearings reached his desk before it was formally released. David decided not to wait until the hearings began, but secretly took the report to liberal senators on the committee to ask for their support. "Oh, they [the committee members] always say we try to lobby—that's what they call it—a senator before he has even seen the information," David explained by way of denial. "They think we sneak around behind their backs with this report before it's finished, trying to beat them to the senator. Hell, we never do that."

The hearings took a back seat to the more detailed critique of Medicare being prepared by Constantine, Vail, and Robert Fullerton of the Ways and Means staff. Constantine was surprised that much of the information he wanted had not been kept by the Medicare officials. This was especially important since the Finance Committee is now largely dependent on the agencies under scrutiny for the data necessary to perform its oversight. David claims that he drafted "cost effectiveness amendments" designed to bring the skyrocketing Medicare costs of the program under control, but could not get the members of the Finance Committee interested in them until after the staff report was completed.

In February 1970 Constantine's staff report was finally released. Most of its proposals dealt with better supervision of increased medical costs (and therefore Medicare payments), cost cutting, and efficiency in accounting procedures. David, who takes credit for the report's data, was critical of the committee's grandstanding:

If you look at that report, most of the specific criticisms are of Medicare, even though Medicaid had far more serious problems. One of the problems was that they didn't know what was wrong with their own program, and we did. We knew where the problems were. We compiled the data that was "exposed" by the Finance staff. They had no compunctions about asking us about everything imaginable, then they went running out to the press showing what they'd found, and we'd given it to them! The fact that we were in good enough shape to know what was wrong is why we were so condemned.

BHI officials had been somewhat reluctant to turn over critical information to Constantine, believing that their data would be slanted and misrepresented. This incident seemed to confirm their fears.

Constantine did send out an independent questionnaire to state governors, insurance intermediaries, and various contractors, but the survey was a debatable oversight tool because of its generally biased questions. Most of the questions dealt with the clarity and usefulness of HEW regulations and asked for examples of friction and malfeasance in the program. Some of the questions to the governors were leading. For example: "In your opinion, to what extent has the requirement that all states move toward the goal of comprehensive benefits by 1975 caused your state to establish a program with broader rules of eligibility and benefits than your state might have preferred?" Constantine seemed to be inviting a political answer that had little bearing on the *quality* of the Medicare program.

The effectiveness of Constantine's questionnaire was limited by the breadth, depth, and honesty of the answers. Most of those he received were incomplete, too facile, or slanted by the respondent's point of view. Constantine was still dependent on the data and opinions of the administrator of the programs, the BHI. Rettig asserts, "Medicare and Medicaid are a different kind of animal. You have to be much more oriented to the program in action rather than the theory if you're going to understand the program."

By alienating many sources, Constantine had forfeited much valuable information, including the daily complaints and comments of the staff in BHI and in the field.

Discussing his view of Congress' oversight of Medicare, Wolkstein said that "Congress is preeminently interested in politics. You might say Finance should be interested in taxes or health care, but they're not. They're interested in politics more generally." This view seemed borne out by the committee's response to the barrage of complaints from constituents, in which the elderly and the poor were joined by middle-income families, complaining vociferously about the costs of all medical care and blaming the crisis on Medicare. In turn, the committee shifted the blame from their oversight procedures onto BHI.

The committee's staff report, prepared in unusual secrecy and aimed at creating a major news impact, was entitled *Medicare and Medicaid: Issues, Problems and Answers*. It offered issues and problems but few answers, and it began with stern assessments: "The Medicare and Medicaid programs are in serious financial trouble. The two programs are also adversely affecting health care costs and financing for the general population."[3]

The report questioned the judgment behind HEW regulations and their application. For example, it charged that intermediate care facilities, mainly nursing homes, were being designated without sufficient inspection; that other institutions, from hospitals to out-patient care facilities, were being given participatory status despite substandard ratings from HEW; and that participating institutions were given no inducements by HEW to limit their costs. Payments were made too quickly and the general level of supervision exercised by HEW was inadequate to prevent abuses.

Although the report was based on technical data, it also had pointed a finger at obstinate Medicare administrators who had plagued Constantine with their delays:

> While the Medical Services Administration [in HEW] probably requires additional personnel if effective Federal

> supervision is to be realized, it appears vital that any addi-
> tional and present personnel—including officials—operate
> with a greater sense of responsibility and direct involvement
> than has been manifested heretofore.[4]

This statement, though couched in impersonal "bureaucratese,"
leveled the blame in no uncertain terms. This and similar comments were taken by the career civil servants in BHI as unjustified personal insults. "I've never forgiven them for that phrase
'lackluster administration,'" Tierney said.

The HEW liaisons in Washington, Edwards and Trout, were
also stunned, but their strongest objection was to the secrecy in
preparing the report. Knowing that it would have repercussions,
Constantine had tried to keep the report "entirely under our hats"
to prevent any preliminary lobbying by those he criticized. So
he kept the report from Trout and Edwards, who were responsible for a public reply, but not from Wolkstein and Tierney, who
saw the report while it was in progress—as was customary. And
Robert Ball of the Social Security Administration evaluated the
report before it was released.

At public oversight hearings, convened by the Finance Committee in February 1970 to explore the recommendations of the
staff, HEW made a point-by-point reply to the report. After
HEW replied, Under Secretary John Venemen and several Medicare administrators, including Tierney and Wolkstein, were
invited to testify. Confronted by data and analyses in both the
staff report and HEW's reply, the senators could have come to an
understanding of the complex problems in the program and pro-
ceeded with the difficult work of formulating solutions, which had
thus far evaded the staff. Instead, Senators Ribicoff and Byrd
joined in Senator Hartke's demand that HEW Secretary Elliot
Richardson appear before them to take responsibility for the
"litany of shortcomings in the Medicare program," as Long put it.

The oversight hearings degenerated into bickering. Hartke
announced that "there is a charge of sabotage now in the operation of the program." With some of the most knowledgeable men
in the Medicare field at the hearing, committee members com-

plained that HEW had not responded to their requests for explanations. And Senator Gore, more than a little angry at the peevish conduct of his colleagues, turned on the Republicans for their approach to the hearings:

It is a fact, as Senator Bennett has said, that the Democrats created this financial problem by making medical services available to needy people. That is a weakness of Democrats. We look after people. And one of the strong points of the Republicans, they want to look after that dollar, raising the interest rates every time the moon comes up.[5]

At this point, after grinding axes and accomplishing little else, Long was ready to leave. But before his departure he tried once more to make the oversight hearings seem more ambitious than they were:

This Medicare program is completely out of hand and it appears that no one but the Senate Finance Committee is doing anything about it. I believe the committee is acting courageously and in the best public interest in trying to get some order into this program and to fix some limit on the amounts that will be paid under this program.[6]

The chairman and other committee members, such as Anderson, were then content to leave oversight to their staff once more, and Long put Constantine in charge of questioning the witnesses. "We hate to do this," Senator Anderson lamented, "but would you mind if the staff continued to ask some questions if the members were not here?" Straightfaced, Tierney replied, "Not at all, the staff has been asking me questions for two years now, Senator."

An opportunity for real reform had quickly slipped away when the senators left as uninformed as they had come. They had not used the opportunity to analyze the Medicare program thoroughly or to criticize it constructively. The Senate Finance Committee had gone through the formal process of oversight, but its interest was in headlines, not reform. Constantine later returned to his small and cluttered office to draft what legislation he could.

Tierney and Wolkstein retreated to Baltimore resolved to institute the suggestions they had received and avoid another set of hearings in Washington.

Since the members did not seem to want to oversee the Medicare program actively, the greatest hope for improving Medicare lay as before with the unmonitored administrators of the plan. Over the next eighteen months, administrators' implementation of some of the suggested reforms substantially improved the program. In a conciliatory mood, Tierney will say that the congressional report and hearings probably helped. "That report really cleared the air," he explains, "so that now I think we have very good relations with Jay and the committee." The heat generated by the controversial hearings permeated to uncooperative doctors and insurance carriers who feared that Congress might be cracking down and that the time had come to play the game fairly or be penalized. BHI reinforced that feeling by increasing the vigilance and manpower of its regional offices around the country.

In 1972 the Finance Committee finally tried to alter Medicare with Section 216 of H.R. 1, the omnibus welfare bill. Introduced by Senator Ribicoff, the section would establish the office of Inspector General to report to the committee on health programs administered by HEW. The inspector would handle all the oversight duties, including judging Medicare's "efficiency and economy . . . consonance with provisions of law, and the attainment of the objectives and purposes" of the program. He would have access to all records, reports, and financial documents from any agency relating to the program. Authority would be granted to the inspector to suspend any "regulation, practice, or procedure" of the health care programs for the purpose of attaining the stated objectives. He would notify the Secretary of HEW and the Ways and Means and Finance committees when suspending any phase of Medicare. The Senate Finance Committee felt that the office of Inspector General would make a major contribution to the efficiency of the massive Federal health programs. Tierney, however, held to his belief that the Medicare administrators were aware of their problems and could deal with them without interference.

Tierney, Wolkstein, and David are not seduced by the relative calm in their relations with the Finance Committee. They know that their most important ally is Constantine and that their most powerful enemy could also be Constantine. "Everything he recommends to the senators gets included in legislation," says Tierney. In stating his case for improved congressional oversight, Tierney said, "I'm [still] not satisfied with our influence with Finance."

It is apparent that the Finance committee has been delinquent in its approach to overseeing the Medicare/Medicaid program. Whether the reason is lack of interest in an unglamorous task or a lack of subcommittees (on Finance until 1973 and even now on Ways and Means), the job of oversight has been left almost entirely to an already overburdened staff. The types of technical and administrative problems that developed in the Medicare program cannot be discovered and solved simply by the committee members' reliance on complaints from constituents.

Until congressional committees take a real interest in systematic and comprehensive oversight, the taxpayers' money will be used ineffectively on government programs, and the individuals who need service from such programs will suffer. Congress' response to the Tax Expenditure Budget serves as another major illustration of the tax committees' obstructionist role in oversight proceedings.

THE HIDDEN SPENDERS

When the Congress sets a deficit of $10 billion and a budget of $250 billion for a given year, the tax system must raise $240 billion. But there are many kinds of income Congress had decided *not* to tax, often called "tax incentives," "subsidies," or "loopholes." These tax concessions are the equivalent of direct public expenditures. By passing a law that allows a certain group of taxpayers to avoid paying $1,000 they would otherwise owe,

Congress is in effect giving each of these taxpayers $1,000 from the U.S. Treasury. And to reach the $240 billion in needed revenues, the rest of us provide the extra $1,000 by paying $1,000 more in taxes.

These tax expenditures are now used on programs to encourage harvesting timber, digging clam shells, and drilling for oil; to increase purchasing of machinery, building of apartment houses, and the corporate training of unskilled people. There are enormous programs to foster home ownership, encourage stock purchasing, finance state and local governments, and help exporters. These funds also finance programs for the lame, the blind, the aged, the young, the military, the insured, the uninsured, the sick, banks, railroad companies, coal and iron companies, farmers, and polluters. They help pay for political campaigns as well as research and development.

The total amount spent through tax expenditures now amounts to more than $50 billion each year, or 20 percent of the total direct budget. This enormous spending beyond the $250 billion in the direct budget continues year after year with very little oversight and very little regard for governmental priorities. There is no attempt to analyze tax expenditures and their relationship to direct spending programs, even though in many budget areas more is spent through the tax system than by direct outlays. Unlike appropriations, these tax expenditures are not automatically reviewed each year. They do not lapse automatically, but continue indefinitely, and new expenditures are approved every year by the Ways and Means and Finance committees. These amounts have always been voted on in secret, and because of incomplete and often misleading bill reports, members of Congress are not always sure how much they are spending through the tax expenditure mechanism and to whom those expenditures are going.

Unanswered Questions

Spending money through the tax system instead of the appropriations system raises special questions. In the case of an appropriation, the entity getting the money is reasonably identifiable, but a tax expenditure usually works by allowing people or corporations to pay no tax on a given kind of income, to deduct certain amounts from their taxable income for doing what the tax system wants to encourage, or to receive a "tax credit" or a straight reduction of taxes for spending in a particular area. And the taxpayer himself determines whether he receives the aid. For example, in an effort to expand production and jobs, the government allows a corporation to receive a tax credit if it buys a new piece of equipment. The corporation receives that tax break merely by buying a machine, regardless of whether it was necessary to increase production or to increase jobs.

The tax expenditure mechanism also tends to be highly regressive; that is, a poor taxpayer benefits less from these tax expenditures than a rich one. Many members of Congress annually propose to allow parents to deduct $1,000 or more per year for money spent on their child's college education. Such a tax expenditure sounds fine, but it would work like this: the taxpayer in the 25 percent bracket would save $250, while the very wealthy taxpayer in the 70 percent bracket would save $700. The tax system would spend almost three times as much subsidizing the education of the rich taxpayer's child as on helping the average taxpayer's child.

Citing another example, former Assistant Secretary of the Treasury Stanley S. Surrey asks:

> What HEW secretary would propose a medical assistance program for the aged that cost $200 million, and under which $90 million go to persons with incomes under $5,000? The tax proposal to remove the 3 percent floor under the medical expense deduction of persons over 65 would have just that effect.[7]

Another example of a regressive tax mechanism is the deduction for charitable contributions, the tax provision used to lend public assistance to private philanthropy. The wealthier the giver, the more the philanthropy gets, because of the freeing of otherwise taxable cash. When a taxpayer in the 70 percent bracket contributes $10,000 to his favorite charity, it costs him only $3,000 and the Treasury, in effect, kicks in $7,000. At the other end of the rate scale, the government through this system decreases aid to the favorite charities of the less well-off taxpayer. Those who contribute smaller amounts and who do not itemize their deductions receive no benefits at all.

Tax expenditures through a tax credit raise related questions. If, for example, we allow a $1,000 tax credit for parental spending on a child's college education, then taxpayers can subtract $1,000 from their tax bill. This particular tax mechanism expends $1,000 on the rich or poor taxpayer equally. But there are millions of people (roughly 30 percent of the population) who are so poor they have no tax liability. The credit system would benefit them not at all.

For those below the taxable rates, the $25 tax credit for political contributions is no incentive to contribute. A struggling business or a tax-exempt organization does not benefit from provisions such as manpower training tax incentives: it has no taxes to credit against the subsidy. One answer would be to make the credits refundable—each person who took on the expense would be reimbursed by the credit even if no taxes were owed.

Another problem with tax subsidies is that while billed as incentives, they often provide windfalls to taxpayers for doing what they would do anyway. The DISC is a tax expenditure that provides such a windfall. Yet at the Treasury Department's request both the Senate and the Senate-House conference junked a House-passed provision that would have limited the benefits to exports *in excess* of previous levels. A recent government-commissioned study indicates that a $1.4 billion tax expenditure to stimulate oil exploration resulted in only $150 million worth of additional exploration.[8] And in many cases tax expenditures go to employers who hire the unskilled as part of a manpower program, even though they would have hired such employees in any event.

Furthermore, there is the fact that tax incentives/subsidies/expenditures increase the burden of taxes on the rest of us. This is an upshot of the "erosion of the tax base" which the economists Joseph Pechman of the Brookings Institution and Benjamin Okner have decried. They calculate that if all tax subsidies were eliminated, income tax rates could be cut 43 percent across the board.

Because tax expenditures are open-ended, determined by numerous contingencies, and subject to the vagaries of private decision making and market mechanisms, their total impact is difficult to foresee. And yet these expenditures have a plain relation to budget planning, not only in the analysis of total resource allocation but in forecasts of the revenues available for government spending.

The Tax Preference Committees

As important as these questions are, the tax committees have substantially ignored them. Tax expenditures are enacted informally, many of them at the request of special interests and in secret session. They are not periodically reviewed or structured to lapse after any number of years. They are not carefully studied to determine who benefits. More basically, even the fundamental question asked of any appropriations measure is rarely raised: is the expenditure producing the effects intended and at what cost?

Indeed, instead of running a given tax expenditure program through the congressional committees working with the particular area getting the tax break—education, health, natural resources, commerce, housing, or whatever—all tax expenditure programs are deliberated and passed upon by the tax committee. As Surrey points out, a similar situation would prevail if these other committees "were suddenly to legislate on technical tax matters."[9] Thus with tax committees in charge, debate and deliberation on tax expenditures are characteristically cruder and more perfunctory than debate on an analogous direct expenditure program.

The tax committees have even gone so far as to resist publication of a budget on the tax expenditures, so that the Congress and people cannot regularly see how much subsidy is being applied to what. In fact the committees have stifled the attempts of the rest of Congress to at least *reveal* these expenditures.

The Back Door

Attempts to bring tax expenditures out into the open began in the 1950s. In the 1955 study, *Federal Tax Policy for Economic Growth and Stability*, launched by the Joint Economic Committee under Chairman Paul Douglas and Congressman Wilbur Mills, an economist cautioned:

> If it be decided to subsidize a certain activity, we should be hesitant about administering the subsidy by way of a tax preference. Subsidies in this form vary directly in amount with the tax brackets of the recipients; they are invariably hidden and do not show up in the budget; their cost frequently is difficult to calculate; and their accomplishments are even more difficult to assess. Partly for those very reasons they are likely to become fixtures which are not easily removed.[10]

In a 1959 paper that was part of a landmark compendium of tax studies (initiated by Mills when he became chairman of Ways and Means), Walter Heller, economist and later chairman of the Council of Economic Advisers, explained the back door or catacomb nature of tax expenditures:

> The back door to government subsidies marked "tax relief" is easier to push open than the front door marked "loans, guarantees, and insurance." Rather than run the gauntlet of the Budget Bureau and the congressional Appropriations Committees, groups seeking subsidies turn to the tax committees of Congress for government support without government interference. Often, they do so with the tacit or expressed support of the substantive committees dealing with small business, agriculture, foreign investments, natural resources, and the like. . . . The very groups that use this back door are often among the most insistent advocates of responsible and informed Government budgeting. Yet here is a whole catacomb of Government benefits which are

largely hidden from public view, let alone periodic review. Once embedded in the tax structure, the preferential provisions are treated as inalienable vested rights, impervious to change in tax rates, economic policy and technology.[11]

In the first half of the 1960s tax reformers placed tax expenditures low on their list of priorities. But notice came of an assault on tax expenditures in President Johnson's 1966 Economic Report:

> In a fully employed economy, special tax benefits to stimulate some activities or investments means that we have less of other activities. Benefits that the Government extends through direct expenditures are periodically reviewed and often altered in the budget-appropriations process, but too little attention is given to reviewing particular tax benefits. These benefits, like all other activities of the government, must stand up to the tests of efficiency and fairness.[12]

In reference to tax expenditures in a 1967 speech to money marketers, Assistant Treasury Secretary Surrey said, "We need a full accounting for these effects of the tax system." He proposed to treat these expenditures as line items in the federal budget, so they could come under the scrutiny of the Congress, the Bureau of the Budget (now the Office of Management and Budget), and the public. Surrey noted that tax expenditures had become an easy and unexamined way to spend billions for domestic purposes without a direct tax increase. Surrey insisted that alternatives to proposed tax incentives—in the form of direct expenditures, loans, subsidies, and other direct programs—be thoroughly explored. The new approach would be productive:

> Indeed, the Treasury has found that the way to obtain imaginative and broad thinking about these social problems —to obtain real brainstorming—is to tell the groups concerned to forget their stereotype, first impulse solution of tax incentive, to close the Internal Revenue Code, to bar their tax lawyers from the meeting—and then get down to the real task of analyzing the problems and thinking about solutions. The results are always positive.[13]

A month after Surrey's speech, Chairman Mills delivered a speech on the House floor about "back-door spending":

> What I would like to emphasize is that the expenditures we turn away from the front door we must not allow to enter through the back door. If we decide that certain programs, however worthy their purpose, cannot be financed at this time by increased spending, because other needs have priority, we should not turn around and sanction some form of indirect subsidy—in the form of special tax relief—for these programs.[14]

And by mid-February 1968, Surrey was challenging the broader business community about the non-contract tax incentives:

> It is hard to see why the individual who becomes a tax millionaire through the after-tax benefits accorded low-income housing or some other tax-benefited activity is really different from the defense contractor, and why the latter is subjected to renegotiation while the former need not meet any overall limits on the rewards of tax subsidies.[15]

Tax Expenditure Budgets

In 1968 Surrey began to prepare as full an accounting of tax expenditures as he could. The first Tax Expenditure Budget (TEB), accompanied by a conceptual analysis entitled "Tax Expenditures: Government Expenditures Made Through the Income Tax System," came in the Annual Report of the Secretary of the Treasury on the State of Finances for fiscal 1968.* The TEB breakdown allows for a comparison of tax provisions with direct expenditures in the same category. The first TEB was a "minimum listing," the report said, based on "widely accepted definitions of income and standards of business accounting and . . . the generally accepted structure of an income tax." It excluded some tax expenditures because of inadequate evidence

---

* In a supplement to his famous "Taxpayers' Revolt" statement to the Joint Economic Committee, Secretary Joseph W. Barr updated the revenue cost figures to cover fiscal years 1968, 1969, and 1970.

of their magnitude, technical considerations, or the insignificant amounts involved. It ignored other taxes, such as estate and gift taxes, excises, and tariffs, and confined itself to "items that would be generally recognized as more or less intended use of the tax system to achieve results commonly obtained by Government expenditures."

As a presidential candidate, Richard M. Nixon called tax incentives a suitable way to solve social problems. But in late April 1969, when the President finally sent tax legislation proposals to Ways and Means, he showed signs of advocating a public Tax Expenditure Budget, the public itemization of all tax expenditures:

> Tax dollars the Government deliberately waives should be viewed as a form of expenditure, and weighed against the priority of other expenditures. When the preference device provides more social benefit than Government collection and spending, that "incentive" should be expanded; when the preference is inefficient or subject to abuse, it should be ended.[16]

But by summer's end the President fully supported the practice whereby the federal government exploited tax expenditures as a tool to spend without seeming to spend. So at Treasury's suggestion and encouragement, and without any study at all, in its 1969 Tax Reform Act Congress committed the government to a $500-million tax expenditure for pollution control facilities to encourage industries to clean themselves up, and a $300 million one for rehabilitation of low-rent housing.[17] At Treasury's behest it also mandated smaller tax expenditures for railroad cars and mine-safety equipment. In 1969 and 1970 the Treasury Department tried in vain to ram through a huge tax expenditure, the DISC provision, that would have lost $600 million to $1 billion in revenue annually. It was finally obtained in 1971.

During the 1960s, as tax expenditures increased in amount and complexity, the executive branch made at least tentative gestures toward examining or sometimes reducing tax expenditures. But the tax committees did nothing: they neither evaluated nor measured the spending, and only in 1969 were a few of the loopholes limited.

The year 1971 saw a wide variety of costly tax expenditures passing in Congress: a restored investment credit, estimated to cost $4.5 billion annually; the ADR system (with an estimated annual cost of $2.9 billion); the DISC (estimated at $400 million annually); rapid five-year amortization of employer on-the-job training and child care facilities; a tax credit to employers of welfare recipients in the Work Incentive Program (estimated cost, $25 million); increased deductions for child and dependent care expenses (estimated cost, $145 million); a tax credit and deduction for political campaigns (estimated cost, $90 million); and a slight liberalization of the use of industrial development bonds. Senate amendments attempting further tax expenditures (relating to college education costs, senior citizens' property taxes, disabled persons, and business investments) were rejected only in last-minute conferences between the houses.

Primarily through former Under Secretary Charles Walker and Deputy Assistant Secretary John Nolan, the executive branch was instrumental in securing passage of the ADR, the DISC, and the investment credit, as well as successfully opposing a Senate amendment to have the TEB published annually as part of the federal budget. One Treasury official explained Nolan's opposition: Secretary John Connally opposed publishing the TEB because "if you publish the numbers, people will aim at them." Nolan was not satisfied with what Congress had done, however. For while the secret wheeling and dealing had brought the administration its loopholes, the committees had enriched their own clientele as well. In an interview he candidly remarked: "There were lots of stinking little appendages in the '71 Act that the Treasury didn't want and that don't belong in the tax laws."

Nevertheless, the administration did not campaign for reducing or evaluating *any* of the hundreds of growing tax expenditures in 1970 or 1971, and Congress did not consider doing it.

Former Assistant Secretary Surrey comments on the tax expenditure boom of the last three legislative sessions:

> With respect to these new subsidies it can generally be said that less critical analysis is paid to these tax subsidies than to almost any direct expenditure program one can mention. The tax subsidies tumble into the law without supporting studies, being propelled instead by clichés, debating points, and scraps of data and tables that are passed off as serious evidence. A tax system that is so vulnerable to this injection of extraneous, costly and ill-considered expenditure programs is in a precarious state from the standpoint of the basic tax goals of providing adequate revenues and maintaining tax equity.[18]

But as the 1970s began, the Congress continued as before with only one slight revision: Senator Jacob Javits (R., N.Y.) acted to make the amounts of the tax subsidies public through the published Tax Expenditure Budget. He proposed an amendment to the Tax Reform Act of 1969 to require the Treasury to publish an annual tax expenditure budget, relating tax expenditures to specific budget outlays. Introducing the bill the New York senator said: "This information must be publicly available if the public is to intelligently call the attention of Congress to take appropriate action where needed."[19] Banking on Chairman Long's assurances that the Secretary of the Treasury had already committed himself to publishing the information in all future annual reports, Javits withdrew his bill from consideration. Secretary of Treasury Barr did give some separate compilations of tax expenditures for fiscal years 1968, 1969, and 1970; but they were very rudimentary. They were not tied into the budget process in any way, and the tax committees ignored them. There has been no coordination with the budgetary process, no review of present expenditures, and no effort to measure the cost benefits of tax expenditures.

Since the agitation of economists and Surrey's tax policy officials for tax expenditure budget began, the committees have added massive new expenditures in complex areas with no evidence or judgment. Remarking on a typical expenditure, the incentive for housing rehabilitation in the 1969 Reform Act, Surrey notes:

> Without any study at all the Treasury induced the Committee to commit the Government to an expenditure of over $300 million for the rehabilitation of rental housing. [This] action was taken with [out] any regard to the overall priorities . . . in the housing area.[20]

THE HARD WORK OF IRRESPONSIBILITY

The nonfeasance of the committees during the early 1970s has not been accomplished without some effort. Working hard to avoid oversight, the tax committees defeated the early efforts of Senator Gore to require a tax expenditure budget, ignored a Joint Economic Committee Report on the effects of some of the known subsidies, beat back attempts by Senators Javits and Percy to include tax expenditures in the budgetary process—despite the vote of the full Senate in favor of the measure—and allowed tax expenditures to slip out the back door as they had always done.

In June 1970 Senator Gore introduced "The Tax Expenditure Information Act of 1970," a bill calling for a TEB and correlating the estimates to budget outlays set forth in the annual budget. The bill died in the Finance Committee.[21]

The JEC's minority report on the President's February 1971 Economic Report recommended the following:

> A program budget should be drawn up to show not only direct budget outlays, but also revenue forgone by the Treasury as a result of special provision in the Internal Revenue Code and Government assisted credit programs. . . . These outlays and subsidies should be matched against the estimated economic and social benefits that flow from them. . . .[22]

Following the next TEB proposal by Senator Javits in 1971, Joint Economic Committee staff member Jerry Jasinowski studied the issue to lay the foundation for congressional analysis. The staff report, *The Economics of Federal Subsidy Programs*, published in January 1972, showed that of the four major forms of subsidies —cash, tax, credit, and benefit-in-kind—tax subsidies were nearly twice as costly as all the others combined. In releasing the first volume of study papers Senator Proxmire noted:

> At present, there is absolutely no way of gauging their worth or effectiveness. While subsidies may be good or bad, there has been virtually no analysis of who gets the benefits from these subsidies or if they achieve in any way the goals they were originally designed to obtain.

Here are a few of the findings of this ground-breaking report:

> —Beneficiaries of tax expenditures in real estate included high tax bracket investors, renters, demolition companies, and landowners. To subsidize low and moderate income housing, the government should provide a direct, specific subsidy "rather than using a tax law provision that applies to all rental housing."[23]
> —By exempting state and local bond interest the federal government lost $2.6 billion while states and localities saved only $1.9 billion.[24]
> —Of tax expenditures affecting the petroleum industry, the report states the "consensus of professional economic opinion is relatively certain that the special tax provisions result in an inefficient allocation of resources, a smaller national income and questionable income redistribution effects."[25]
> —The timber industry's tax expenditures favor the large, integrated timber company, giving almost nothing to the "small woodlot farmer, without increasing supplies of timber or encouraging conservation."
> —Timber industry preferences alone cost the government $130 to $140 million per year.[26]
> —Though they entail less bureaucratic difficulties than direct grant, some tax expenditures involve a lot of red tape.
> —Tax expenditure treatment of U.S. firms operating abroad probably *reduced* U.S. productivity, held down the real wages of labor, and exported jobs abroad.[27]

In May 1971, Senator Javits, with Senator Percy as co-sponsor, made another attempt to get the TEB published. His bill was "to amend the Budget and Accounting Act to require that the budget contain information with respect to losses incurred and indirect expenditures made through the Federal tax system." Javits asked that the bill be referred to the Committee on Government Operations, where he and Percy sat.[28]

Over the course of the next few months the bill gained some important co-sponsors, including the committee's chairman, Senator John McClellan (D., Ark.) and Senators Harris, Hatfield, Humphrey, and Chiles. During the floor debate, Finance chairman Long became testy, resenting the fact that the Government Operations Committee had not held hearings on the bill before several of its members, including Senator Chiles, tried to tack the same measure onto a Finance Committee *tax bill* as an amendment (to the 1971 Revenue Act) and thus "waste time." There were already ninety amendments to the tax bill, Javits pointed out, so that one more wouldn't be anything "to get exercised about." As for Long's and the Treasury's opposition to publishing the TEB, Javits countered:

> In the same way that we see the budget, and what people are going to have to pay to support it, we ought to see what the tax indulgences are; it is as simple as that, and I cannot see why the Treasury Department would want to obfuscate on it, unless they have something to hide, or they are ashamed of these tax indulgences, or do not want people to know about them. That, it seems to me, is the only reason there can be.[29]

Long lost on his motion to table the amendment, and the Javits measure passed by a vote of 48 to 23.[30] Later, however, the Senate-passed measure was sabotaged in conference, although the conferees did require Treasury to supply TEB data annually to the tax committees.

WHO KNOWS? WHO CARES?

Behind the scenes, tax committee members have certain strong but unstated reasons for avoiding a tax expenditure budget, for failing to add to public and congressional knowledge of tax loopholes, and for ignoring the oversight responsibilities that normally go with spending. TEB would make it more difficult for client groups to obtain special favors. It would entail the need to research or at least justify the expenditures before other members of Congress. It might even mean a loss of jurisdiction, since spending for copper mining or building construction might be claimed by the committees covering those substantive areas.

The stated reasons for nonfeasance in this enormously important area of oversight are not quite as coherent or understandable as those generally presumed to be at work. Senator Long told us that he "didn't agree with Mr. Surrey on that," referring to the whole notion of a tax expenditure. As far as he is concerned, "The government has the power to tax it all off of you . . . and if we don't tax something, that's it, it's not a favor, we just don't tax it and that should be the end of it." If these preferences "result in a lot of people making tax-free money, then jack up the minimum tax (not at 10 percent)."

Other Finance members went along with their chairman. Ranking Republican Finance Committee member Wallace Bennett gave us basically the Treasury argument he had delivered in the debate on Javits' bill.[31] Bennett was all for keeping track of expenditures but didn't want the Treasury tied down by the task. Bennett hinted that he was more than a little suspicious of the motives of those seeking the TEB. As for oversight, he said the executive agencies monitored tax expenditures and "would resent our intrusion." The Finance Committee shouldn't be an overseer, in his view, but simply a legislator. Bennett didn't see the tax expenditures as being topsy-turvy: since we have a progressive tax system, the benefits should be "progressive" as well. Senator Talmadge's legislative assistant, Dan Tate, said it was "not a boiling issue" and he knew little about it. "The first I heard about it was when Javits brought it up and I didn't understand it then."

An aide to former Senator Jordan didn't know who was analyzing tax expenditures but thought they should be scrutinized more closely. However, he said, "ongoing study of them would be up to individual senators and private interests." He felt tax expenditures had been handled "irresponsibly" on the floor: "In 1971, when the tax bill hit the floor, it was like a gang of piranha. All the amendments would have reduced federal revenues by $55 billion in three years. They would have done this with direct expenditures."

Senator Griffin's man was against tax expenditures and knew of nothing being done about them, but stressed that "the Senator always asks what it costs." Senator Hartke's aide was not sure what Hartke thought about the tax expenditure question, but added that the level of economic thinking on Capitol Hill was not very high, so problems were not looked at in those terms.

On the House side, staff members were generally uninformed and unconcerned about the tax expenditure issue. One exception, Dr. Woodworth of the JCIRT staff, believes that Congress is not "geared" to do the sort of effectiveness study we were inquiring about; it "almost needs an executive willing to carry the ball." A JEC minority staffer did not consider TEB to be much of an issue on the committee. Those demanding the TEB "haven't made it hot enough for other members to get excited over it," and most members don't feel they have to take a position. The minority staff has not sought out executive agencies to pin them down on how they are evaluating tax expenditures. The staff could do this without a directive or permission from a member, he admitted, but "we don't want to get into it prematurely and get ahead of the whim of Proxmire."

The General Accounting Office informed us it had done no work in this area and had no plans to do any, although the JEC had asked them to. (Senator Proxmire contends that GAO has the capacity to look at costs and benefits of tax expenditures.) The GAO was unaware of any efforts being made, and said one problem might be that the benefits could prove evasive and intangible.

A sampling of the congressional committees in whose substantive areas major tax expenditures are made uncovered slightly more critical views. The Senate Interior Committee, we were told, was not interested in the effects of expenditures on natural resources, and did not involve itself in consideration of new legislation and oversight in this area.* The response from the Senate Banking, Housing, and Urban Affairs Committee was similar: some concern, but no capability or time to conduct studies. And we noted a reluctance on their part to suggest altering the tax incentive system; housing has thrived on the back-door approach, and if this were closed down, "we might not be able to get all these resources out the front door." In the fields of labor, health, education, poverty, and manpower development, our inquiries again met with negative responses. It was felt that the question should be raised and something done about it, but the Treasury Department was frequently mentioned as the body responsible for generating the data.

As for executive branch awareness and activity in this area, Surrey had told us he doubted that any of the agencies were doing significant cost-effectiveness analysis on the tax expenditures, although he referred to one small study coming out of the Department of Agriculture showing that a farm used as a tax shelter was worthless unless the taxpayer was in the 70 percent bracket. And James Smith, assistant Treasury secretary for congressional relations, acknowledged that in the area of tax expenditure analysis the executive branch was doing little.

We sought to verify these initial soundings, sampling executive agencies under whose aegis various tax subsidies would fall if cast

* However, in an ongoing staff study of the energy crisis some attention is being paid to relevant tax expenditures. The staff has avoided seeking help from Treasury's Tax Analysis Office because the issue has become "polarized, ideologized, and politicized." The staff complained that the real fault lay in the absence of rational decision making by the committees. In the face of inadequate staff and computer facilities, such issues as the cost effectiveness of tax expenditures can be sophisticated niceties.

as direct expenditures. The response was very familiar. HEW was not doing anything on the matter, with the exception of some gross estimates on health insurance done only in conjunction with legislative proposals from the Ninety-third Congress. One spokesman explained that "HEW can't take on the world"; that tax expenditures were not in HEW's budget, and in any case were just facts of life; and that maybe Treasury was doing something, but it was often very difficult to get information from it. The Deputy Assistant HEW Secretary for Program Systems confessed, "One would assume there should be a relationship . . . but I haven't thought about it very much at all." As for the Commerce Department, we were told that no one was "riding herd on it," and that it was unclear whether a cost-effectiveness model even existed. Commerce was doing very little analysis of several recent pieces of legislation affecting its domain, including DISC and the investment credit.

The Department of Housing and Urban Development had nothing significant to report, even though housing enjoys some handsome tax expenditures. One official told us that the big tax subsidies for housing weren't too important to HUD, as it concerned itself mainly with starts and completions which the subsidies had little to do with. He felt that HUD could probably get the job done without the two principal tax expenditures, the mortgage interest and property tax deductions. The presently responsible executive agency, Treasury, seems to be unable to perform cost-benefit studies of tax expenditures.

There are no known tests of cost-effectiveness of tax expenditures. Treasury Under Secretary Edwin Cohen contends, "It is next to impossible to determine the effect they have—how in the hell can we determine the effect they have? It's like appraising a work of art: you get different opinions from different sides."

Does anybody know what we're getting for all that money? Jasinowski says the Joint Economic Committee has estimated that 75 percent of the tax expenditures do not achieve their intended objectives. But this is only a rough preliminary determination, and Surrey says there is "damned little" research going on in the academic world regarding cost effectiveness of tax expenditures. This is a "nonglamorous field," he thinks, and there is a lack of money for tax research.

One beginning was a series of studies collected by the Tax Institute of America in 1970 and used for a "Tax Incentive Symposium."[32] It featured some of the familiar personages of the TEB struggle and discussed in a broad fashion the tax expenditures in such areas as natural resources, real estate, training the unemployed, and investment credit. There is considerable overlap in contributors to the symposium and to the JEC studies, which suggests that serious concern in this area is restricted to a small core of dedicated analysts, and since the tax committees ignore their expertise in favor of executive branch personnel, such analysts have hardly anything to do directly with the tax committees.

In effect, Congress has given over to the executive branch one of its most important constitutional powers, the power to tax and spend. Congress' nonfeasance in fulfilling its responsibility has been so great that some members seem unaware that it is contrary to the Constitution to leave these matters to the executive. In the meantime, the massive tax expenditure system feeds itself on the subclause labyrinth of a complicated thousand-part Internal Revenue Code. Unmonitored and unexamined, tax expenditures are thrown out like confetti upon special interests who merely have to request aid from the right people at the back door. One rural senator, more familiar with tax expenditure issues than most, expressed the feelings we heard repeatedly from those who are familiar with the lack of tax expenditure oversight: "They all got their damn snouts in the trough on those committees. They got to have someone come around and kick some snout. They can only see a few inches in front of themselves, you know, you gotta kick them hard."

The tax committees overlook oversight, somehow assuming that their undermanned staffs or the very agencies administering their legislative programs can handle the massive monitoring job. Should the committees ever decide to enter the realm of government and not be content with making laws for which they feel no responsibility, laws which crassly pander to special interests, then there may someday be a fair and honest tax structure, or a well-run and humane government health and social security program. Until then the indentured bureaucrats will reign, the special interests will smile, and the committees will do little for the average taxpayer.

4

Money Talks

In every community, those who feel the burdens of taxation are naturally prone to relieve themselves from it if they can. . . . One class struggles to throw the burden off its shoulders. If they succeed, of course, it must fall upon others. They also, in their turn, labor to get rid of it, and finally the load falls upon those who will not, or cannot, make a successful effort for relief. . . . This is, in general, a one-sided struggle, in which the rich only engage and . . . in which the poor always go to the wall.

—*Attorney James C. Carter defending the constitutionality of the income tax before the Supreme Court, 1895*

Ways and Means is the money committee, and it and business are like two goddamned magnets coming together. Common Cause, Nader and the AFL-CIO together can't do a tenth what industry can in that committee.

—*a Washington lobbyist*

Since 1913 and the graduated income tax, the theory of American taxation has been to make taxes equitable and fair: to tax citizens, but to tax more those who can afford to pay more. But those who can afford to pay the most are also those who have most access to the authors of tax laws—the members of Congress and, in particular, the members of the Ways and Means and Finance committees. A desire to protect their special interests usually makes members of Congress and lobbyists alike flock to the revenue committees. One lobbyist noted that "everyone is on there to protect some interest or other." Using a former member to illustrate his point, he said that "John Watts was there to protect tobacco and bourbon and that is what he accomplished in life." About Ways and Means, another lobbyist said, "You'd think the President of the United States was holding a press conference— you can't get through all the lobbyists around that committee." The lobbyists *don't* come running because of pending social security and welfare legislation: "The people affected are not that well organized," Ways and Means staff member James Kelly explained. And though they are immensely concerned with trade, the industry lobbyists *don't* take positions *en bloc*. "In 99 percent of cases, you get all sides of opinion," said John Martin, the man who plans Ways and Means hearings. "It's rare to have the business community all on one side." Instead, each lobbyist fights for a tax cut for his particular client. As Louis Eisenstein, a corporate attorney, said in *The Ideologies of Taxation*, "Our taxes reflect a continuing struggle among contending interests for the privilege of paying the least."[1]

Until recently there was a lobbyist for virtually every well-financed interest group in the country, and one for every current (or even antiquated) tax idea—except that of tax reform. Ways and Means member Richard Fulton lamented, "Unfortunately, we don't hear from the general public. The AFL-CIO is the best representative of the average taxpayer. There are no other general groups for tax reform, except perhaps the Liberty Lobby."

The significance of the committee members' dependence on a relatively small and very partisan group for its information is discussed by Roy Blough:

> The conception of producer interests and particularly of business interests, in the proposals brought to Congress . . .

make it difficult for the members of the taxing committees to secure a balanced view of either of what is the general interest, what the public wants or what the public would want if it were informed of the facts.[2]

MEMBER'S BILLS: THE BEST HIDEOUT

One way committee members can satisfy the special interests that constantly pester them for favors is through "member's bills," or what Representative Barber Conable optimistically called a "safety valve for inequities."[3] Several times a year the committee's regular business is suspended and the subcommittee considers member's bills. Designed to correct minor technical flaws and blatant inequities in tax laws, the member's bills are usually supposed to be approved unanimously by committee members and then reported to the floor. In Ways and Means, such bills are often tossed into the hopper late in the legislative session, when confusion and pressure to adjourn prevail. With no debate and few representatives present, they are routinely summarized and passed.

Member's bills usually aid the special interests closest to the particular committee. Sometimes this includes interests within the member's home district. As Representative Rostenkowski's legislative aide said when discussing the congressman's attitude toward member's bills: "If any constituent comes from Illinois with a legitimate gripe, Dan will consider it with the [Ways and Means] committee. If it is not an obvious giveaway, he feels bound to introduce it." While any representative might introduce such a tax relief bill, the fortunate taxpayer must have special "clout" for the member to fight for the bill behind closed committee doors.

A cagy lobbyist knows a member's orientation to his district or state and will subtly exploit it. Former Representative Betts said that "the average lobbyist does not drip around here and try to convince me. He is smart enough to know some of my constituents and tell them, 'You better call Betts.'" A lobbyist for the Independent Petroleum Association of America, Minor Jamison, agreed with Betts. The most effective method, he said, is to first have a congressman's constituents pressure their representative, then the Washington lobbyist will be listened to "because they know we represent friends of theirs back home." Campaign contributions help too, as Jamison well knows. Former IPAA President Harold McClure has been quoted as saying he contributed $90,000 to political campaigns in 1968 alone. Other oil interests contribute much more in each election.

Former Senator Paul Douglas regards tax favoritism as "one of the worst evils of our tax system. It not only fosters injustice, but also has made our tax laws unintelligible to all but a few initiates, who are highly paid for their knowledge and influence. Some Washington attorneys have grown rich by engineering such legislation."[4] Not only Washington lawyers have grown fat by squeezing member's bills through Congress—the campaign chests of incumbent members of Congress have swelled from them, too. One member of the Finance Committee unabashedly admitted that "this is the way we finance our campaigns."[5]

Unlike major legislation, member's bills are not subjected to the public scrutiny of open hearings. It "saves time to deal with the bills behind closed doors," Ways and Means member Jerry Pettis said, "especially since they don't deserve full hearings as they don't affect the entire economy." Though bills may be withdrawn when they jeopardize the committee's harmony, this situation almost never occurs. In the clublike atmosphere of the committee room, mutual esteem and cooperation are the norm and members barely examine their colleagues' member's bills so that their own may receive the same superficial treatment.

When a committee member violates the unwritten rules of courtesy and opposes a member's bill—as Thomas Curtis (D., Mo.) often did in the mid-1960s because he thought the bills were making substantive and not technical changes in the law—the bill may still be reported out. Unless, as one Treasury official said, the committee members and the representatives in the relevant executive departments "jump up and down," then the committee will pass the bills. One bill was reported out of Ways and Means in

1965 even after Curtis had objected and four executive departments had opposed it.[6]

And it is even rarer that a member's bill is opposed by the Treasury Department. It too must cultivate cooperation from the committee members. It would prefer not to object to a minor bill so that it could charm the vote from a member on a major proposal from the administration. Gerald Brannon, a former Treasury official, conceded, "We'd lose ground on the whole if we acted like a virgin on every piddle-ass thing that comes along. It's a complex tactical game."

Just how complex the game is, and how the Treasury Department can compromise, is illustrated by the handling of Ways and Means member Herman Schneebeli's bill to give foundations a tax break. Under the 1969 Tax Reform Act, foundations were required for the first time to contribute to charity at least 6 percent of their assets. The 6 percent rule was inserted to restrain foundations from simply investing in low-income or no-income assets without performing the charitable purposes for which they had been given tax exemption. The 1969 act gave the foundations until 1975 to reach the 6 percent level. The families that owned the Sun Oil Company and the cereal giant, the W. K. Kellogg Company, lobbied to change the 1969 act. Both foundation funds are heavily invested in family stock.

Schneebeli, anxious to assist the Pew family, which owned Sun Oil and included some of his largest campaign contributors,* introduced a bill that would ease the tax "burden" on these foundations.

The Schneebeli bill was originally written to benefit only the Pew and Kellogg foundations,[7] and the Treasury Department was under intense pressure from the White House not to fight it, partly because the Pew family had given more than $142,000 to

---

* For instance, in 1970 at least $7,000 came from the Pew family for Schneebeli's campaign: $2,000 from Mary Ethel Pew; $2,000 from Mabel Pew Myrin; and $3,000 from J. Howard Pew, chairman of Sun Oil's executive committee.

national Republican organizations in 1968. Treasury proposed an alternative that the Ways and Means Committee adopted. Under the new bill, the maximum required charitable payout would be 5 percent, which foundations would not have to reach until 1978. The required payouts would start at a meager 3.5 percent in 1971 and increase by half a percentage point every two years. Thus Congressman Schneebeli could tell the Congress Project that his bill would benefit "hundreds of foundations" as well as the Pew and Kellogg trusts. Even so, the average taxpayer was not gaining by the proposed shift in tax burden; rather, charitable causes could lose up to half a billion dollars under the new bill.

Though the Treasury Department had been conciliatory and broadened the bill so that foundations besides Pew and Kellogg would benefit, the House defeated it. It also defeated Schneebeli's determined resurrection of the bill in 1972.

The heralded 1969 Tax Reform Act also contained several Senate special interest amendments, many relating to repeal of the investment credit. Uniroyal, Inc., secured an exception worth $3 million, Lockheed one worth $11 million, McDonnell-Douglas $6.5 million and Howard Hughes also received a handsome break. Another exception was written for the benefit of three shipping lines, Lykes Brothers Steamship Co., Prudential Lines, and Pacific Far East Lines. One obscure provision was applicable only to two firms, the American Reciprocal Insurance Company and the Commerce and Industry Insurance Company. Kennecott, Anaconda, Phelps-Dodge, and the American Smelting and Refining Company were the principal recipients of another tax favor. Senator Wallace Bennett secured a break for three of his corporate constituents, the Great Salt Lake Mineral and Chemical Corporation, the National Lead Company, and Kaiser Aluminum. Bennett also obtained a special amendment for the Browning Arms Company. A member of the Irvine family secured a stricter amendment than that applying to other foundations, to help her in a dispute with her fellow directors of the foundation. The JCIRT staff draftsmen memorialized the recipient of one special interest provision, radio station WWL of Loyola University, in New Orleans, by making the initial letters of the three clauses of the provision spell out the call letters WWL.

In October 1971, Jackson Betts introduced a member's bill that would have helped just one company, Insurance Securities Incorporated, a mutual fund. ISI was starting a new mutual fund whose stockholders would all be tax-exempt. Though the new fund would almost certainly be nontaxable, Betts's bill would have amended the tax code to formally exempt the type of fund that ISI planned. The Washington lawyer who handled the matter for ISI was Mitchell Rogovin, chief of the Justice Department's Tax Division and a member of the Common Cause Tax Reform Advisory Group. The bill became notorious when the news media discovered that Treasury Secretary John Connally owned more than $50,000 in ISI stock.

The reformers in Congress have tried to temper Ways and Means's enthusiasm for such bills. On February 29, 1972, Wright Patman (D., Tex.), chairman of the House Banking and Currency Committee, attacked the congressional process that almost automatically approves member's bills:

> These bills contain broad questions of public policy as well as parliamentary procedure of a representative government. . . . We must not have bills like this, with no hearings, no adequate reports, no compliance with rules. . . . Members of Congress do not know how far-reaching they are and what they will do. It is costing us billions and billions of dollars. . . . Now is the time we must stop this procedure.[8]

Some in the House agreed with Patman. Between October 12 and 14, 1972, Ways and Means had approved forty-one member's bills. One that Mills sponsored would have postponed some of the provisions of the 1969 Tax Reform Act and saved the banking industry about $70 million. Second-ranking Democrat Al Ullman sponsored another that would have saved four lumber companies more than $25 million annually. Third-ranking Democrat James Burke sponsored a bill to cut cigar industry taxes by over $162 million during the first ten years and $21 million annually after that. In reaction against this quantity, the House put these and nineteen other member's bills over to the next session.

At the second session three of Ways and Means's member's bills were defeated. Mills then withdrew fifteen others rather than have them defeated also. Next, in June 1972, came an omnibus bill—the Technical Amendments Act of 1972—with twenty member's bills. After that ploy was criticized by taxpayers and newspapers in his home state of Arkansas, Mills abandoned the bill,[9] but again it was only a tactical retreat. The same day Mills gave up on the Technical Amendments Act, Ways and Means chief counsel John Martin sent a confidential memorandum to committee members asking them to list additional member's bills for Members' Day 1972.[10]

The chairman of the Senate Finance Committee is no less a champion of special interest bills. In the rush at the end of the session, on October 11, 1971, the committee spent a two-hour executive session approving thirteen member's bills worth about $240 million in concessions and benefits to special interests. One member's bill would have saved Lockheed Aircraft Corporation as well as other aircraft manufacturers and airlines $145 million. Another would have given the AVCO conglomerate an expensive tax break.

As a result of floor action by tax reform senators, most of these bills were defeated, but at the same time a few tax relief amendments were added.* One that passed was a bill that Frank Church (D., Idaho) intended to aid the arts. Since the tax deduction for contributions of paintings and manuscripts had been reduced three years before, Church was aware of the problems that museums and libraries had in obtaining donations from artists and writers. He introduced the bill (S.1212) to partly reinstate the deduction for charitable contributions by artists and writers.

On October 16, Church successfully added his bill to H.R. 7577. He said on the floor that "this amendment is restricted to

---

* Unlike most Ways and Means bills, which come to the floor with a closed rule, those of the Finance Committee may be amended by the Senate.

artists, composers, and writers, those who create. . . . It is antici-pated that it would not have consequential effect upon Federal revenue." Yet the next day the JCIRT's staff report to the House-Senate conferees dealing with H.R. 7577 refuted Church's claim: it estimated that the bill would cut revenues by $60 million annually. The major beneficiaries of the amendment would not be writers and artists but, rather, the major pharmaceu-tical companies that donate excess inventory to hospitals and relief organizations. The high markup of drugs—often 100 percent—would make such "contributions" profitable under Church's amendment. Church's legislative aide, Mike Wetherall, explained that "the Senator said at the time that was not how he intended it and requested that the language be modified to limit it to artists and writers."

Such tax relief bills and floor amendments previously cleared by the Finance Committee have given rise to a tax code shot full of loopholes. One of the classic tax relief provisions is the "Louis B. Mayer amendment," which saved the former movie magnate and head of Metro-Goldwyn-Mayer about $2 million in taxes.[11] As president of MGM, Mayer had a contract which gave him a share of the company's profits for five years after his retirement. When he left the company in 1951, though, he decided to take a lump-sum settlement that would have been heavily taxed by the govern-ment. Mayer's lawyer, Elsworth C. Alvord, chief tax lobbyist for the U.S. Chamber of Commerce, convinced the Finance Commit-tee to report an amendment to the tax code (eventually known as Section 1240) to have Mayer's settlement taxed as capital gains (25 percent of Mayer's settlement) and not personal income (at that time 91 percent). The amendment described the contract in such detail that the tax privilege would be applicable only to Mayer's contract with MGM.*

---

* Section 1240 of the U.S. Tax Code reads:

"Amounts received from the assignment or release by an employee, after more than 20 years' employment, of all his rights to receive, after termina-tion of his employment and for a period of not less than 5 years (or for a period ending with his death), a percentage of future profits or receipts of

Another special amendment that coddled the wealthy was introduced in 1956 by Robert Kerr, a member of the Finance Committee. During World War II an Oklahoma City general contractor, Leo Sanders, had received $955,000 from the federal government for a contract.[12] After government prodding, he finally included this small fortune on his tax report, but as capital gains instead of personal income. He filed no tax returns for the next three years. The government finally filed suit against Sanders for $729,446 in tax deficiencies and $226,258 for delinquency. The Tax Court upheld the government's decision, and the Supreme Court denied Sanders' appeal in February 1956. Less than four months later Congress passed Kerr's provision that reversed the Court's decision, made the maximum tax that could be applied against Sanders' government contract settlement only 33 percent, and excused him from the delinquency charges.

The amendments tacked onto the Foreign Investors Tax Act at the end of 1966 were among the most infamous. The act was eventually so burdened with extra amendments that some amateur poet wrote:

> 'Twas the night before Christmas,
> When all through the House,
> Not a creature was stirring,
> Not even a mouse.
> When across in the Senate,
> There arose such a clatter:

---

his employer shall be considered an amount received from the sale or exchange of a capital asset held for more than 6 months if—

(1) such rights were included in the terms of the employment of such employee for not less than 12 years,

(2) such rights were included in the terms of the employment of such employee before the date of enactment of this title, and

(3) the total of the amounts received for such assignment or release is received in one taxable year and after the termination of such employment."

Subparts one and two limit the section's applicability to employees who had the sort of contract defined by the section at least twelve years before the section was enacted. The only way that the provision could be more explicit would be if it mentioned Mayer by name.

Russell Long was inserting
Extraneous matter.[13]

Long tossed in an amendment that would triple the depletion allowance from 5 to 15 percent for clam and oyster shells used in making cement and chicken food. Senator Frank Carlson (R., Kans.) then did the same for his state's clay, shale, and slate industries. Then, as the *Washington Post* put it:

> The $200 million-a-year clay pipe industry, feeling left out, appealed to [Vance] Hartke. He trimmed the Christmas tree (as the bill was called because of all the amendments that adorned it) on behalf of clay pipes with a floor amendment tripling their depletion allowance.[14]

The House-Senate conference later shrank the depletion for clay, shale, and slate to 7.5 percent, but kept Long's 15 percent for mollusks.

Hartke had also introduced an amendment that would save the Harvey Aluminum Company of Torrance, California, about $2 million. An investment credit program adopted in 1962 let businessmen deduct from their corporate taxes 7 percent of the funds spent on new plants and machinery in the fifty states and the District of Columbia. Though Congress had just suspended the credit to stem inflation, Hartke extended its coverage to include U.S. possessions, so that Harvey Aluminum could deduct 7 percent of its new plant in the Virgin Islands. Since the amendment as passed was retroactive to January 1, the firm would not have lost a cent under the investment credit plan that had expired on October 1. Although Harvey Aluminum had no plants in Hartke's home state, Indiana, the senator was a good friend of S. Keith Linden, one of the company's vice-presidents and its chief Washington lobbyist. Linden had sponsored a fund-raising dinner for Democratic members of Congress and had been the treasurer of the Senate Democratic Campaign Committee while Hartke was its chairman.[15]

Hartke was also generous enough to offer as an amendment from the Senate floor a bill that had originally cropped up in Ways and Means. Most of its benefits would have gone to doctors, lawyers, and other professionals earning more than $25,000 a year, since it gave them tax deductions of up to $2,500 a year for income put into personal pension plans. It would have cost the government about $60 million annually in reduced taxes. The Finance Committee had refused to add the amendment to the bill after Long argued that it discriminated against those who could not deduct their pension funds (in the form of social security) from their taxes. But Hartke, along with the American Medical Association, the American Bar Association, the American Dental Association, the American Institute of Certified Public Accountants, and the National Society of Professional Engineers, gladly supported it.

Some of the biggest and most effective lobbyists are the railroads. In 1969 the railroads secured a $100-million package of benefits for themselves. Pleading that there was a freight car shortage, they insisted that the investment credit—which was about to be repealed—be kept in effect for railroads. Assistant Treasury Secretary Edwin Cohen's meetings with railroad lobbyists produced a five-year depreciation write-off for "rolling stock." It also included amortization for rail roadbeds and tunnel bases, which permitted the railroads, according to one former Treasury official, to "depreciate the undepreciable by calling it amortization —wholly unjustifiable on any grounds of tax logic."

VOICES OF THE PUBLIC

If Patrick Henry thought that taxation without representation was bad, he should see how bad it is with representation.
—Farmer's Almanac, 1966

Most members of Congress are indignant at any accusation of pandering to special interests and forsaking the welfare of the general public. Ways and Means member Phil Landrum (D., Ga.) says, "Every one of us represents the public interest." To most members of Congress, though, the "public interest" means responding to those groups or individuals who are most vocal and persistent, invariably those that can afford to be.

The few groups that do speak for the general public are hampered by the government and have limited influence compared to campaign supporters and fund raisers. For example, the tax laws themselves discriminate against public interest organizations. Most expenses for lobbying by business—the cost of material, travel, personnel, and entertainment—are tax deductible. But contributions by an individual to a lobbying organization—the financial staple of public interest groups—are taxable. And many on the revenue committees resent claims by the public interest groups that they represent the entire public. Committee members are inclined to give more credence to the representatives from private industry—not because they have greater knowledge or expertise, but simply because they speak for power and money.

The respect given to lobbyists from private industry is reflected by the great courtesy shown them when they testify before the revenue committees. They are generally allowed to give their entire testimony without interruptions, and when they have finished testifying, members thank them and praise them for their logic. For instance, when the president of the American Iron and Steel Institute, John P. Roche, testified on President Nixon's economic recovery program before the Senate Finance Committee, in October 1971, Senator Bennett complimented Roche for making "a pretty good argument" and paternally advised him, "don't throw it away."[16] But when Thomas Stanton of the Public Interest Research Group testified, he was repeatedly harassed by Bennett and Senator Paul Fannin (R., Ariz.). When Stanton called Treasury Secretary Connally's figures on the capital cost index "deceptive and misleading," Fannin rushed in to defend Connally. Before Stanton could "explain in detail" what he meant, Fannin cross-examined him:

> Let me ask you this. What is your background and experience in business and government?
> MR. STANTON: Well, sir, relatively little. I have simply studied—

SENATOR FANNIN: Still, you are criticizing people with long experience in government affairs, and I accept your testimony on that basis. Mr. Chairman, I have no further question.[17]

Despite the hostility that public interest tax groups encounter from Congress, a number have sprung up in the last few years. Their effectiveness is hard to gauge, but their dedication cannot be denied. Among these groups is Common Cause. For about a year and a half during 1970 and 1971, the citizens' lobby had a Tax Reform Advisory Group headed by Harvard economics professor and former Assistant Treasury Secretary Stanley Surrey to handle research and suggest revenue areas where Common Cause might be effective. The board, which included Mortimer Caplin, former director of the IRS, and Bernard Wolfman, dean of the University of Pennsylvania Law School, was most active during Common Cause's fight against Assets Depreciation Range and the Domestic International Sales Corporation. Since then Common Cause's sixty-member board of directors has decided to concentrate on recouping about $10 billion from the loopholes in the tax codes. It is also concerned with opening the shutters that surround the revenue committees. For instance, it convinced the 1972 Democratic National Convention to adopt a plank demanding the abolition of Ways and Means's closed rule. Whatever direction Common Cause's fight for reform takes, its membership of 200,000 should provide it with considerable political clout.

The unions are another tax reform group. Both the AFL-CIO and the United Auto Workers have tried to ease the tax burden on lower-income people and make it more equitable. Their regular newsletters, which occasionally treat tax and welfare reform issues, have great potential to mobilize their millions of members. For years the unions have fought the tax reform battle almost alone.

Created in January 1972 by Public Citizens, the Tax Reform Research Group is another public interest group. It has three lawyers, an economist, and a professional organizer. Its goal is to reform the tax system by presenting people, votes, clout, pressure, and anger at the local and national levels. It has attacked the Asset Depreciation Range regulations, the Domestic International Sales Corporation, member's bills, IRS auditing and ruling procedures, and local property taxes. In its first two years Tax Reform has started a periodical, *People and Taxes*, published a citizen's tax bibliography, and helped organize citizen taxpayer leagues around the country.

A tax reform coalition called Taxation with Representation/ Tax Analysts/ Tax Advocates has also developed. Attorney Thomas Field, formerly with the Justice and Treasury Departments, is its head. Taxation with Representation, incorporated in July 1970, is basically a mediator that aims to "assist public-spirited tax experts who wish to testify as members of the general public" on tax issues before Congress or the IRS. TWR takes no stands. It keeps its members posted on developing issues and distributes their testimony in its periodical, *Complete Documents Service*. Tax Analysts and Tax Advocates, begun in the fall of 1972, are both supported by the Stern Fund, other foundations, private contributions, and the sale of a weekly publication. Tax Analysts is headed by Dr. Gerard Brannon, former director of the Treasury Department's Office of Tax Analysis. It has three hundred consulting experts available to consult with and help journalists do revenue research. They also monitor tax legislation on the recommendation of the group's Legal Activities Policy Board, and counsel other public interest law firms on tax matters. They publish *Tax Notes*, a weekly newsletter containing special reports on tax issues, discussion of congressional and administration activity, and analyses of pending tax legislation. As the action arm, Tax Advocates has filed a suit to make public all the rulings of the IRS and to reveal congressional correspondence with the Treasury Department. It plans action on the lobbying restrictions imposed on certain tax-exempt organizations, the Tax Expenditure Budget, and on certain Securities and Exchange Commission procedures.

The power of grass-roots pressure is significant, particularly when harnessed by a powerful industry to protect "its" money. Public interest advocates would do well to observe the timing and tactics of the Savings and Loan League's assault against an early Kennedy administration proposal.

MISREPRESENTATION TO THE PUBLIC

For years withholding of income taxes on wages and salaries has been the established order, protecting workers from having to pay huge lump sums at the end of the year, and resulting in no more than 3 percent of such income going unreported and untaxed. The same check had never been applied on dividends and interest —income on stocks, bonds, and interest on savings deposits, and the like—largely income to the more affluent. They were expected to declare voluntarily and pay the required taxes. Although a 1959 Treasury study showed that this burden was not being shouldered in a very responsible fashion—the total unreported income of this type was estimated to be $3,777,000,000, at an annual revenue loss to the government of $864,000,000,[18] a burden to be borne in part by wage and salary earners—the Eisenhower Treasury Department was cool to the idea of withholding on interest and dividends.[19] But others had been advocating such withholding, among them Senator Paul Douglas and Professor Stanley S. Surrey of Harvard Law School, a former Treasury official. When John Kennedy was elected president, Surrey headed a task force to formulate recommendations on taxes. The report has never been made public, but one of its suggestions was that the new administration go after withholding on dividends, an item included in President Kennedy's subsequent tax message to the Congress on April 21, 1961. (Surrey in the meantime had become Assistant Secretary of the Treasury for Tax Policy, after stormy Senate Finance Committee nomination hearings.)[20]

Unfortunately, the Treasury had not discussed its 1961 tax package with anyone in Congress, which made for difficult sledding, and withholding was one of the most controversial of the provisions.[21] Economist Joseph Pechman of Brookings played a major role in designing the withholding plan, which required the institution paying out the dividend or interest to deduct automatically the current 20 percent basic rate of income tax from all such payments made. The recipients of the income could file quarterly for any amount paid over that which they owed. Based on the experience with withholding on wages and salaries, it was anticipated that this would be an efficient system.

In the House, there was apprehension over the provision, whipped up in part by the testimony of banking and savings and loan institutions at the hearings. The testimony, muted by comparison to what was to come later, was cast in terms of red tape and widows and orphans who would have money withheld which was not owed. Chairman Mills strongly supported the 20 percent measure, although the committee reported it out at 16⅔ percent, to deal with the danger of overwithholding. The real issue to the banks and the savings and loan organizations was not the widows and orphans, but the loss of reserves and loanable funds they would experience under withholding. Most depositors let their interest build up in their accounts, and this money could be used by the institutions for their own purposes. Twenty percent of it would be a large cut in the resources they had available to run their businesses, earn other money, and expand.

For tactical reasons the opposition to the withholding plan waited to make its full assault in the Senate, but the administration was taking no chances. The limited debate on the House floor saw the Democrats arguing that withholding was the only way to collect the real $1 billion owed, and that nontaxpayers could be protected by appropriate administrative measures. Republicans for their part looked to modern data processing and publicity to do the same job. A former aide to Ways and Means member Al Ullman describes the pressure put on the House to pass the measure:

> Boggs [the majority whip] dragged a Wisconsin Democrat, who was threatening to defect because of the withholding section, off the floor to the Speaker's office where [Speaker]

McCormack was on the phone to the President. Thrusting the phone toward the Wisconsinite, the Speaker said, "Tell the President all about it!"[22]

All Wisconsin's representatives voted for the bill, and it passed the House 219-196 on March 29, 1962.

As the bill moved on to the Senate, both JCIRT chief of staff Colin Stam and the chairman of the Finance Committee, Senator Harry F. Byrd, Sr., were opposed, especially to the withholding provision. Byrd and the administration both agreed that Senator Bob Kerr might more happily manage the bill, which he did with the help of Stam's assistant, Dr. Laurence Woodworth. At the hearings, individuals, organizations, banks, corporations, and savings and loan associations testified against withholding. The administration had since agreed to use a system of exemption certificates to protect the widows and orphans but this failed to conciliate opponents.

The real flak came through the mails. A few days before the bill had passed the House, the executive committee of the United States Savings and Loan League had decided to try a massive letter-writing campaign against withholding.[23] It sent out letters to its 4,800 local association members asking that they and their depositors, borrowers, and other clients send the Senate a message. The message came. Former Senator Douglas received more than 75,000 letters in three weeks' time in what he termed "a letter-writing blitz. . . . The deluge of concentrated opposition we received was even bigger than when Truman fired MacArthur."[24] A former aide to Finance Committee member Eugene McCarthy estimates that for weeks his mail ran over a thousand letters a day on withholding, and this was the case for many senators.[25]

Former Douglas aide Howard Schuman says, "The savings and loan people were putting out a lot of crap about withholding"; the letter writers seemed to think that the tax would be on their principal, not the interest, and that dividends and interest had not been taxable before. Douglas said that messages were coming through to his office with arguments that interest was not income and hence not subject to taxation, or that it should not be taxable because it was the fruit of saving. The 20 percent levy on the total was a recurrent theme, "attached as part of a Communist scheme to confiscate all private capital. A high rate of patriotic indignation was thus injected into the discussion, and we were branded as sinister villains seeking to undermine the republic." Douglas added, "During the whole discussion, which went on for weeks, I do not remember ever receiving a single letter from an economist supporting our efforts. The tax academicians were so absorbed in promoting dubious economic growth that they were ready to ignore tax injustice."[26]

Although many banks joined in the campaign, the American Banking Association and the National Association of Mutual Savings Banks both refrained from officially supporting the "grass-roots" pressure. According to one close observer, "Both thought the United States Savings and Loan League's well-publicized efforts were an almost vulgar display of political muscle-flexing which might in time react unfavorably upon the savings and loan industry." Treasury Secretary C. Douglas Dillon was disgusted, charging that the letter-writing campaign had "set new records for distortion of the facts and . . . created widespread misunderstanding."[27] Dillon sent letters of clarification to individual senators, proponents replied to their letter-writing constituents, insertions were made in the *Congressional Record,* and the president discussed the matter in a press conference—all with little success in undoing the mischief. As Douglas put it, "the tide was irresistible."[28] Too late, the League called off its letter-writing campaign. The assault had had a profound "shock value" on senatorial offices and sensitivities, and by early June a majority appeared to oppose withholding.[29]

In an attempt to salvage the plan, Treasury and *ad hoc* chairman Kerr worked out a compromise with a series of exemptions, which had the effect of reducing anticipated revenues from $780 to $620 million. But the damage had been done. On July 11 the Finance Committee rejected withholding, ten to five. The only faithful administration supporters were Kerr, Anderson, Douglas, Gore, and Hartke. An informal floor pool showed that a maximum of thirty-eight votes was all the administration could hope for on the floor in an amendment fight. It was a major defeat; in deep trouble with the rest of its tax package, the administration abandoned its long tussle with the banks and savings and loan institutions and gave up on withholding.

The committee then unanimously passed a substitute proposed by Chairman Byrd requiring that the payers of interest and dividends report to the Treasury Department all payments over $10 in a calendar year and to whom they were paid, and that they notify the recipients of the amounts paid them.

VOICES OF INDUSTRY

The revenue committees are prey to more lobbying groups than any other committee on Capitol Hill. Whether they are lobbyists for unions, industry, or the public interest, their influence on the laws that flow from the committees is significant, and the laws that are produced are important ones.

The oil and gas industry is well represented in Washington, with over sixty organizations of varying sizes and degrees of strength keeping an eye on government developments, educating, persuading, representing, and the like. Oil production goes on in thirty-two states, with over 1,200,000 employees directly involved, and constitutes a $15 billion business. The largest Washington petroleum lobby is the American Petroleum Institute, primarily a spokesman for the "major" companies in the "Six Sisters" (Texaco, Gulf, Shell, Mobil, Standard, and Atlantic-Richfield), although it claims to be an "umbrella" group with nearly eight thousand corporate and individual members. It employs 230 lobbyists, economists, lawyers, geologists, public relations specialists, researchers, and clerical people in a lavish complex in Washington. It has been operating since 1919, and is organized as a nonprofit organization. API is headed by Frank Ikard, a former member of the Ways and Means Committee.

The Independent Petroleum Association of America represents smaller producers and firms, wildcatters, and individual businessmen and professionals. It has a total staff of about twenty, less than the API has in its public affairs and governmental relations divisions alone. IPAA's membership has been on the decline, down from around 7,200 in 1956 to about four thousand today, reflecting the increasing dominance of "the majors." IPAA's vice-president for public affairs, Lloyd Unsell, is its chief lobbyist. Formerly a moonlighting speech writer for the late Senator Robert Kerr of Oklahoma, the Finance Committee's staunchest oil protector, Unsell now performs similar chores for Finance member Cliff Hansen of Wyoming, the latter-day "Mr. Oil" (a title shared with Chairman Long). Unsell was instrumental in orchestrating the independents' efforts to protect their flanks in 1969, although the IPAA generally seeks to avoid conflict with its big brother, API, and its big sister oil companies. IPAA has been in existence since 1930 and until recently was based in Tulsa, Oklahoma.

A third organization is the American Chemical Society, set up by Congress in 1937 to foster research. Among the largest members of ACS are the major petroleum companies, which in 1944 created the Petroleum Research Fund, a trust now worth over $100 million and administered by the ACS as a tax-exempt unit dedicated to research in petroleum and petroleum products. The ACS's organ is the *Chemical and Engineering News*, which champions the petrochemical industry and inveighs against its detractors, be they environmentalists or tax reformers.

Numerous other groups abound, including the American Petroleum Refiners Association, a much smaller operation than IPAA. A powerful regional group is the Mid-Continent Oil and Gas Association, representing industry components mainly in Kansas, Oklahoma, Texas, and Louisiana. Its Washington office is headed by a close associate of former President Johnson and former Treasury Secretary Connally. Other regional organizations include the Rocky Mountain Oil and Gas Association, the Texas Independent Petroleum Refiners Association, the Kansas Independent Oil and Gas Association, and the Independent Oil and Gas Association of West Virginia.

Coordination of the complex "industry" is said to be loose and often ineffectual. One aide to Long explained this by referring to the highly individualistic "bastards" at the top of companies being represented. His experience has been that the industry's lobbying is seldom a united effort, but rather is characterized by "incessant infighting—their biggest problem is in their own ranks." And if the issue is not in a particular company's direct interest, "they won't use up their green stamps and will sit it out," though they may be under pressure to join in.

One industry lobbyist claimed the trade associations have a hard time lining up support because many of the companies are "paranoid, scared that other companies are in there stabbing them."

The petroleum industry over the years has been able to maintain its tax preferences by a variety of strategic courtships. These included for many years the congressional leadership, most especially the Johnson-Rayburn-Kerr axis; the revenue-raising committees, long open almost exclusively to industry supporters who display a certain longevity and devotion of service, and who on the Finance Committee tended to come from the principal oil-producing states; the Treasury, in its key personalities and specific divisions, including units in the IRS; and the presidency, except for Kennedy, who was insecure about his standing with the business community, dependent on some oil campaign money, and willing to sacrifice oil reforms for other tax measures and reforms.

The oil industry is perhaps the most universal constituent force and pressure for every member of Congress, as well as a campaign funding source for many. In addition to these relationships, the industry has been able to sell a set of myths centering on the energy crisis, national security, the tremendous risk involved in the industry, the widows and orphans with small holdings of stock as the main beneficiaries of the preferences, and in general the sheer patriotism of the industry.

But at the same time a small band of willful tax reformers has been crying in the wilderness over the gross inequities inherent in oil industry tax breaks. Such public figures as Douglas, Gore, Proxmire, Williams, Humphrey, and Vanick have long sought to burst the oil bubble. Academics and Treasury reformers have tried to do the same, but with no greater success. A slight adjustment was made in the 1963 tax bill, but not a substantial diminution by any means. Yet by 1969 the oil depletion allowance had, through various means, become a symbol of inequities. The recruitment criteria for the tax committees were changing, and not all the new members had been "cleared" on the oil question. By then any tax reform effort which did not attempt some inroads into the industry's favored position would have been seen as a sham. The comprehensive Treasury tax reform studies that provided the basis of the 1969 Tax Reform Act did not include recommendations on the petroleum industry, but study of the industry had been commissioned as part of the overall study. Although one of its major findings was that the cost of producing an additional $150 million worth of revenues was $1.4 billion, Treasury officials felt that the data were inadequate to make sound predictions about the effect of changes in the system of tax preferences.

But the sentiment was there and the industry knew it. However, it was not quite prepared to have its benefits pared as they were by its apparently self-appointed in-house representative, Hale Boggs, the Ways and Means member from petroleum-rich Louisiana. It was his motion that ultimately prevailed in committee, knocking the depletion allowance down from 27.5 to 20 percent. He reasoned that this would remove the industry as a congressional "whipping boy" and called upon "progressive members" of the industry "to accept these reasonable reforms and thus remove the issue as one of national controversy."[30] This was the rate passed by the House, under closed rule, and the industry had to turn to the Senate for relief. Although expecting to get the rate back up to the sanctified 27.5 level, the best it was able to get from the Senate was a raise to 23 percent, which Chairman Long requested to bargain with in conference. The compromise worked out in conference was 22 percent.

The depletion allowance is only one of the industry's tax preferences, and is more beneficial to the major oil companies than to the smaller and independent ones. More helpful to small oil companies is the "expensing" of intangible drilling costs. This tax preference permits the immediate deduction of the costs of drilling, rather than requiring the ordinary business practice of spreading the deduction of such costs over the life of the asset, matching expense and return in a fairly correct reflection of income. But this permits the small producer or wildcatter to sell his rights to a well, immediately deduct the costs from the income, and have a very favorable tax situation as well as the capital necessary for further exploration. Small operators usually need this capital more than the large ones, who of course still take advantage of the expensing provision. The typical small producer will not have a sufficiently high ratio of net to gross income to be able to take advantage of the full 27.5 percent depletion allowance, while the large one will. In short, the allowance was worth more to the majors and the expensing far more to the minors.

The 1969 tax reform hearings did not stem from administration proposals, and when called by the Ways and Means Committee, the industry was unsure of what would be coming and of their strategic position. The initial presentation at the hearings did not focus on the distinctive relative benefits of the allowance. Chairman Mills drew it out of the witnesses,[31] who were somewhat reluctant to acknowledge the difference and create a rupture in the industry's united front. But the delegation, representing the API, the IPAA, the drilling associations, and an oil investment banking firm, scrambled to support the provisions that specifically favored their constituencies. The crack began to form under Mills's well-placed chisel, as he inquired about doing away with the expensing provision and replacing it with a more usual capitalizing requirement.

> CHAIRMAN MILLS: Would that have an impact on industry?
> MR. MC CLURE: It would have a very dramatic impact on we independents. There is no question about that. . . .
> MR. WRIGHT (of Humble Oil): In the larger companies it would not have the impact it would have on the smaller companies.[32]

The following day a group of seven witnesses, representing various regional independent oil associations, told the committee that their companies were too small to take advantage of the full 27.5 percent.[33] They cited figures from polls and educated estimates which ranged 0 to 25.5 percent, with averages hovering around 16 percent.[34] Their arguments implied that a reduction in the depletion allowance would not affect them in any way. However, the smaller witnesses were insistent on the utterly critical necessity to leave the expensing provision alone.

On the Senate side the industry was no longer a united front. The independents, while not neglecting the depletion allowance proposals, strongly stressed that expensing was more important to them.[35] Some big companies went after larger depletion allowances, while others looked more to a favorable compromise on depletion and retention of the existing expensing. Other spokesmen attempted to adjust the mechanisms of the depletion allowance to make it more available to independents, which would also have benefited the majors.

In the end Finance and the Senate-House conference gave some depletion benefits back to the majors and left the expensing alone, to the benefit of both majors and minors. The net loss to the majors, and to the entire industry, may turn out to be more tactical than monetary in the long run. Most of the large companies purchase for processing crude oil extracted by themselves, setting their own prices to themselves. The depletion allowance is calculated on the selling price of crude oil at the wellhead, and so the big, vertically integrated companies have raised their prices to themselves to make up for the cut in the allowance.[36] It all comes out favorably for the integrated majors, but the practice penalizes the independent refineries, who must buy all their crude oil from others. Thus some of the independents have been severely damaged, while the majors have been increasing their after-tax profits. A tax expert has charged that the Antitrust Division of the Justice Department has often requested the IRS to investigate the integrated firms' self-dealing in crude oil but that the IRS "has been reluctant to act."[37] The expert blamed the delay on the questionable loyalties of employees in the Oil and Gas Branch of the IRS Natural Resources Section.

The real damage to the industry from the 1969 cuts came more from the fact that cuts were made at all. The industry's solid bulwark was breached. Legislators can now ask more critical and probing questions and seriously challenge the whole complex of preferences and subsidies enjoyed by the industry. And "the industry" had exposed itself as being divided, both in the public and congressional consciousness and within itself. The rifts of the 1969 season have been institutionalized in the resultant practices of the self-interested components of a once unified special interest group.

RAISING REVENUE AND HAVOC

Few laws, and especially few tax laws, follow the neat demarcations of the charts in civics textbooks that trace a bill from its conception through congressional debate to the president's desk for final signature. If it were so simple, Washington—a city that thrives on intrigues, innuendos, and the sheer joy of complexities —might collapse from boredom. As the economist Joseph Pechman said, "[tax laws] are one of the most interesting, puzzling, and controversial features of the legislative process."[38] Senator Proxmire's administrative aide, Howard Schuman, called Pechman's "legislative process" a "mumbo-jumbo" and even denied that there *is* a process. Getting a bill through, he said, "is an art, not a process." If Schuman is right, the best artists in Washington are those in the executive branch—in the Treasury Department, the Federal Reserve Board, the Office of Management and Budget, and, master of them all, the man who sits in the White House Oval Office. Although the Constitution put the burden for initiating tax policy on the House, for the past twenty years the initiative has often come from the executive branch. The multibillion-dollar 1971 Revenue Act, for example, came from the executive and was rammed through the entire legislative process in four months.

Prominent in the tax policy sent to Congress are two divisions of the Treasury Department—the Office of Tax Analysis and the Office of the Tax Legislative Counsel. The two sections together employ about thirty economists and statisticians and about twenty tax attorneys. The directors of both offices report to the Assistant Secretary for Tax Policy, and the Assistant Secretary for Tax Policy is aided by over one thousand other personnel.

The tax committees have often been content to play a reactive role. They depend upon the executive branch not only for the initial policy proposals but also for the expertise to interpret the proposals at every step of the legislative process: introduction, hearings, executive markup sessions, floor justification, and the House-Senate conferences. At each of these points, Congress cordially opens its doors for lobbyists from the executive branch.

At Ways and Means hearings on legislation proposed by the executive, it is not unusual for the Treasury Secretary or the Assistant Secretary for Tax Policy to testify. He may fill the hearing reports with intricate tables, complex legal and technical explanations, and memoranda to support the government's case. At the committee's executive sessions, these very same representatives from the executive may appear again. John Kennedy's Treasury Secretary, Douglas Dillon, was a frequent visitor to executive sessions. Other Treasury secretaries, like John Connally, preferred to meet with the committee in informal sessions and make their pitches in nonlegislating atmospheres. Lesser representatives from the Treasury Department are always visiting with individual members in their offices to explain the executive branch's policy. At markup sessions, Ways and Means members are frequently outnumbered by administration personnel and the sessions turn into a three-way discussion between the Treasury, Ways and Means, and JCIRT staffs.

After Congress passes the tax laws proposed by the executive branch, the executive branch and its agencies set the regulations for implementing them. The Treasury Department is empowered to "prescribe all needful rules and regulations for the enforcement" of the Internal Revenue Code.[39] Proposed regulations are first published in the government's *Federal Register* for taxpayers' comment. Under the Administrative Procedure Act, hearings may be required.

If private interests cannot convince a member of Congress to favor them with a member's bill or special amendment to a bill, they may be able to wangle a favorable ruling from the IRS. While about 600 rulings are published each year, over 30,000 "private rulings" are not.* These rulings can be expensive. In 1964 the IRS gave away some $400 million in tax benefits to violators of the antitrust laws, notably including General Electric, Westinghouse, and the other major electric companies convicted of price-fixing violations. The ruling: such companies could deduct from taxes the treble-damage payments (for antitrust violations) as "ordinary and necessary" business expenses.

A series of rulings on hard mineral "production payments" between 1966 and 1969 cost the government over $175 million, in the form of tax cuts for large oil companies acquiring coal and other hard mineral companies with tax-free dollars.

In 1972 the IRS issued a ruling allowing American copper companies favorable tax treatment on property expropriated by the Chilean government. The cost: somewhere between $75 million and $175 million in tax cuts for the copper companies.

A few case studies show how congressional tax machinery has interacted with the executive branch, special interests, and public interest representatives. They also show how special IRS rulings have benefited select groups of American business.

Assets Depreciation Range

In a television interview on January 4, 1971, President Nixon discussed his plan for the nation's economy for the coming year. He assured Americans that his administration was going to take an "activist" role in solving the twin problems of inflation and

---

* In June 1973 a federal district court ruled this secrecy violates the Freedom of Information Act and ordered IRS to make even the private rulings open to public examination. As of this writing, IRS has appealed the case.

unemployment. But he warned "this year I do not think it realistic to propose a new tax—either new taxes or tax reform."⁴⁰

Most Americans thought the President's statement also meant that he wouldn't back any tax cuts for 1971. But exactly a week later the President announced that he had approved Treasury actions to establish the Asset Depreciation Range System to allow businesses to deduct their equipment costs at a greater rate than previously. The administration originally announced that this would cut business taxes by $2.7 billion annually.⁴¹ It later revised this figure to $3.9 billion, more than the combined 1972 budgets of the Environmental Protection Agency, the State Department, and the entire federal judiciary system.⁴² According to this new estimate, the ADR tax giveaways to business would cost each taxpayer about $50 each year.

ADR represented more than a 10 percent cut in corporate income tax rates. Just a year before, when Congress passed the Tax Reform Act of 1969, it had refused to shrink corporate income taxes by even 2 percent. But ADR clearly showed that the administration sided with business. Though ADR would cost the government nearly $4 billion a year, the President had recently vetoed a $453 million education bill and a $514 million housing bill. The cost of ADR was greater than some of the administration's major social programs, such as its proposed $2.1 billion welfare reform or the $3.6 billion total of federal aid to preschool, elementary, and secondary education.

Under Section 167 of the Tax Code, businesses can deduct a part of the cost of their assets—equipment and machinery—from their income each year. The deduction must be based on the expected life of the equipment deducted for, so that they eventually recover its full cost minus the amount they would receive for it as "salvage." Several methods can be used to compute the "depreciation." Under the straight-line technique, owners can deduct an equal amount on the time each year. Or more can be deducted during the first years and less deducted later.

As originally announced by the administration, ADR allowed firms to shorten by 20 percent the expected life of a fixed asset acquired after January 1, 1971. This meant that machinery previously slated for depreciation over a ten-year span could now be depreciated over eight years. Using ADR a businessman could deduct more from his gross income—and his tax bill. For example, under the original depreciation schedule, a machine costing $1 million with a ten-year life span would give the owner a $100,000 deduction for ten years. But under ADR, $125,000 could be deducted for eight years. To promulgate this tax relief, the Treasury proposed to abandon its "reserve ratio test." Since 1962, this had required that owners relate the tax or depreciable life of their equipment to its useful or active life. The administration said it was junking the reserve ratio test because of alleged problems in administering it.

But the one hitch in the administration's plan was the law it was sworn to uphold. A 1968 Treasury Department study concluded that changes in the depreciation rate would have to be legislated by Congress. A September 1970 report by the Presidential Task Force on Business Taxation, headed by a former law partner of President Nixon and Attorney General John Mitchell, agreed. It included an even more generous ADR proposal, but noted that shifting from depreciation to cost recovery unrelated to useful life "does require amendment of the present law." As the Treasury's former Assistant Secretary Stanley Surrey said of the Treasury Department under the Nixon administration, "On substantive issues, its arguments border on dishonesty. This was especially true of the ADR."*[43] And a December 11, 1970, memo from Acting Assistant Treasury Secretary John Nolan advised, "We would . . . have reservations as to our administrative authority to abandon the reserve ratio test completely without legislation." Nolan warned:

> Before any decisions are made, the matter should first be
> discussed with John Byrnes and Senator Bennett, then with

* In fact, the IRS is budgeted about one and a half billion dollars annually to administer all provisions of the tax laws. Treasury was trying to say that the $4 billion ADR System was needed just to help administer a small part of the tax laws.

Wilbur Mills and Senator Long and if it then seems appropriate with the Joint Committee on Internal Revenue Taxation. In effect, we would feel that they should have almost the equivalent of a veto over any such liberalization.[44]

Yet despite the recommendations of some of his closest advisers, the President adamantly refused to submit ADR to Congress:

Now I, as President, and I may say, too, formerly one who had practiced a good deal of tax law, I considered that I had the responsibility to decide what the law is. And my view is that while they had expressed a different view, that the correct legal view . . . was to order the depreciation allowances.[45]

In his January 11 press conference, Treasury Secretary David Kennedy asserted that the executive branch had the "power and the authority" to adopt ADR, especially considering "the uncertainties which we would have" if it were submitted to Congress.

Three young lawyers with the Public Interest Research Group reacted to a January 10 article on the drift of Nixon's ADR policies. Working through the night, they prepared a brief to file a motion for a temporary restraining order on ADR. The tax reform lawyers wanted enforcement of the Administrative Procedures Act, which requires agencies like the Treasury Department to give formal notice of proposed rule changes and to allow thirty days for the public to submit its views on the change. On January 11 a federal court not only rejected a motion from the Tax Division of the Justice Department to dismiss PIRG's tax reform suit, but also refused to grant PIRG a temporary restraining order until it had more information than the newspaper report.

Full hearings on the public interest group's motion for a temporary restraining order were set for January 26. Shortly after the January 11 decision, President Nixon announced from his San Clemente bluffs that he himself had approved ADR.

Treasury Department officials were confused in the wake of the President's announcement and the pending court hearing.

On January 12 Edwin Cohen, the Assistant Secretary for Tax Policy, told the press that Treasury had intended to hold the hearings—it had simply forgotten to announce the fact. The next day he refuted his previous day's statement that hearings were required by the Administrative Procedures Act but said that they would be held anyway—just to be "fair."[46] But he privately said, "After opinions are heard, Treasury doubtless will still want to adopt the basic systems."

In an affidavit filed by the Justice Department three days before the PIRG hearing, IRS Commissioner Randolph W. Thrower said that public hearings would be held after publication and formal notice. Before the final regulations were drawn, he said, "consideration will be given" to public comments. On the eve of the hearing, Cohen also submitted a similar affidavit promising hearings on ADR. When Justice Department lawyers gave the same assurance in court, the PIRG lawyers withdrew their suit.[47]

Though the Treasury had capitulated to PIRG's pressures to hold the hearings, it had done so most reluctantly. The day PIRG withdrew its suit, Cohen said of the hearings, "So far as I know, we're not going to hear any arguments that we haven't thought of, though, of course, we'll listen. We don't anticipate changing our mind. As a very practical matter, a businessman can rely on this going into effect in its broad outline."[48] Angered at Cohen's attitude, PIRG attorney Tom Stanton (later director of the Tax Reform Research Group) accused the assistant secretary of displaying "an arrogant attitude that the Treasury Department had nothing to learn from public participation."[49] Cohen's mood was contagious. The Treasury Department's deputy assistant secretary said, "We will listen to everybody who has something to say. I will add that it is highly unlikely we will change the concept of what we recommend."[50]

Once the administration had announced that it would hold hearings, anti-ADR forces began to mobilize. PIRG and Taxation with Representation solicited analyses and comments from tax experts. Common Cause charged that the administration was trying to make "an end run around Congress. It is another example of the executive branch granting to itself powers it does not possess."[51] Two former IRS commissioners, Sheldon Cohen and Mortimer Caplin, assailed Nixon's action as exceeding his authority over taxes.[52] And Ralph Nader promised further legal action if the regulations were approved without being submitted to Congress. He charged that "a policy change of this magnitude is a matter for the Congress to prescribe through our constitutional procedures, rather than for the executive to dictate."[53]

Yale law professor Boris Bittker believed the Treasury was exceeding its statutory authority by permitting depreciation of assets over the ranges proposed.[54] Walter Heller cautioned that they were "the wrong tax cuts in the wrong way at the wrong time." They could be inflationary, Heller warned, and would actually hurt investments. And Northwestern University's Robert Eisner, an economist who has devoted much of his career to studying the determinants of capital investments, concluded that ADR would probably produce "a considerably smaller increase in capital expenditures than the loss in tax revenues associated with the increased depreciation." He criticized the administration's deferral argument, which contended that ADR was not a tax break but merely postponed taxes. "There is no knowledgeable expert in the Treasury or out of it who can stand by this statement. It is unfortunate that such a flat contradiction of what is an unambiguous matter of arithmetic and mathematics was issued in the name of the President of the United States." The President's and the Treasury's actions were "at worst . . . a conscious effort on the part of some to deceive the public. At best they represent a confusion."[55]

The Treasury Department had tried to notify the four ranking members of the two tax committees of the January 11 presidential edict. The reason for this courtesy was that during a Ways and Means executive session on the 1969 Tax Reform Act, Cohen had assured the committee members that if they approved the investment credit repeal, the administration would not attempt to meddle with depreciation rates.

On Friday, January 8—just three days before the new regulations were to be announced as accomplished fact by President Nixon—Treasury Secretary David Kennedy, Cohen, and Dr. Laurence Woodworth of the JCIRT staff flew to Arkansas to brief Mills on their plans. The Treasury cleared the proposal with ranking Finance Republican Bennett by a phone call, but were unable to locate either Chairman Long or ranking Ways and Means Republican Byrnes, who were both vacationing in the Caribbean. Finance chief counsel Tom Vail gave the green light for Long, and Ways and Means minority counsel Richard Wilbur did the same for Byrnes.

On January 11, the day President Nixon announced the regulations, Cohen told the press, "We did discuss this with Chairman Mills. . . . He agreed with the deduction," but the official transcript of the press conference issued by the Treasury's public relations office omitted the assistant secretary's statement. Mills, expressing doubt that the move would accomplish the economy-stimulating objectives alleged by the administration, fought the move behind committee doors.

Members of Congress jumped into the fray. Senators Edmund Muskie and George McGovern supported the public interest groups. The third-ranking Republican on the Senate Finance Committee, Jack Miller of Iowa, announced his opposition to the administration's proposal. Forty-five Democrats in the House, led by Ways and Means member Sam Gibbons, urged the IRS to withdraw its proposals:

> Only the Congress, as elected representatives of the American people, is able through a comprehensive legislative process to properly evaluate the type of tax legislation that is most beneficial to the country as a whole. In this way benefits on behalf of one segment of the society at the expense of the general taxpayer can be avoided.[56]

Sam Ervin, chairman of the Senate Judiciary Committee, threatened to have his Subcommittee on Separation of Powers investigate the Treasury's encroachment on Congress' jurisdiction over taxation. Cohen to this day is mystified at all the fuss:

> What the hell was there that could be new? We had piles of memorandums a foot thick, from studies done over a ten-year period. Everything was well known to people in the field. All the legal arguments had been made. It could only be a matter of judgment. I had signed the necessary papers, so I must have believed that what we were doing was correct. What the hell is there that's new?

While the opposition was marshaling, the administration was lining up its troops, businesses that stood to benefit from ADR. The Tax Council, a Washington-based tax policy organization supported by business, praised the regulations as "soundly conceived and . . . needed to quicken business interest in new capital outlays as they develop." The National Machine Tool Builders Association declared that the Treasury had both the legal authority and the precedents to put the new rules into effect.[57] On the other hand, economist Dale Jorbenson, hired to speak for AT&T, conceded that ADR would not have any impact for at least eighteen months.

The Treasury chose the machine tool industry, one of ADR's major beneficiaries, as one of its main spokesmen for ADR outside the administration. It provided opponent's statements to the industry's legal and lobbying representative, John Ellicott, of Washington's largest law firm, Covington and Burling. Ellicott's forty-two page rebuttal to the statements of Yale law professor Bittker and Robert Damress, *Harvard Law Review* editor, was signed by another Covington and Burling partner, Joel Barlow, one of Washington's most powerful tax lobbyists. The Barlow-Ellicott memo was used verbatim by the House Republican Conference as a policy statement on ADR.

An outline of testimony for the May 3 hearings had to be submitted by early April. But once the administration saw the opposition force, it extended the deadline for prospective witnesses. The *New York Times* reported:

> [T]he Administration has decided that some statements in support of the liberalization were needed from academics and others with no personal axes to grind and that it needed time to find persons who would write and submit such statements. Ordinarily, such comment from distinterested persons is not solicited by either side on proposed tax regulations but the opponents have flooded the revenue service with critical statements.[58]

When the hearings finally convened, Treasury was so locked into its position that it was unable to listen. On one side of the witness table were ITT, the U.S. Chamber of Commerce, the Council of State Chambers of Commerce, AT&T, the Association of American Railroads, the American Mining Congress, the Machine Tool Builders Association, the Manufacturing Chemists Association, the American Textile Manufacturers Institute, and the National Association of Manufacturers. On the other side were Senator Birch Bayh, Representatives Charles Vanik and Henry Reuss, the National Welfare Rights Organization, the National Council on Hunger and Malnutrition, Ralph Nader, Common Cause, and the AFL-CIO. But these witnesses did not receive the same treatment as their opponents.

The *Wall Street Journal* reported:

> The treatment accorded the witnesses differed sharply, however. Critics of the Administration proposals frequently were peppered with technical questions, particularly by Mr. Cohen and Mr. K. Morton Worthy [IRS chief counsel]. But advocates of the change were often praised for their definitive analyses or for being recognized experts on the subject and often were asked to elaborate on the benefits of the liberalized depreciations guidelines.[59]

One seasoned financial reporter called the hearing a "kangaroo court."

On June 22 the administration announced that ADR would take effect on January 1, 1973. But two weeks later a brief prepared against ADR by Charles Halpern's Center for Law and

Social Policy was filed by Ralph Nader, Common Cause, the United Auto Workers, the National Rural Electric Cooperative Association, a building contractor, and Representative Henry Reuss. It asked a permanent injunction against ADR and noted that by the Treasury Department's own estimates the new act would cost the Treasury $39 billion over the next ten years.

The administration was apprehensive about the suit. The Treasury's September motion to dismiss the case was based entirely on procedural grounds: it met the plaintiffs' substantive charges only in a lone footnote. And a member of the President's Task Force on Business Taxation took the extraordinary step of warning an astonished attorney at a prestigious law firm not to assist the plaintiffs. He said that two firms had already "defected" from the government's position on the issue.

The beneficiaries of the administration's tax break—the nation's largest businesses—were anxious to use ADR, but they feared that the courts would strike it down. The Nixon administration first tried to soothe businessmen's nerves by sending a spokesman, Treasury Secretary John Connally. He denied before a meeting of the U. S. Chamber of Commerce that ADR was a giveaway. "This charge," he said, "would be a mystery to me if it were not for the fact that political candidates can cause otherwise reasonable people who really know better to let their rhetoric rule their reason."[60] The chairman of the House Republican Conference, John Anderson, agreed with Connally. The Illinois representative, whose Rockford district is a center for the machine tool industry, accused the Democrats of "playing politics by their opposition."[61]

But the Republicans' arguments didn't convince the business-financial community. The *Kiplinger Tax Letter*, the nation's most widely read tax advisory service, wrote: "Liberalized depreciation rules are turning into a major fracas. Outcome will have a hefty impact on business profits for years to come. But for now, companies are caught in the middle—showing uncertainty about whether to go forward with the new rules or stand pat with the old."[62]

This attitude was reflected by another business newsletter, *Tax Planning Ideas*, published by the Institute of Business Planning. It warned its readers that the administration had the weaker arguments in the ADR court case and advised them "that the safest course is not to make purchases or investments on these assumptions. At this stage, look on ADR as offering a possible windfall. That's all."[63]

Realizing that ADR would not be used until its legality was established and that the court case could take years, the administration finally decided to take ADR to Congress, where it belonged in the first place. It attached ADR to a bill that was almost guaranteed to pass, the 1971 Revenue Act (H.R. 19047). This tax package served as a complement to the President's August 15, 1971, wage-price freeze.

After three weeks of hearings on the revenue bill, the Ways and Means Act pared ADR to $2.6 billion a year. The Revenue Bill was then sent to the House floor where it was debated for one hour and thirty-nine minutes. It was approved the next day —October 6—by a voice vote with no dissention and with only 30 representatives present.

During the truncated House debate, Wilbur Mills justified the windfall to business:

> The tax reductions provided by the Revenue Act of 1971 represent balanced personal and business income tax relief. This balance is required not only on equity grounds but also by the fact that the restoration of sound and vigorous economic conditions requires not only investment by business but also the stimulation of consumption by individuals as well.[64]

Committee member Sam Gibbons, who had opposed the bill in Ways and Means, conceded that he favored some sections of the act but reminded his colleagues that someone would have to make up for the lost revenue if it passed:

> One man's tax incentive is another man's tax handicap in this country. The dollars we take out of the U. S. Treasury

must eventually be made up elsewhere—either in spending reductions or in somebody's increased taxes. Or, alternatively, by just increasing the size of the national debt—as we have done with great regularity. Increasing the debt just takes revenue out of the pockets of those who are on a fixed income because it is inflationary. On September 24 of this year, when I last computed it, the U. S. Treasury was $32,200 million-plus worse off at that date than it was just the year before.[65]

The Senate took its responsibility to debate this important bill a bit more seriously and spent several days debating the Revenue Act. On November 12, Birch Bayh moved that the ADR be eliminated from the bill. Bayh contended that the Nixon administration had made two major mistakes in trying to deal with underemployment and underproduction through ADR:

First, it is proposing permanent changes in our tax laws to deal with problems which are temporary in nature. . . . [With ADR] we have a far-reaching change in our tax laws which will not only not have its full impact until the mid-1970s, but is no real incentive to investment at all. Yet this change is being pushed by the administration as an answer to our short-run economic problems.

The second big mistake being made by the administration is its belief that the most direct way to spark a recovery is to give tax breaks for investment. But the problem we face is not an insufficient tax incentive for business investment. Investment in plant and equipment has fallen off because the economy was in a recession—and we still have not recovered. Once consumers regain their confidence and spending picks up and we can begin to cut into that intolerable unemployment rate, investment on new plant and equipment will occur naturally. So what we need to do, it seems to me, is to design a tax package that would spark a recovery of consumer spending now and into next year, but without creating any permanent revenue losses.[66]

To spur consumer spending, Bayh proposed a temporary income tax credit of $50 for individuals and $100 for joint returns:

> This . . . would eliminate an annual revenue loss of about
> $2 billion, it would redress the imbalance that now exists in
> the bill between the large tax cuts for business and the
> meager cuts for individuals, and it would prove an even
> greater fiscal stimulus to our stagnant economy than the
> present bill.[67]

A few minutes later, Bayh got into a fairly heated debate with
John Pastore (D., R.I.). Pastore was concerned that if Bayh's
motion passed, "the little mill in Rhode Island" would not be
able to reap the benefits that it might receive from ADR.

> MR. PASTORE: Mr. President . . . We instituted a Marshall
> plan where we peddled more than $20 billion all over the
> world to modernize our competitors abroad. We did it will-
> ingly. We find today, as we look around, that our machin-
> ery is archaic. We need modernization. They tell us we
> cannot compete because we have not modernized and we
> have not been able to get the money to do so. . . .
> MR. BAYH: . . . The investment tax credit [another tax
> break] permits a great incentive for buying new machinery
> and building new apartments, thus providing jobs, but the
> accelerated depreciation range means that everybody who
> already has a machine is going to get an additional tax
> break. It seems to me that kind of benefit is not going to
> help the economy of this country. It is giving a special tax
> break to those who do not need it.
> MR. PASTORE: Why does the Senator bring an apartment
> house into the picture? Why does he not bring into the pic-
> ture the little mill in Rhode Island?
> MR. BAYH: I will be glad to yield—
> MR. PASTORE: I do not care who yields, but I would like an
> answer.
> MR. BAYH: The little mill in Rhode Island is going to be
> brought into the picture under the investment credit.
> MR. PASTORE: Provided it has the money to buy the ma-
> chinery. Where is it going to get the money if it does not
> have the cash flow? That is the question. I have looked at
> this question over a long time, and I am not buying philos-
> ophy tonight: I am buying realism tonight.

MR. BAYH: I think the Senator from Rhode Island is sincere in what he says. I am looking at it as realistically as he is.
MR. PASTORE: That is right. The Senator comes from Indiana and I come from Rhode Island.[68]

When a vote was finally taken, the allies of that "little mill in Rhode Island" managed to keep ADR in the bill—by two votes, 35 to 37. A slim majority of the Finance Committee had joined the majority opposing Bayh's motion. Nine of the committee's sixteen members voted against it, seven for it, and one—Carl Curtis—did not vote. Those who voted to keep ADR were Bennett, Fannin, Griffin, Hansen, Jordan, Miller, Byrd, Ribicoff, and Talmadge; Anderson, Fulbright, Harris, Hartke, Long, and Nelson voted with Bayh.[69]

Ten days after Bayh's motion was defeated, the entire package was passed—64-30—sent to a House-Senate conference, and signed by a grateful President. Though the President had yielded to pressure from Congress, public interest groups, and unions to send ADR to Capitol Hill, he and the business-financial community were the victors in the end. The original Treasury regulations were withdrawn and the lawsuit thereby made moot. As usual, the alliance between the party in the White House and the financial establishment was too strong for labor and public interest groups to break. And the administration had the indispensable support of Wilbur Mills, without whom it would have had little success.*

Flying the DISC

Another giveaway in the 1971 Revenue Act was the Domestic International Sales Corporation. Designed by the Treasury Department, DISC was sold to the White House and the business community, then almost literally shoved down the throats of the members of the Ways and Means and Finance committees as well as the rest of Congress.

---

* So far, ADR has failed to live up to expectations. Businesses, especially smaller businesses, have not used ADR to nearly the extent predicted by overoptimistic Treasury and big business advocates.

DISC is a special corporate entity used for exporting products. The enticement to establish a DISC is that it can be used to "defer" taxes on up to one-half of export profits. Many tax experts, though, thought that DISC would actually excuse taxes rather than defer them, since a DISC can use its tax-free income for other business investments. It can reinvest in its own export business or in certain Export-Import Bank obligations; or it can make loans to foreign importers for the purchase of American imports or make loans to its parent company or to another U.S. export producer. "Deferral" will continue as long as the DISC's earnings are used for these purposes. DISC's profits are taxed only after they have been distributed to their shareholders. In addition to products, it can also export services, such as engineering and architecture for foreign construction projects.

To be eligible for DISC status, a corporation (or its subsidiaries) must be duly incorporated, offer a single class of stock, maintain at least $2,500 of outstanding capital stock, keep its own bank account and banking records, and have its DISC status approved by its stockholders. A DISC need not have its own employees, and its stock can be owned by nonresident aliens and foreign corporations. In short, an exporter can get DISC tax benefits by setting up a paper corporation.

The Treasury Department hoped that DISC would help to ameliorate the deficit-of-payments crisis. Paul Volcker, a Treasury official, said that he was convinced that DISC would "help direct the attention of American industry—particularly smaller and medium-sized firms—to the opportunities available in foreign markets. It should induce fresh corporate planning and marketing efforts to develop these markets."[70] Treasury also hoped that DISC would put domestic exporters on par with American corporations abroad. The foreign-based corporations did not have to pay taxes on their earnings till they were repatriated, and DISC would put domestic exporters on an equal footing while keeping jobs and capital at home.

The Treasury Department had been considering DISC for several years. A strong advocate of tax incentives to boost exports was John Petty, the assistant secretary for international affairs, who had long proselytized businessmen and other members of the department and had gathered data demonstrating that DISC would aid exports. But Surrey, as well as many other Treasury economists and Petty's own staff, disagreed. Surrey warned that DISC would be "a complete waste of government funds," especially since the Treasury Department itself had computed that DISC would cost the government about $600 million to $1 billion in revenue each year. (When Congress was finally sold on DISC, Surrey observed angrily that "the Treasury was feeding Congress a lot of crap on DISC.")

Once Richard Nixon entered the White House, Surrey, a Democrat, left the Treasury and DISC was pushed by the Treasury Department. In 1969 the department moved for DISC legislation over the opposition of many of its technicians and economists. Armed with what Woodworth called "very raw data" and a draft from the Tax Analysis Division of the Treasury Department, Treasury representatives went to the Finance Committee's last executive session on the 1969 Tax Reform Act to formally propose DISC. But Paul McDaniel, an aide to Finance member Albert Gore and a Treasury official until August 1969, stymied Treasury's move to get DISC into the bill by resurrecting an old bill of Gore's that would repeal existing provisions allowing deferred taxes for corporations on earnings from foreign-based subsidiaries. Caught between issuing new deferrals and entirely prohibiting them, the Finance Committee preferred to do neither. Senator John Williams candidly said, "I see this on this end and that on that end: let's drop the whole thing!"

Thwarted in the committee, the Treasury Department continued to court the business community through scores of meetings around the country with businessmen, trying to sell the idea of DISC while soliciting data that might support the *a priori* arguments that Treasury had been using so far. But most businessmen were skeptical that DISC would actually cut their taxes. Some companies realized that the proposal would not necessarily help them increase their exports. Others saw the idea as a revenue bonanza for themselves but a misalignment of national priorities. Several firms, including the Libby, McNeill and Libby Company, Du Pont, and the Zenith Sales Company, publicly expressed their doubts about DISC's virtues.[71]

The Treasury Department next proposed DISC at a May 12, 1970, Ways and Means hearing on tariff and trade proposals, and Nolan told the committee that DISC would "provide a satisfactory basis for taxing export income."[72] As Stanley Surrey later told the *Wall Street Journal*, the other concerns of Ways and Means—tariffs for shoes, mink skins, textiles, and oil quotas—permitted the DISC proposal to pass through the House, almost unseen and certainly not understood."[73] But in good part thanks to Surrey the few mavericks on Ways and Means did notice and protest the provision. Gibbons attacked DISC as "just a damned tax preference"; Vanik criticized it as a "tax giveaway that doesn't even really increase tax incentives,"[74] and Corman and Gibbons released a long dissent to the proposal, saying that DISC was

> appropriately named as far as the American taxpayer is concerned. For it will run him around in circles to the tune of $600 million or $1 billion a year, which Treasury and our committee staff estimate this proposal will cost us in lost revenue.
>
> . . . The committee consideration of the DISC proposal is an unfortunate example of how tax loopholes are born—a special provision is created and labeled a tax incentive in the hope that it may do some good, despite little if any evidence that it will be effective, and also despite the prospect that it will be difficult to remove. We spent last year [1969] trying to cut back or eliminate tax incentives that for the most part were created in a similar manner.[75]

Arguing against Corman's and Gibbons' remarks, Conable and Pettis—while admitting that DISC would cost the government close to $1 billion annually—concluded that it was still worthwhile. "Although DISC is a tax loophole, we believe it to be a modest one which will have the desired effect of stimulating exports at this time," they said.[76]

The expected roster of witnesses appeared at the hearings. Speaking for DISC were representatives of the National Association of Manufacturers, the U.S. Chamber of Commerce, the Machinery and Allied Products Institute, and many others eager to reap the DISC windfall.

Two sets of data that Treasury began to distribute to illustrate the advantages of a DISC came from Union Carbide and the Hewlett-Packard Company. Treasury officials admitted relying "quite heavily" on them, especially the Hewlett-Packard letter. In 1971 these documents were presented as clinchers, in response to a specific request for hard data by Senator Nelson, a new member of Finance. He had the JCIRT staff analyze the data, and subsequently published the response in the *Congressional Record*. The staff found the data insufficient to prove that a DISC program would result in increased exports, and the Hewlett-Packard letter, in fact, indicated that "it would be more advantageous to the company to retain the additional funds provided by a DISC corporation rather than to expand exports." Even using Treasury's prized examples, the staff found that the wishbone simply would not work.

Joining the AFL-CIO in its opposition was an economist, Dr. Elliott Morss, an economics professor at George Washington University. Speaking for Taxation with Representation, he contended that no one had produced any evidence that DISC would actually stimulate exports. He recommended a "healthy skepticism" toward Treasury claims that DISC was needed to eliminate inequalities in the government's tax treatment of earnings from exportation. His major criticism of the proposal was that it was based on faith instead of objective data:

> Treasury Secretary Kennedy has stated that enactment of the DISC proposal will increase exports "over time" by a "billion dollars or more" at a cost of up to $600 million in lost tax revenues. These are the only figures available from the Treasury regarding the DISC proposal. No information is available regarding the economic assumptions and methodology that underlie these estimates, nor has Treasury

indicated the data sources that it used when making these estimates. . . . The result is that we must accept the Treasury revenue and export estimates on faith. . . .

Certainly no program in the field of social welfare would be proposed by a federal agency on the basis of analysis as superficial as that produced to date in support of the DISC proposal.[77]

But before the committee's final vote, a JCIRT confidential report to Ways and Means scathingly denounced DISC.[78] The JCIRT staff concluded that DISC would be a virtual tax *exemption* provision, not a tax *deferral* provision. It would grant tax benefits to exporters for simply continuing what they had been doing; it would favor exporters over those who produced only for domestic markets. The staff contended that a DISC that was a subsidiary of a parent company would have substantially greater benefits under the provision than an independent export firm. A few large exporters would gain much more from DISC than their many small competitors. JCIRT observed that the decline in the trade balance was not caused by a decline in exports but an increase in imports. DISC would do little to stem the decline in the American trade surplus, which had plummeted from $6.8 billion in 1964 to $690 million in 1969. The report cited a study by a member of the President's Council of Economic Advisors, Dr. Hendrick S. Houthakker, which indicated that for the $600 million revenue loss, exports would be increased by only $300 million.

But the committee disregarded JCIRT's report and added DISC to the foreign trade bill. Woodworth later said, "We had the analysis—the committee didn't want to hear it." DISC was "not subjected to economic analysis; there was wooly thinking" done on it, and the committee eventually approved it because it wanted to do something for exports.

After the House passed DISC, other countries began to protest the provision. One official at the Common Market's headquarters in Brussels commented, "Your government says that this is a tax deferral, but in reality it is a straight tax exemption for a big part

of a company's profits." Europeans believed that DISC would violate the General Agreement on Tariffs and Trades ban against
government subsidy of exports, he said, and it could start a
"fiscal world war."

Ironically, the Treasury Department's assistant secretary for
congressional relations, James W. Smith, later contended that this
reaction by Western Europe—their "naïve activity on their own
behalf," their "complaining and squealing"—helped convince the
Finance Committee to approve DISC in 1971. Some of the committee members, according to Smith, assumed that if Europeans
disliked DISC so much, then it must be good for the United
States.

Regardless of European opinion, DISC never made it through
the Finance Committee in 1970. Ralph Nader labeled it "a billion dollar boondoggle."[79] Tom Field of Taxation with Representation stressed that there would be increased administrative
costs and suggested other ways to stimulate exports.[80] Lee Metcalf (D., Mont.) warned:

> DISC could lead to the sort of Frankenstein corporate mon-
> ster that led to the recent bankruptcy of the Penn-Central
> Railroad. . . .
>
> The autopsy on the Penn-Central, a subsidiary of a
> network of financial manipulations that almost defies un-
> tangling, must indicate that a combination of bigness, mis-
> management, and greed can end with an extended palm at
> the door of the U. S. Treasury.
>
> Most people do not know that DISC would allow large
> oil companies, for example, to receive tax benefits from their
> coal subsidiaries' exports to other countries. The tax advan-
> tage would be immediate—regardless of whether exports
> expand. Furthermore, many foreign countries have quotas
> on U. S. coal so DISC could not possibly spur exports of
> coal to these countries, but the U. S. taxpayer would still
> pay the subsidy.
>
> Congress has been given a very simplified concept; a tax
> benefit for companies that export will, by its very nature,
> spur the export of U.S.-made products. The world of trade

does not move in such simple straightline relationships. It could, instead, become a maze of financial intricacies that will take years for lawyers to untangle.[81]

To counter the committee's strong opposition to DISC, the Treasury Department lined up support from such industrial giants as Union Carbide, Gulf Oil, Du Pont, Mobil Oil, Humble Oil and the Manufacturing Chemists Association. But despite all its efforts to sway the committee, its members remained adamant against DISC. Treasury officials were not even invited to the executive session on DISC—the first time they had been excluded from a Finance executive session in 1970. The committee rejected DISC, because it contended that Treasury had not proven that DISC would improve the balance between American and European trade. Chairman Long pointed to the JCIRT staff report to explain: "We think it would cost a lot more than the Administration estimates and wouldn't do nearly as much good as the Administration hopes."[82]

In the first part of 1971 Treasury's main priority in legislation was the administration's revenue-sharing plan. The DISC was on the shelf waiting for a more opportune time. In mid-July, as part of the administration's gearing up for another try at DISC, the U. S. ambassador to the Netherlands, J. William Middendorf, suddenly appeared in Washington and visited various people to revive their interest.[83] An aide to special presidential assistant Peter Peterson assured the ambassador that Peterson was all for DISC but "wanted to be sure that when the Administration goes to the Hill with any proposals in the trade area it is better prepared than it was last fall."

Middendorf lobbied various top State Department officials and all expressed support. Mentioned in many of the conversations, however, was the opposition of organized labor. Treasury official Petty told him labor's opposition was "unreasonable" and expressed hope of adding a "carrot" to the bill as an enticement. Secretary of Commerce Maurice Stans expressed strong support, as did Senators Charles Percy and Lowell Weicker. Senator Ribicoff "indicated that if the DISC proposal were to come before the

Finance Committee today he could certainly support it and he believed it would receive the approval of the Committee," but added that Treasury and State had not recently been doing much to push it.

On the House side, ranking Republican John Byrnes echoed Ribicoff's complaint, and said that the committeemen would want to know how the DISC would fit into the administration's overall plans to deal with the balance-of-payments problem, preferring a single package to deal with all of them. He was confident, however, that if Secretary Connally or Peterson came to Mills and himself with a DISC proposal "something might be worked out." Ways and Means member Betts revealed that that very morning at a Republican breakfast meeting Secretary Connally had referred to the need for a DISC program. Betts warned that it would be difficult to get the committee to focus on it, because Chairman Mills "was busy with a variety of things in and out of the Congress and that it would take a strong Administration push to get action."

Pressure continued to build over the next few months. The new Treasury secretary, John Connally, favored it; the American ambassador to the Netherlands had come to Washington to lobby for it; Commerce Secretary Maurice Stans strongly supported it; Republican Senators Charles Percy and Lowell Weicker came out for it; and Finance Committee member Abraham Ribicoff said that he would approve it if it came before the committee again.

In September the Ways and Means Committee held hearings on DISC, this time as part of the 1971 Revenue Act. Treasury Secretary Connally now claimed that DISC would raise exports by $1.5 billion, while still costing the government only $600 million annually.[84] Among those testifying for the DISC were the American Bankers Association, the National Association of Manufacturers, the U. S. Chamber of Commerce, the American Mining Congress, the National Coal Association, the Tax Council, and, again, the Hewlett-Packard Corporation, a huge California conglomerate co-owned by Deputy Secretary of Defense David Parker. On the other side were labor and public interest groups: the AFL-CIO, Common Cause, Ralph Nader, Stanley Surrey, and Taxation with Representation.

The committee held only three days of executive hearings on the administration's entire economic recovery program. Deputy Assistant Treasury Secretary Nolan thought the committee might have debated DISC longer to be completely certain of its ramifications and details, but the members felt obligated to act on the balance-of-payments problem, even if the action was a big business windfall instead of a solution.

During the executive session the committee favored a position recommended by the JCIRT staff that would "defer" only that income from exports which exceeded that made before DISC was passed. Though the Treasury contended that this incremental approach would be an administrative nightmare and inherently inequitable, the committee included this variation on DISC. Indicating that whatever was all right with Ways and Means was all right with the full House, the congressmen debated the economic package—which included DISC, ADR, investment credit, and other concessions to business—for one hour and thirty-nine minutes. For final approval a voice vote was used, not a roll call.[85] This was an impressive show of expeditious legislating, but hardly demonstrative of representative democracy. Constituents had no way of holding their representatives accountable for a position on the issue without the roll call tally.

Between House passage of DISC on October 6 and the Senate Finance Committee's six-day hearings on the 1971 Revenue Act on October 7, 12, 13, 14, 15 and 18, the *Wall Street Journal* editorially blasted DISC as a "tax haven" that would fudge "the accepted rules of international trade." It went on to suggest that DISC should be completely scrapped:

> Chairman Mills and his committee took some of the shine out of an administration tax gimmick designed to encourage American business corporations to step up their export activity. If the idea disappears entirely before the tax bill becomes law, it would be no great loss.
> . . . The use of special tax incentives to further public

policy is a doubtful technique in principle to begin with. It soon gets the entire tax structure out of kilter, creating loopholes for some taxpayers and transferring to others the burden that has been lifted from the fortunate. The result is a sense of unfairness and ill will among taxpayers, which is the first step toward wide-scale efforts at evasion. . . .

Treasury Secretary Connally doesn't think this [the Ways and Means version] would be sufficient "incentive" to exporters. In our view, it is a better incentive than the original, since only measurable gains would be rewarded.

But the Ways and Means version still doesn't answer the objection to tax incentives in principle. Nor does it provide the possibility that once DISCs are established they will win further concessions. With that thought in mind, we would be very happy if the full Congress decides to send this particular DISC sailing, far enough that it wouldn't be likely to return.[86]

Secretary Connally stubbornly rejected the advice of the most widely read financial newspaper in the country. On the first day of the Finance Committee hearings he reminded its members:

The House Ways and Means Committee in 1961 considered in detail the possibility of adopting the investment credit on an incremental basis for investments in an effort to respond to similar allegations of windfall benefits in capital goods that would have been made anyway, even without the credit. That committee finally abandoned the idea as inherently inequitable and unworkable. The Senate should reject the incremental DISC concept as equally unworkable, inequitable and damaging to the basic purpose of DISC to retain jobs in the United States.[87]

Questioned by the committee, Connally charged:

Other countries will say, we don't like this DISC proposal, it does this or it violates GATT, or something else, but the truth of the matter is in all of our conversations and negotiations with a great many of these countries at the Treasury Department and in connection with international tax treaties they do at least this and more. . . .[88]

A few days later a Harvard professor of political economy, Richard A. Musgrave, refuted Connally's statement: "[T]he Domestic International Sales Corporation proposal, I believe, contradicts the spirit if not the law of GATT. It invites retaliation, creates ill will and opens new loopholes in the tax structure."[89] Musgrave was supported by an article by Stanley Surrey which was put into the hearing record:

> Presumably the Treasury believes this proposal is not contrary to GATT. It is a strange world, however, if this proposal—seeking completely to exempt the export trade of a country—is not a barred subsidy. It is hard to see what would remain of GATT in the tax area after this step and those taken abroad in retaliation or emulation.[90]

He cited the infamous Hewlett-Packard and Union Carbide letters as convincing evidence for the DISC.

When Senator Nelson asked Connally to respond to some of Surrey's criticisms, the secretary deferred to Nolan, who did not specifically meet any of Surrey's objections.[91] Taxation with Representation presented a panel of experts to discuss DISC, including Musgrave, Lowell Harris of Columbia, Paul Taubman of the University of Pennsylvania, William Davenport (a former tax legislative counsel at the Treasury Department) of the University of California at Davis Law School, Elliott Morss of George Washington, Gary Fromm of American University, and Alan Shanck of Wayne State Law School. After the first witness had briefly summarized his testimony he was warned by ranking Republican Bennett that the whole panel had a mere ten minutes in which to address the committee. The subsequent statements were necessarily speedy. The committee felt no need to question any of the witnesses nor to promote dialogue on the DISC issue.

Assistant Secretary Smith claims that Treasury's capital cost chart had a great influence on the Finance Committee. The consternation of leaders of other countries influenced them as well, a point later emphasized on the floor by Senator Fannin.[92] Tom Vail attributed the committee's turn-around simply to the fact that "the Administration got the votes." Chairman Long said the administration was successful because, "they just wore the committee down." Long still feels the DISC is "by no means the best device" by which to deal with the balance-of-payments problem, but "we're becoming internationally bankrupt, we're destroying our power among the powers of the world by being the world's debtor," and so something had to be done. Quotas are the only way out of the "terrible mess we are in," he thinks. "The administration got the DISC through because it compromised with different senators on different issues, persuading them here and promising help there."

The senators we interviewed were vague about their votes and their reasons, and as usual no record was taken of the committee tally. But in Finance members' votes on floor amendment votes to delete the DISC provision, only Senators Hartke, Fulbright, Harris, and Nelson were willing to delete it.

And Treasury was not at a loss for help from its corporate friends. Smith says he did

> the legwork and ginned up major industrial groups and corporate representatives interested in DISC. I'd tell them which congressmen needed work, and ask, "Who's good with them?" I'd contact the right persons and put them on the congressman, and ask for the benefit of the discussion.

Several senators and staff members indicated that the "right persons" came forth. Wayne Thevenot, Long's legislative assistant, told us that the administration kept up pressure on the staff and got people from Louisiana to telephone Long telling him how important the provision was to the state. This was done with many other senators. Thevenot explained, "The White House finds out who's who and then sics them on you. You can sit back and pick them out, you expect them." Speaking of labor's effort to block DISC, Surrey says they lost "cuz it's damned hard to win." Surrey himself had written an article for the *Washington Post* roundly denouncing the DISC as "A Billion Dollar Tax Loophole Hidden in New Economic Policy."[93] Pro-DISC lobbyists with whom he is friendly told him later that the article served to spur them on in their own efforts.

The Finance Committee in executive session compromised between the House incrementalism and the administration request for deferral of tax on all income, simply by making *half* of the income subject to the deferral. The committee also put a ten-year limitation on the DISC provision. On the floor an amendment sponsored by Senator Fulbright restricting the DISC provision to five years was adopted by a voice vote, but this was deleted in conference. Staff estimates were that the Finance version of DISC would cost $400 million during the first four years and $400 million annually by 1978.[94]

The same day Bennett agreed to take Fulbright's five-year proposal direct to the Senate-House conference, the Senate passed the Revenue Act 64-30. Only five of the Finance Committee joined the minority on the floor and four of these were Republicans voting against their own President's economic program—Fannin, Hansen, Jordan and Miller. The lone Democrat was Gaylord Nelson.[95]

The final conference version of DISC was presented to the House on December 9, 1971, by Wilbur Mills. He told his colleagues that the House conferees had made two concessions on DISC to the Senate conferees, but he refused to limit DISC to five years as Fulbright had suggested. They had agreed to the Senate's version of DISC that limited tax deferral to one-half of a DISC's export profit rather than the incremental plan originally passed by the House. Mills explained, "The conferees concluded that this change is desirable because it achieves the desired objective of providing significant incentive to expand export operations but provides this treatment more simply and equitably than did the House provision."[96] The House conferees also agreed with the Senate to deny tax deferrals to DISC profits invested in foreign plants and equipment. They realized, Mills said, "that to allow tax deferral on amounts invested abroad would be inconsistent with the primary purpose of the DISC provisions which is to encourage our export abroad."[97]

The conference version easily cleared the House—320 to 74, with 37 representatives not voting. Of the twenty-five Ways and Means members, twenty-one voted for the Revenue Act, three opposed it, and one did not vote.*98

While the House was passing the conference report, the Senate was approving it too. Although Long, who led the Senate conferees, admitted, "I cannot say that I view this as a very satisfactory conference agreement from the standpoint of the Senate,"99 many of the Senate bill's original provisions (with the exclusion of most of those on DISC) were severely compromised. The bill easily cleared the upper chamber 71 to 6, with 22 senators not voting. Nine of the Finance Committee members voted for the Conference bill; two voted against it, and five did not vote.†

Now back at his old law practice in Washington, Nolan says that DISC has had a "fantastic" effect. "All sorts of people are coming to them," he says, including people not formerly in the export business. Administration officials are traveling across the country urging businessmen to take advantage of the new tax laws and establish DISCs. By the end of March 1972, 1,146 companies had informed the IRS that they intended to start DISCs. By late June 1972 this figure had swollen to 2,100. Such giants as Ford Motor Company, Dow Chemical, and General Electric Company had indicated that they would form DISCs.

While American business was scrambling to set up DISCs, the Treasury Department was trying to placate the GATT signatories that DISC was not a rebate on "direct" taxes—and even if it was, the department contended, other GATT members were

* Committee members who voted for the Revenue Act were Betts, Brotzman, Broyhill, Burleson, Burke, Byrnes, Carey, Chamberlain, Collier, Conable, Corman, Duncan, Fulton, Griffiths, Karth, Landrum, Mills, Pettis, Schneebeli, Ullman, and Waggonner. The three opposed to the act were Gibbons, Green, and Vanik. And the one member not voting was Rostenkowski.

† The nine committee members who voted for the bill were Curtis, Fulbright, Griffin, Hansen, Hartke, Jordan, Long, Miller, and Ribicoff. Only two of the five committee members who had voted against the original Senate bill voted against the conference bill—Fannin and Nelson. Not voting were Anderson, Bennett, Byrd, Harris, and Talmadge.

doing the same. But the GATT members were not satisfied. One Treasury official admitted that DISC had given the United States "less leverage" in the GATT.

So American business gets richer, the European countries get madder, and the Treasury is poorer by an average of $400 million annually. Unfortunately, an accounting of the benefits and harms of DISC may never be possible. The price controls and dollar devaluation that were part of the entire "economic recovery" package have so altered the original elements of analysis that even if exports rose dramatically, it would be impossible to determine just how much of the increase was caused by DISC.

Congress had acted simply out of a desire to "do something for exports" and was swayed from its original reluctance not by reasonable evidence but by pressure from the Treasury Department and corporate special interests. Though armed with a mechanism for informing itself on the arguments of both sides—committee hearings—Congress forfeited its chance to make a rational decision. The DISC provision, rooted in the absence of data and legislated in the heat of extreme executive branch pressure, may rest in the tax code for a long time, shifting more of the tax burden to the average American taxpayer.

As the histories of DISC and ADR show, the revenue committees and Congress are almost adjuncts of the interests most concerned with tax laws—or, to be more exact, with tax loopholes. While preserving a façade of enacting legislation that will help the national treasury, the revenue committees continually guarantee that business will pay far less than its fair share of the national dues. In short, committee members have succumbed to the intense lobbying of business interests and the campaign handouts at election time.

Roy Blough writes in *The Federal Taxing Process* that the concentration of lobbying for vested interests "makes it difficult for the members of the taxing committees to secure a balanced view of either what is the general interest, what the public wants, or what the public would want if it were informed of the facts."[100] One of the great difficulties of letting the people know what they would want if they were "informed of the facts" is the sheer complexity of the tax code. No less an expert than Wilbur Mills has called the code "a mess and a gyp" and a "house of horrors" in which some taxpayers are "pets" and others are "patsies." Louis Eisenstein has called the tax code a "remarkable essay in sustained obscurity" that has "all the earmarks of a conspiracy in restraint of understanding."[101] And the author of *The Rich and The Super Rich*, Ferdinand Lundberg, a former teacher at New York University, is even more sarcastic. The tax structure, he says, is a "pullulating excrescence negating common sense, a parody of the gruesomely ludicrous, a surrealist zigzag pagoda of pestilent greed, a perverse thing that makes the pre-revolutionary French system seem entirely rational."[102]

If the public is to be responsibly informed and organized on how it will part with its tax money, if it is to be a force that will effectively counter industry's battalions of lobbyists and the millions of dollars pumped into revenue committee members' campaign coffers, then first the tax code itself must be streamlined in substance and wording; it must be made lucid and nonevasive. Then, perhaps, a tax code could evolve that will not pander to special interests, that will be as equitable as the graduated concept of taxation originally intended. But small taxpayers—most of the working people, that is—must resolve to play a part in shaping these changes.* Otherwise the bill for these inequities and loopholes will keep coming to them for payment.

---

* The *Tax Action Manual*, published by the Tax Reform Research Group, tells how to make representatives accountable to all taxpayers, not just special interests, by organizing taxpayers to counter special interest influences.

5

Reforms for the Present to Cope with the Future

Committees like Ways and Means and Finance, which were originally intended to deal with how the government will acquire and appropriate money, have developed a kind of political greed which—as if they were not already powerful enough—makes them thirst for greater jurisdiction, greater power. To compound the revenue committees' problems of dealing with this power, of using it correctly and efficiently, they have given themselves too little staff. So by their own design the committees have made themselves among the most powerful in Congress and yet the weakest, since they cannot effectively control (through oversight) what they have wrought. The following reforms would streamline the committees.

IMPROVED ABILITY TO FUNCTION

Jurisdiction

Jurisdiction can easily be pared down to relieve the committees of matters that properly belong to others, and to allow them to concentrate on equitable revenue raising and tax reform. Welfare, revenue sharing, national health insurance, unemployment compensation, and education can be more effectively handled by committees devoted primarily to such social programs. The non-tax aspects of social security, Medicare, and foreign trade should also be shifted away from the revenue committees.

Redistribution of jurisdiction should include a more precise clarification of the committees' overall jurisdictional responsibilities so that the tendency to assert power over anything that has to do with revenues can be checked. Had the committees not been preoccupied over the last few years with the abortive welfare reform effort, national health insurance, and schemes to aid private education, they might have produced some significant tax reforms, some effective measure to reverse our failing foreign trade posture, or sound fiscal policy controls that would have both checked inflation and retained for Congress its constitutional powers of taxing and spending. Taxing, foreign trade, and fiscal policy control are major sources of domestic disquiet, international disrespect, and concern both at home and abroad over the government's performance. Congress, particularly the Democratic leadership, must relieve the tax committees of some of their more recently acquired responsibilities, to enable them to come to grips with the current national crisis.

Subcommittees

Whether or not they are relieved of some responsibilities, the committees should establish subcommittees, each with strict jurisdictional boundaries and an adequate budget. At the beginning of the Ninety-third Congress the Finance Committee established subcommittees to deal with health, international trade, private pension plans, interstate commerce, foundations, and international finance and resources. Unfortunately, these subcommittees remain powerless to initiate legislation, which is still done only by the full committee. Conspicuously missing are subcommittees for welfare, social security, revenue sharing, fiscal policy, and taxation. It is probably best that the full committees retain jurisdiction over taxation, but certain areas should be assigned to subcommittees, as the Finance Committee has done with private pension plans, foundations, and other issues. These should be full-fledged subcommittees with legislative powers. Subcommittees would enable the committees to analyze and review their responsibilities and to design alternatives to inadequate systems. Such a delegation of duties would not be an abdication by the full committee; instead it would be a rational method to deal with the mind-numbing load. Expertise among individual members of Congress could develop, especially compared to the present monopoly of information by a few members on each committee. The full committee could review the recommendations and considerations of each subcommittee. Any increase in the time necessary to get a measure out of committee would be offset by relieving the full committee of the initial spade work.

Staff

The committees should increase and improve their staff at all levels—personal staffs, the committees' (and subcommittees') staffs, and the JCIRT staff. The JCIRT staff is acknowledged by all to be excellent, but it is too small and overworked to counterbalance the Treasury and special interests effectively. It should be increased in size and capability so that it can do its own accurate revenue estimates, in-depth alternative designing for the committees, and position papers for the members' education. For daily assistance to the committees, the three staffs should be readily accessible, and therefore large enough to meet all the committee members' needs, including those of minority party members. The difference, for example, between the size of the

Finance professional staff (six) and that of the Senate Judiciary Committee (about 100) is shocking.

Members' personal staff should be admitted to the executive sessions. Their present exclusion handicaps members in understanding and keeping up with all the complex issues being discussed. Since the staff receives second hand what is discussed at the executive sessions, it too is at a disadvantage when doing research. If members' personal aides were admitted to the executive sessions, they would have an incentive to secure expert staff for themselves. Hiring experts would not only enormously enhance a member's ability to function on the committee but would also augment the committee staffs' resources.

JCIRT Expansion

The JCIRT should do much more extensive research into existing systems of taxation, to formulate alternative means to meet the country's revenue needs. It should design effective vehicles for better educating the members of the tax committees and all the members of Congress. When tax legislation is proposed by the committees, the JCIRT should be able to present position papers on anticipated discussion topics and reform. The JCIRT pamphlets on drafted legislation should be made available not just to the committtees, but to the entire Congress well before floor consideration of a bill. Members should be able to rely on these JCIRT reports to intelligently debate *alternatives*, as well as the details of the pending legislation. These reports should be intelligible to non-tax committee congressmen. Before hearings begin, the JCIRT should try to instruct the committee members on the topics and issues at hand, so that participation by all members could reach the level where the deliberative process could truly be called a committee effort. The JCIRT should not be permitted to structure and limit the scope of inquiry and consideration; but it could assist members to make informed decisions.

The Congress needs to provide itself with computers, and the JCIRT probably needs this resource most of all.

Broad Hearings

The committees should obtain more representative and diversified opinion and analysis at hearings. Members should make a special effort to request participation from a variety of sources with no direct financial stake in the results. Testimony from academic and professional people in the field, including practicing lawyers, would not only be instructive and a balance to the overwhelming dominance by special interest representatives, but might also inspire more private research. Hearings should be held outside Washington, D. C., especially on social welfare for the committees to get first-hand information from the people who live under the systems they design. The Senate should no longer patiently wait for a bill to come from the House before holding hearings. The Senate now lets itself be restricted by the House both in framing the issues and proposing legislative formulas. An independent consideration of the issues might produce a more creative final product.

Floor Amendment Review

The Senate should require that amendments to be offered on the floor be submitted far enough in advance for the Finance Committee to study and draft reports on them. The staff should then report on the amendments for the rest of the Senate. Along with the report on the entire bill, the reports should be circulated far enough ahead of floor consideration for senators to study them, make inquiries, and plan floor action. Such a process might also place more responsibility on the Senate conferees to defend the Senate version of the bill, since the amendments would have been more fully considered and responsibly endorsed by the full body.

Democratization of Conferences

Former Senator Albert Gore, who was a Finance Committee member and conferee, made several suggestions for improving the conference committee. First, the full membership of each house should select the conferees by ballot. Second, a record of the conference actions should be kept, and the day after the end of a conference all votes during the conference should be published in the *Congressional Record*. Third, the report issued by the conference committee should include a comprehensive statement by the managers of the bill explaining the conference's actions and a statement by the Treasury about its positions on issues raised at the conference. Fourth, statements of conferees disagreeing with the majority on major points should be incorporated in the report, just as minority, individual, or supplemental views are now included in the reports of the other standing committees. Fifth, no vote should be taken in the Senate or House on a conference report until the report has been printed and available to members for at least three days (see Clause 3 of Rule XXVIII of the House).

The Committee on Committees

The Democratic Caucus in the House should replace the Ways and Means Committee as the party's committee on committees (which assigns House Democrats to committees). This task does not involve a great deal of time for the Democratic members of Ways and Means, but it gives them, especially the chairman, an unhealthy amount of power. There are enough pressures on the members of the House for their votes on tax measures without being under the lash of Mills's informal whip system.

Tax and Appropriations Relations

The disjointed relationship in Congress between raising revenue and making appropriations is currently being studied by the Joint Study Committee on Budget Control. Since President Nixon's attempt in October 1972 to take over the power of setting a spending ceiling, it is of critical importance to the continuing viability of Congress as a coequal branch of government to maintain its power of the purse.

The Joint Study Committee on Budget Control, established in the wake of Nixon's move, issued an interim report pointing out the need for permanent legislative committees and staff to implement budget and spending control procedures, early determination of the appropriate revenue-expenditure ratio, and authorizations in advance of the year they will become effective. The committee hoped that these general recommendations would eventually lead to a mechanism for Congress to (a) determine the proper level of expenditures for the coming fiscal year after full consideration of the fiscal, economic, monetary and other factors involved; (b) provide an overall ceiling on expenditures and on budget authority for each year; and (c) determine the aggregate revenue and debt levels which appropriately should be associated with the expenditure and budget authority limits. It is essential that tax expenditures be subjected to the same budgetary controls as direct expenditures. Otherwise direct budget controls will create even more intense inducements for "back door" tax subsidy programs.

Executive-Branch Lobbying

The members of the revenue committee should insist that the Treasury Department adhere to the law (8 USC S.1913) which forbids the use of any appropriated funds by an executive agency to propagandize and lobby members of Congress. In the taxation area, the intimate involvement of Treasury in policy formulation makes this a difficult provision to enforce, but the members must be vigilant. The line is often fairly clear, as when Treasury does a concentrated selling job on a particular provision or bill to an industry or a home-state business so that it will do the lobbying. With grossly disproportionate resources at its disposal, Treasury can be simply overwhelming when it wants to: the country is saddled with such reminders as the DISC and the ADR. It is up to the members of the revenue committees to protect themselves and their peers from such infractions by enforcing the laws which they have sworn to uphold and by gathering staff and other resources to diminish their dependence on executive branch information.

INCREASED ACCOUNTABILITY

The revenue committees have the security of power and prestige in their respective houses. From protracted secret sessions they hand down massive pieces of legislation, to be duly accepted by their peers. Or they dispense tax favors to the powerful, as they shackle the powerless with punitive welfare systems. Yet for all their power, the revenue committees are now comfortably beyond accountability. Implementing the following recommendations would establish some conditions under which an accounting could be demanded.

Party Responsibility for Membership

The party caucuses in each house should accept full responsibility for the composition of the revenue committees. If the committee members are too cautious or oversolicitous of special interests, empty complaints are not the appropriate response. Party irresponsibility was perhaps most pronounced among Senate tax reformers before some of their band were assigned to the Finance Committee recently. Members should be required to rotate committee assignments, with a maximum number of years set for service on one committee. This would help to revitalize congressional committtees.

Party Caucus to Select Committee Chairman

The party caucus should also be responsible for the chairman of the revenue committees. Early in the Ninety-third Congress the House Democratic Caucus decided that the party caucus would elect all committee chairmen every two years. The results were as they would have been under the old seniority system. But in future caucus elections, with time for advance planning and campaigning, it is possible that new members, whether they have seniority or not, will come forward in various committees. It is, of course, hard to conceive of a set of circumstances that would dislodge the redoubtable Wilbur Mills. But the opportunity is now available, and the party has the full burden of responsibility for his actions in leading the committee. Moreover, Mills has considered retirement for physical reasons, and his likely successor, Al Ullman, would have much less power. The Senate has not yet moved to the House Democratic system, but the Democratic majority is not thereby absolved from responsibility for the activities of Chairman Long. It has the power to call for caucus election of chairmen, and by foregoing this the majority implicitly shoulders that responsibility. The Senate should institute the system of electing committee chairmen by party caucus vote.

All Committee Meetings Open

Meetings of the committees and their subcommittees, including markup sessions, should all be open to the public. In the Ninety-third Congress the House passed a measure establishing the premise that all meetings *should* be open. They can be closed only by an open vote by the committee at the beginning of the meeting. The Senate rejected such a rule, although Senate Rule 25.7(6) provides that "any such closed session may be open to the public if the committee by rule or by majority vote so determines." The House provision permits a vote to close a meeting to be taken before the meeting, and it is also possible to close the meetings one by one, as long as the vote is a public roll-call vote. Thus Ways and Means could continue its present practice of closed executive and markup sessions simply by voting ahead of time. Things will not change much unless the committee disciplines itself to abide by the spirit of the rule. The committee voted overwhelmingly for closed sessions in early- and mid-1973 tests of the new rule.

All Votes Recorded

All votes taken in committee should be recorded votes and should be published in committee reports with adequate descriptions. The House and Senate should institute rules to tighten the present provisions regarding recorded votes. Attendance at all meetings of the committees or subcommittees—whether open or closed—should be published for public review. Verbatim transcripts of all committee meetings should be made public before floor consideration, so the members of the parent body can study them and form their own judgments of the committees' actions. Members will be more informed voters when they are armed with the information and options that the committee used to arrive at its recommendations. The transcripts necessarily would be more comprehensive than the current bare-bones minutes taken by the Finance Committee's chief counsel (and unavailable even to committee members), and broader than the Ways and Means record so jealously guarded by the committee staff.

Opening the Closed Rule

The traditional closed rule under which all Ways and Means legislation goes to the floor of the House became a symbol of the lack of democracy in Congress. The House Democratic Caucus recently voted a change that begins to pry open the closed rule. Any chairman desiring a closed rule for a bill must give notice in the *Congressional Record*. No action will be taken on this request for four days. If during this period fifty Democrats indicate in writing that they wish to add a specific amendment to the bill, the party will caucus within three days to determine whether the full House should consider the amendment. The caucus decision would not be formally binding on the Democratic members of the Rules Committee when the rule on the bill is given, but they would be expected to go along.

This cumbersome procedure may be usable by the Democrats in the House, but it is not much help to the 192 Republicans. An alternative would permit any amendment from the floor that would delete a provision of a bill, but none that would add one. The committee chairman would have the option of withdrawing the bill if such amendments unacceptably emasculated it. This alternative has been advocated during the past few years and could coexist with the new Democratic Caucus rule. Another compromise between a strict closed rule and a completely open rule would have the Ways and Means Committee conduct its hearing, hammer out a legislative draft, and then publish it for the full House with the implication that it would consider amendments suggested by the other members. The bill would then be reported out under the modified closed rule permitting deletions but not additions.

While any of the above procedures would be preferable to the current strict closed rule, a completely open rule is the only effective circuitbreaker for the overload of special interest influence. True, special interests have made great inroads in legislative areas where an open rule is permitted, but in taxation there is a natural political check: assuming a more or less constant deficit level, reductions in special interest taxes will have to be offset by increases in the taxes of everyone else. The issue of a tax increase, and what kind of increase, could be fought hard and well by members on both sides of the question, if there were no buck passing to the entrenched members of Ways and Means. Each representative would be accountable on each floor amendment because of the public voting on the floor. As it is now, representatives pass the buck to twenty-five Ways and Means members especially selected for their entrenched seats. It's time to make all members of Congress completely accountable on tax issues by opening the closed rule.

Concentrated Tax Bills

The committees should scale down the scope of the taxation measures they report out. The practice under Chairman Mills has been to dish up huge, complex omnibus bills with a little bit for everybody. This method of compromise has enabled him to have an almost perfect record for passing committee bills. But while there is something for everyone, few understand the whole. If the committee legislates more single-issue bills, the rest of Congress might grasp the issues and vote more responsibly. With simpler legislation, the closed rule might not be the threat it is at present, when bills run to hundreds of pages on the most arcane and intricate schemes. The members' sophistication about tax matters might be appreciably advanced.

Hearings for All Bills

Public hearings should be held on *all* proposed legislation before the committees, including "minor" amendments and member's bills. If an adjustment is sought regarding some wrinkle in the Internal Revenue Code, the proponent of the change (whether a private party or the Treasury or another executive agency) should be required to defend it publicly. If such a measure is not enacted in both houses of Congress, members in each house should block such bills and demand that they be examined and openly deliberated. After such hearings the committee should issue a report to the full Congress explaining the measure and its revenue effect and identifying the particular beneficiaries, as the House Judiciary Committee does for its "private relief bills." Adoption of this procedure by the revenue committees would considerably clean up the inequitable practice of permitting the taxation legislative process to be manipulated by those able to purchase access to the members of the revenue committees or the Treasury.

Effective Oversight

The committees should immediately institute effective systems to conduct oversight of the jurisdictions assigned them. Establishing subcommittees would aid in facilitating this. Such oversight as now exists is largely a matter of chance. If it is true that the problem is one of committee time for serious oversight, perhaps the only solution is to pare down the committees' jurisdictions and/or develop adequate staffing. A portion of each committee's staff should be devoted solely to oversight, and the committees should not rely merely on federal agencies for data instead of conducting independent investigations. They could also make more extensive use of the General Accounting Office, set up to "review and analyze" government programs. The need for an equitable tax system, our grave foreign trade position, and the scandal of rising health care costs are matters for the revenue committees to oversee and remedy, but these problems have been allowed to fester unchecked because oversight is conducted so haphazardly.

Publication of the Tax Expenditure Budget

The Tax Expenditure Budget is one area where legislative inquiry and oversight is required immediately. The scandal of nearly $60 billion in revenues being forgone in order to achieve certain policy objectives—with few in Congress or the executive having a clear idea of what the nation is receiving in return—is an issue that the revenue committees must address immediately. The Tax Expenditure Budget should be published in coordination with the direct expenditure budget, so that members of Congress can readily determine the total allocation of resources in a given area. No new tax expenditure should be legislated until a joint task force (comprised of revenue committee members, members of the committee usually responsible for the particular substantive area, the Treasury, and any other executive agency responsible for the substantive area) studies the various approaches to the desired goal and decides that the tax expenditure approach is actually the best way of achieving it. As for existing tax expenditures already lodged in the Internal Revenue Code, the committees should launch a joint congressional-Treasury group to study their effectiveness. The study group should be charged with suggesting alternatives for achieving the specific policy objectives. The undertaking would be massive, but the nation cannot afford the luxury of $60 billion in expenditures, many of which may be worthless in terms of policy. The tax expenditure budget is one area in which accountability is long overdue. The Senate and House budget committees, organized in late 1974, may serve to remedy some of these problems.

Publication of Campaign Contributions

The clerk of the House should be required to run printouts, from already reported data, of campaign contributions to all committee members from special interest groups (or their representatives) whose interests are legislated by the committees. There should be one place where a citizen can immediately review all the special interest contributions to committee members. Under the present system of reporting campaign contributions, citizens can cull this information only after days of poring through hundreds of reporting forms. The ready availability of such information would make it harder for special interest groups to exert pressure on committee members in private. Members' personal financial interests (stockholdings, for example) and incomes (from outside law practice, for example) should also be published.

BEYOND THE FORMAL LEGISLATIVE PROCESS

Tax Code Recommendation Board

The revenue committees should spearhead a drive to create a national commission of laymen, experts, and public officials from all three branches of the federal government to conduct a thorough study of the Internal Revenue Code and suggest how to simplify and reform it.

Better Media Coverage

The news media should take far more seriously their responsibilities to report tax news. Their performance so far has been woefully inadequate. The news media must translate the mysteries of taxes for the public, and present them clearly and comprehensibly. Taxation and welfare inequities are not matters for occasional, cursory coverage during a legislative struggle; they should be the topic of continual comment and review. The $60 billion tax expenditure program, for example, is rarely discussed in the press. This might be contrasted with the media splash given the government guarantee of a $250 million loan to the Lockheed Aircraft Corporation. The press has tremendous power to mold public opinion in this area, as is proved by the explosion of editorial support that followed former Secretary of the Treasury Joe Barr's remark about an imminent "taxpayers' revolt" and the resulting Tax Reform Act of 1969. Media members who lack experienced personnel to cover tax matters might use the professional services of the new Tax Analysts group for assistance.

More Active Scholars

Scholars and professionals in the fields of taxation, economics, public finance, business, and the social sciences should stop abdicating responsibility for contributing to the legislative process. For example, there are hundreds of professors of tax law in the country, yet only a handful—usually the same ones over and over—ever come before the revenue committees with the fruits of their research and reflection. The same observation applies to practicing tax lawyers. And legislation considered by the Ways and Means Committee during the Ninety-second Congress and endorsed by the Treasury to permit certain kinds of tax-exempt organizations to testify before the committees should be enacted. At present, for example, even the distinguished Brookings Institution is not allowed to testify unless specifically requested by the committees.

Increased Citizen Participation

Labor unions especially have a great potential for launching a reform drive with their membership as a power base. Grass-roots pressure on members of Congress, especially those on the revenue committees, would be extremely effective. The various citizens' organizations listed in Chapter Three are eager to work with local groups, to forward them educational materials, to put them in touch with other interested groups, and to lobby on their behalf in Washington. All the scholarly articles and testimony in the world do not have the effect on the members of Congress that a clear message from their constituents does. A good deal of citizen effort must be expended to counterbalance the enticements that the special interests offer members of Congress.

Appendices

APPENDIX 1.
Senate Record

---

1. People vs. Corporations

Last year Senator Birch Bayh (D., Ind.) led a fight to cut back ADR corporate depreciation benefits in the Revenue Act of 1971. (*See Congressional Record*, November 15, 1971, pp. S.18612–18.) Senator Bayh and other tax reform senators opposed ADR as a high-priced and inefficient way to stimulate the economy. Bayh proposed to use the money saved from the corporate tax cut to reduce individual taxes by $25 per taxpayer. The Bayh amendment was narrowly defeated, 40–39. A "+" indicates a vote *for* the Bayh amendment. A "−" indicates a vote to keep ADR at an annual cost of $2.9 billion. "O" means no vote.

2. Minimum Tax

This fall Senator Gaylord Nelson (D., Wis.) led a fight to increase the minimum tax on the wealthy. Loopholes have enabled very wealthy taxpayers to escape most or all of income taxes. In 1969 Congress enacted a "minimum tax" on such taxpayers, but this measure was itself so full of loopholes that the average actual rate is only 4 percent. Senator Nelson's amendment to strengthen this "minimum tax" lost by a lopsided 47–28 vote. (See *Congressional Record*, October 5, 1972, pp. S.16996–99.) A "+" indicates a vote for the Nelson amendment. A "−" indicates a vote against strengthening the minimum tax on the wealthy. "O" means no vote.

3. *Personal Tax Credit*

Senator Jack Miller (R., Iowa) led a fight to replace the increase in personal exemption with a personal tax credit in the Revenue Act of 1971. (See *Congressional Record*, November 15, 1971, pp. S.18618– 21.) The vote on this issue was possibly obscured because the Miller amendment also reduced the size of the overall individual benefits. Senator Miller pointed out that the tax credit was fairer than the exemption because it gave each taxpayer the same amount, while an exemption would give high income taxpayers much more than low or middle income taxpayers. A "+" shows a vote for the Miller tax credit. A "−" is a vote to increase the inequitable personal exemption instead. "O" means no vote.

4. *Tax Reform Bill*

Last spring Senator Gaylord Nelson (D., Wis.) introduced a comprehensive tax reform bill, S.3378. (See *Congressional Record*, March 21, 1972, pp. S.4287–4307.) This bill is similar to the Corman Bill (H.R. 11058) in the House. A "+" indicates the Senator cosponsored this bill; a "O" means he did not.

	1	2	3	4
Alabama				
Allen, James (D)	−	+	−	O
Sparkman, John (D)	+	−	−	O
Alaska				
Gravel, Mike (D)	+	+	+	O
Stevens, Ted (R)	O	+	O	O
Arizona				
Fannin, Paul (R)	−	−	+	O
Goldwater, Barry (R)	−	O	O	O
Arkansas				
Fulbright, J. W. (D)	+	−	−	O
McClellan, John (D)	O	−	O	O

	1	2	3	4
California				
Cranston, Alan (D)	+	+	−	O
Tunney, John (D)	+	−	+	+
Colorado				
Allott, Gordon (R)	O	O	O	O
Dominick, Peter (R)	−	−	+	O
Connecticut				
Ribicoff, Abraham (D)	O	O	+	O
Weicker, Lowell (R)	−	−	−	O
Delaware				
Boggs, J. Caleb (R)	−	O	+	O
Roth, Wm. (R)	−	−	−	O

	1	2	3	4
Florida				
Chiles, Lawton (D)	+	+	+	o
Gurney, Edw. (R)	−	−	+	o
Georgia				
Gambrell, David (D)	+	−	−	o
Talmadge, Herman (D)	o	−	−	o
Hawaii				
Inouye, Daniel (D)	+	+	−	o
Fong, Hiram (R)	−	−	−	o
Idaho				
Church, Frank (D)	+	o	−	+
Jordan, Len (R)	o	−	o	o
Illinois				
Stevenson, Adlai (D)	+	−	+	o
Percy, Chas. (R)	−	+	−	o
Indiana				
Bayh, Birch (D)	+	+	o	o
Hartke, Vance (D)	o	−	o	o
Iowa				
Hughes, Harold (D)	o	+	o	+
Miller, Jack (R)	−	−	+	o
Kansas				
Dole, Robt. (R)	−	−	−	o
Pearson, James (R)	−	−	−	o
Kentucky				
Cook, Marlow (R)	−	−	−	o
Cooper, John S. (R)	−	−	+	o
Louisiana				
Ellender, Allen (D)#	o	o	−	o
Long, Russell (D)	+	−	−	o
Maine				
Muskie, Edmund (D)	+	+	o	+
Smith, Margaret (R)	−	+	−	o

	1	2	3	4
Maryland				
Beall, J. Glenn (R)	−	−	−	o
Mathias, Chas. (R)	−	+	−	o
Massachusetts				
Kennedy, Edw. (D)	+	o	+	+
Brooke, Edw. (R)	o	+	o	o
Michigan				
Hart, Philip (D)	+	+	−	+
Griffin, Robt. (R)	−	+	−	o
Minnesota				
Humphrey, Hubert (D)	o	o		o	+
Mondale, Walter (D)	+	+	+	+
Mississippi				
Eastland, James (D)	−	o	−	o
Stennis, John (D)	+	−	−	o
Missouri				
Eagleton, Thomas (D)	+	o	−	+
Symington, Stuart (D)	+	−	−	o

LEGEND
1. People vs. Corporations
2. Minimum Tax
3. Personal Tax Credit
4. Tax Reform Bill
+ Supported *People & Taxes* position
− Opposed *People & Taxes* position
o No action
Died or resigned during the session
* Elected to fill a vacancy during the session

	1	2	3	4
Montana				
Mansfield, Mike (D)	+	+	−	o
Metcalf, Lee (D)	+	o	−	+
Nebraska				
Curtis, Carl (R)	o	o	o	o
Hruska, Roman (R)	−	−	−	o
Nevada				
Bible, Alan (D)	+	−	−	o
Cannon, Howard (D)	+	+	−	o
New Hampshire				
McIntyre, Thomas (D)	+	o	−	o
Cotton, Norris (R)	−	−	−	o
New Jersey				
Williams, Harrison (D)	+	+	−	o
Case, Clifford (R)	+	+	−	o
New Mexico				
Anderson, Clinton (D)	−	o	−	o
Montoya, Jos. (D)	o	−	o	o
New York				
Buckley, Jas. (R-Con.)	−	−	−	o
Javits, Jacob (R)	o	−	o	o
North Carolina				
Ervin, Sam (D)	−	−	−	o
Jordan, Everett (D)	−	−	−	o
North Dakota				
Burdick, Quentin (D)	+	−	−	o
Young, Milton (R)	−	−	−	o
Ohio				
Saxbe, Wm. (R)	o	+	o	o
Taft, Robt. (R)	−	−	−	o

	1	2	3	4
Oklahoma				
Harris, Fred (D)	+	o	+	+
Bellmon, Henry (R)	−	−	−	o
Oregon				
Hatfield, Mark (R)	−	o	−	o
Packwood, Robt. (R)	o	−	o	o
Pennsylvania				
Schweiker, Richard (R)	−	+	o	o
Scott, Hugh (R)	−	−	−	o
Rhode Island				
Pastore, John (D)	o	−	+	o
Pell, Claiborne (D)	+	o	+	o
South Carolina				
Hollings, Ernest (D)	+	o	−	o
Thurmond, Strom (R)	−	−	+	o
South Dakota				
McGovern, Geo. (D)	o	o	o	+
Mundt, Karl (R)	o	o	o	o
Tennessee				
Baker, Howard (R)	−	o	+	o
Brock, Bill (R)	−	−	−	o
Texas				
Bentsen, Lloyd (D)	+	o	−	o
Tower, John (R)	o	o	o	o
Utah				
Moss, Frank (D)	+	+	−	+
Bennett, Wallace (R)	−	−	−	o
Vermont				
Aiken, Geo. (R)	−	−	−	o
Stafford, Robt.* (R)	−	−	−	o

	1	2	3	4
Virginia				
Byrd,				
Harry (Ind.-D)	–	–	–	o
Spong, Wm. (D)	+	o	–	o
Washington				
Jackson, Henry (D)	o	+	o	o
Magnuson,				
Warren (D)	+	+	–	o
West Virginia				
Byrd, Robt. (D)	+	+	–	o
Randolph,				
Jennings (D)	+	–	–	o
Wisconsin				
Nelson,				
Gaylord (D)	+	+	+	+
Proxmire, Wm. (D)	+	+	–	o

	1	2	3	4
Wyoming				
McGee, Gale (D)	+	o	–	o
Hansen,				
Clifford (R)	–	–	+	o

LEGEND
1. People vs. Corporations
2. Minimum Tax
3. Personal Tax Credit
4. Tax Reform Bill
+ Supported *People & Taxes* position
– Opposed *People & Taxes* position
o No action
Died or resigned during the session
* Elected to fill a vacancy during the session

APPENDIX 2.
House of Representatives Record

1. Timber Bill
On November 15, 1971, Congressman Jerome Waldie (D., Calif.) led a successful floor fight to stop a $25 million special tax break for four large timber companies. This classic special interest legislation, sponsored by Al Ullman (D., Oreg.), was defeated 148–203. A "+" indicates a vote against the Ullman bill, and a "−" indicates a vote for the bill. "O" indicates no vote. (See the *Congressional Record*, November 15, 1971, pp. H.11048–52.)

2. ADR Regulations
In early 1971 President Nixon's Treasury Department attempted to cut corporate taxes by $3.9 billion annually through a device called ADR. The Treasury wrote special ADR regulations allowing businesses inflated depreciation deductions, without regard for Section 167 of the tax laws, dealing with depreciation. Prominent law professors opposed ADR as an illegal Treasury encroachment on the congressional power over taxes guaranteed by the Constitution. Many members of Congress were also concerned about this intrusion on their constitutional power. Congressman Sam Gibbons (D., Fla.) got 44 colleagues to cosign a public letter opposing the Treasury action, and Congressmen Henry Reuss (D., Wis.) and Charles Vanik (D., Ohio) publicly protested it. (The Revenue Act of 1971 mooted the question by writing an ADR system into law.) A "+" indicates that the member of Congress opposed Treasury's attempt to usurp the taxing powers of Congress in behalf of special interests.

3. Closed Rule
This summer, Congressman Henry Reuss (D., Wis.) led a fight to allow House floor amendments to a bill from the House Ways and Means Committee. (See *Congressional Record*, June 27, 1972, pp. H.6174–77.) Ways and Means uses a "closed rule" to prevent amendments from representatives not lucky enough to be on the committee. This effectively cuts most members of Congress out of tax policy decisions.

In this case, Congressman Reuss fought the closed rule because the Ways and Means Committee refused to allow even a vote on his tax reform proposal. Reuss was joined by tax reformers and by others who want to release the Ways and Means grip on our tax laws. The Reuss effort met defeat by a narrow 206–180 margin. A "+" indicates a vote against the closed rule. A "−" indicates a vote to keep tax power undemocratically concentrated in the secretive House Ways and Means Committee. "O" means no vote.

4. *Tax Reform Bill*

In this Congress, two major tax reform bills have received wide support. H.R. 11058, sponsored by Congressman James Corman (D., Calif.) and 48 cosponsors, would raise over $11 billion annually by reducing or eliminating many inequities in present law. (For an analysis of the bill, see the *Congressional Record*, October 5, 1971, pp. H.90208–13.) Congressman Henry Reuss (D., Wis.) sponsored a "quick yield" tax reform package to reduce the nation's budget deficit by over $7 billion annually by ending unfair tax provisions and strengthening the minimum tax on loophole income. (For an analysis, see the *Congressional Record*, March 16, 1972, pp. H.2183–88.) A "+" indicates the member of Congress cosponsored either of these bills.

	1	2	3	4
Alabama				
Edwards, Jack (R)	−	O	−	O
Dickinson, Wm. (R)	+	O	O	O
Andrews, Geo.# (D)	−	O	−	O
Nichols, Bill (D)	+	O	+	O
Flowers, Walter (D)	+	O	−	O
Buchanan, John (R)	+	O	−	O
Bevill, Tom (D)	+	O	+	O
Jones, Robt. (D)	O	O	+	O
Alaska				
Begich, Nick (D)	+	+	+	+
Arizona				
Rhodes, John (R)	−	O	−	O
Udall, Morris (D)	+	+	+	O
Steiger, Sam (R)	−	O	−	O
Arkansas				
Alexander, Bill (D)	O	O	−	O
Mills, Wilbur (D)	O	O	−	O

	1	2	3	4
Hammerschmidt, J. (R)	−	O	−	O
Pryor, David (D)	+	O	−	O

LEGEND
1. Timber Bill
2. ADR Regulations
3. Closed Rule
4. Tax Reform Bill
SOURCE: *People and Taxes*, published by the Tax Reform Group, 1972.
+ Supported *People & Taxes* position
− Opposed *People & Taxes* position
O No action
\# Died or resigned during the session
* Elected to fill a vacancy during the session

	1	2	3	4
California				
Clausen, Don (R)	o	o	−	o
Johnson,				
Harold (D)	−	o	−	+
Moss, John (D)	o	+	o	+
Leggett, Robt. (D)	o	o	+	+
Burton, Phillip (D)	+	+	+	+
Mailliard, Wm. (R)	−	o	−	o
Dellums, Ronald (D)	o	o	+	+
Miller, George (D)	o	o	+	o
Edwards, Don (D)	+	+	+	+
Gubser, Chas. (R)	−	o	−	o
McCloskey,				
Paul (R)	o	o	−	o
Talcott, Burt (R)	−	o	−	o
Teague, Chas. (R)	−	o	−	o
Waldie, Jerome (D)	+	o	+	+
McFall, John (D)	−	o	−	+
Sisk, B. F. (D)	−	o	−	+
Anderson,				
Glenn (D)	+	o	+	o
Mathias, Robt. (R)	o	o	−	o
Holifield, Chet (D)	+	o	o	o
Smith, H. Allen (R)	−	o	−	o
Hawkins,				
Augustus (D)	o	o	+	+
Corman, James (D)	o	+	−	+
Clawson, Del (R)	−	o	+	o
Rousselot, John (R)	o	o	+	o
Wiggins, Chas. (R)	+	o	−	o
Rees, Thomas (D)	+	o	+	+
Goldwater,				
Barry (R)	−	o	−	o
Bell, Alphonzo (R)	o	o	−	o
Danielson, Geo. (D)	o	o	+	+
Roybal, Edward (D)	+	+	+	+
Wilson, Chas. (D)	o	o	+	+
Hosmer, Craig (R)	−	o	−	o
Pettis, Jerry (R)	−	o	−	o
Hanna, Richard (D)	+	o	+	o
Schmitz, John (R)	−	o	+	o
Wilson, Bob (R)	−	o	−	o
Van Deerlin,				
Lionel (D)	+	o	+	+
Veysey, Victor (R)	−	o	−	o

	1	2	3	4
Colorado				
McKevitt,				
James (R)	o	o	−	o
Brotzman,				
Donald (R)	−	o	−	o
Evans, Frank (D)	o	o	+	o
Aspinall,				
Wayne (D)	−	o	−	o
Connecticut				
Cotter, Wm. (D)	+	+	+	o
Steele, Robt. (R)	+	o	+	o
Giaimo, Robt. (D)	+	o	+	o
McKinney,				
Stewart (R)	+	o	o	o
Monagan, John (D)	+	o	−	o
Grasso, Ella (D)	+	o	+	o
Delaware				
duPont, Pierre (R)	o	o	−	o
Florida				
Sikes, Robt. (D)	−	o	+	o
Fuqua, Don (D)	−	o	−	o
Bennett, Chas. (D)	+	o	+	o
Chappell, Bill (D)	o	o	−	o
Frey, Louis (R)	+	o	−	o
Gibbons, Sam (D)	o	+	+	+
Haley, James (D)	−	o	+	o
Young, C. W. (R)	+	o	+	o
Rogers, Paul (D)	+	o	+	o
Burke,				
J. Herbert (R)	+	o	o	o
Pepper, Claude (D)	−	o	−	+
Fascell, Dante (D)	−	o	+	o
Georgia				
Hagan,				
G. Elliott (D)	−	o	o	o
Mathis, Dawson (D)	o	o	+	o
Brinkley, Jack (D)	+	o	+	o
Blackburn, Ben (R)	o	o	−	o
Thompson,				
Fletcher (R)	−	o	−	o
Flynt, John (D)	−	o	+	o
Davis, John (D)	−	o	−	o
Stuckey,				

	1	2	3	4
W. S. (D)	0	0	+	0
Landrum, Phil (D)	−	0	−	0
Stephens, Robt. (D)	−	0	−	0

Hawaii

	1	2	3	4
Matsunaga, Spark (D)	+	0	+	0
Mink, Patsy (D)	+	+	+	0

Idaho

	1	2	3	4
McClure, James (R)	0	0	+	0
Hansen, Orval (R)	0	0	−	0

Illinois

	1	2	3	4
Metcalfe, Ralph (D)	0	0	+	+
Mikva, Abner (D)	0	+	+	+
Murphy, Morgan (D)	+	0	+	0
Derwinski, Edward (R)	0	0	+	0
Kluczynski, John (D)	−	0	−	0
Collins, George (D)	0	0	+	0
Annunzio, Frank (D)	+	0	+	0
Rostenkowski, D. (D)	−	0	−	0
Yates, Sidney (D)	+	0	+	0
Collier, Harold (R)	−	0	−	0
Pucinski, Roman (D)	+	0	+	0
McClory, Robt. (R)	+	0	−	0
Crane, Philip (R)	−	0	+	0
Erlenborn, John (R)	+	0	0	0
Reid, Charlotte# (R)	0	0	0	0
Carlson, Cliffard* (R)	0	0	−	0
Anderson, John (R)	−	0	−	0
Arends, Leslie (R)	−	0	−	0
Michel, Robt. (R)	−	0	−	0
Railsback, Tom (R)	−	0	−	0
Findley, Paul (R)	−	0	+	0

	1	2	3	4
Gray, Kenneth (D)	+	0	−	0
Springer, Wm. (R)	+	0	−	0
Shipley, Geo. (D)	+	0	+	0
Price, Melvin (D)	+	0	+	+

Indiana

	1	2	3	4
Madden, Ray (D)	+	+	+	+
Landgrebe, Earl (R)	+	0	+	0
Brademas, John (D)	+	0	+	0
Roush, J. Edward (D)	+	0	+	0
Hillis, Elwood (R)	+	0	−	0
Bray, William (R)	+	0	−	0
Myers, John (R)	−	0	+	0
Zion, Roger (R)	+	0	−	0
Hamilton, Lee (D)	+	0	+	0
Dennis, David (R)	+	0	+	0
Jacobs, Andrew (D)	+	+	+	+

Iowa

	1	2	3	4
Schwengel, Fred (R)	−	0	0	+
Culver, John (D)	+	0	+	0
Gross, H. R. (R)	+	0	+	0
Kyl, John (R)	−	0	0	0
Smith, Neal (D)	+	0	+	0
Mayne, Wiley (R)	−	0	−	0
Scherle, Wm. (R)	+	0	+	0

LEGEND
1. Timber Bill
2. ADR Regulations
3. Closed Rule
4. Tax Reform Bill
SOURCE: *People and Taxes*, published by the Tax Reform Group, 1972.
+ Supported *People & Taxes* position
− Opposed *People & Taxes* position
0 No action
Died or resigned during the session
* Elected to fill a vacancy during the session

	1	2	3	4
Kansas				
Sebelius, Keith (R)	+	o	−	o
Roy, William (D)	+	+	+	+
Winn, Larry (R)	+	o	−	o
Shriver, Garner (R)	−	o	−	o
Skubitz, Joe (R)	o	o	−	o
Kentucky				
Stubblefield, Frank (D)	+	o	−	o
Natcher, Wm. (D)	−	o	+	o
Mazzoli, Romano (D)	+	o	+	+
Snyder, M. G. (R)	+	o	+	o
Carter, Tim (R)	+	o	−	o
Curlin, Wm. P.* (D)	o	o	o	o
Perkins, Carl (D)	+	o	−	o
Louisiana				
Hebert, F. Edward (D)	o	o	o	o
Boggs, Hale (D)	−	o	o	o
Caffery, Patrick (D)	+	o	o	o
Waggonner, Joe (D)	−	o	−	o
Passman, Otto (D)	−	o	−	o
Rarick, John (D)	+	o	+	o
Edwards, Edwin (D)	o	o	o	o
Long, Speedy (D)	o	o	−	o
Maine				
Kyros, Peter (D)	+	o	+	+
Hathaway, Wm. (D)	+	+	+	o
Maryland				
Mills, Wm. O.* (R)	o	o	−	o
Long, Clarence (D)	+	+	+	+
Garmatz, Edw. (D)	−	o	−	+
Sarbanes, Paul (D)	+	+	o	+
Hogan, Lawrence (R)	−	o	−	o
Byron, Goodloe (D)	+	o	−	o
Mitchell, Parren (D)	o	+	+	+
Gude, Gilbert (R)	+	o	+	o

	1	2	3	4
Massachusetts				
Conte, Silvio (R)	+	o	−	o
Boland, Edw. (D)	+	o	+	o
Drinan, Robt. (D)	+	+	+	+
Donohue, Harold (D)	+	o	+	o
Morse, F. B.# (R)	+	o	o	o
Harrington, Michael (D)	+	+	+	+
Macdonald, Torbert (D)	−	o	−	o
O'Neill, Thomas (D)	+	o	−	o
Hicks, Louise Day (D)	+	o	+	o
Heckler, Margaret (R)	o	o	+	o
Burke, James (D)	−	o	−	o
Keith, Hastings (R)	+	o	−	o
Michigan				
Conyers, John (D)	o	o	+	+
Esch, Marvin (R)	−	o	o	o
Brown, Garry (R)	−	o	−	o
Hutchinson, Edw. (R)	+	o	+	o
Ford, Gerald (R)	o	o	o	o
Chamberlain, Chas. (R)	−	o	−	o
Riegle, Donald (R)	+	o	−	o
Harvey, James (R)	−	o	−	o
Vander Jagt, Guy (R)	+	o	−	o
Cederberg, Elford (R)	−	o	−	o
Ruppe, Philip (R)	o	o	−	o
O'Hara, James (D)	+	o	+	+
Diggs, Chas. (D)	o	o	+	+
Nedzi, Lucien (D)	+	o	+	+
Ford, William (D)	+	o	o	+
Dingell, John (D)	−	+	+	+
Griffiths, Martha (D)	−	o	−	o
Broomfield, Wm. (R)	−	o	o	o
McDonald, Jack (R)	−	o	o	o

	1	2	3	4
Minnesota				
Quie, Albert (R)	−	0	−	0
Nelsen, Ancher (R)	−	0	−	0
Frenzel, Bill (R)	−	0	−	0
Karth, Jos. (D)	−	0	0	0
Fraser, Donald (D)	+	+	+	+
Zwach, John (R)	0	0	+	0
Bergland, Bob (D)	+	0	+	+
Blatnik, John (D)	0	0	+	0
Mississippi				
Abernethy, Thomas (D)	−	0	0	0
Whitten, Jamie (D)	+	0	−	0
Griffin, Chas. (D)	−	0	0	0
Montgomery, G. V. (D)	−	0	−	0
Colmer, Wm. (D)	−	0	0	0
Missouri				
Clay, Wm. (D)	0	0	+	0
Symington, James (D)	+	0	+	0
Sullivan, Leonor (D)	+	0	+	0
Randall, Wm. (D)	+	0	+	0
Bolling, Richard (D)	0	0	−	+
Hull, W. R. (D)	+	0	+	0
Hall, Durward (R)	+	0	0	0
Ichord, Richard (D)	+	0	−	0
Hungate, Wm. (D)	+	0	+	0
Burlison, Bill (D)	−	0	+	0
Montana				
Shoup, Richard (R)	+	0	−	0
Melcher, John (D)	0	0	+	0
Nebraska				
Thone, Chas. (R)	+	0	−	0
McCollister, John (R)	+	0	−	0
Martin, Dave (R)	+	0	−	0
Nevada				
Baring, Walter (D)	−	0	0	0
New Hampshire				
Wyman, Louis (R)	+	0	+	0
Cleveland, James (R)	+	0	+	0

	1	2	3	4
New Jersey				
Hunt, John (R)	+	0	+	0
Sandman, Chas. (R)	+	0	−	0
Howard, James (D)	+	0	+	0
Thompson, Frank (D)	+	0	+	+
Frelinghuysen, P. (R)	−	0	−	0
Forsythe, Edwin (R)	+	0	−	0
Widnall, Wm. (R)	0	0	−	0
Roe, Robt. (D)	+	0	+	0
Helstoski, Henry (D)	+	+	+	+
Rodino, Peter (D)	+	+	+	+
Minish, Joseph (D)	+	0	+	0
Dwyer, Florence (R)	+	0	−	0
Gallagher, C. (D)	+	0	0	0
Daniels, Dominick (D)	+	0	+	0
Patten, Edward (D)	−	0	+	0
New Mexico				
Lujan, Manuel (R)	+	0	+	0
Runnels, Harold (D)	0	0	−	0
New York				
Pike, Otis (D)	−	0	+	+
Grover, James (R)	+	0	−	0
Wolff, Lester (D)	+	0	−	0

LEGEND
1. Timber Bill
2. ADR Regulations
3. Closed Rule
4. Tax Reform Bill

SOURCE: *People and Taxes*, published by the Tax Reform Group, 1972.

\+ Supported *People & Taxes* position

− Opposed *People & Taxes* position

0 No action

Died or resigned during the session

* Elected to fill a vacancy during the session

	1	2	3	4
Wydler, John (R)	+	0	−	0
Lent, Norman (R)	0	0	−	0
Halpern, Seymour (R)	0	0	−	+
Addabbo, Joseph (D)	+	+	+	+
Rosenthal, Benj. (D)	0	+	+	+
Delaney, James (D)	+	0	−	0
Celler, Emanuel (D)	+	0	0	0
Brasco, Frank (D)	+	0	+	0
Chisholm, Shirley (D)	0	+	0	+
Podell, Bertram (D)	+	0	+	+
Rooney, John (D)	+	0	−	0
Carey, Hugh (D)	−	0	−	0
Murphy, John (D)	+	0	+	0
Koch, Edward (D)	+	+	+	+
Rangel, Chas. (D)	0	+	+	+
Abzug, Bella (D)	+	0	+	+
Ryan, Wm.# (D)	+	+	+	+
Badillo, Herman (D)	+	+	+	+
Scheuer, James (D)	+	+	+	+
Bingham, Jonathan (D)	+	+	+	+
Biaggi, Mario (D)	+	+	+	0
Peyser, Peter (R)	+	0	−	0
Reid, Ogden (D)	−	0	+	0
Dow, John (D)	+	0	+	+
Fish, Hamilton (R)	0	0	−	0
Stratton, Samuel (D)	−	0	−	0
King, Carleton (R)	+	0	−	0
McEwen, Robt. (R)	−	0	−	0
Pirnie, Alexander (R)	+	0	0	0
Robison, Howard (R)	−	0	−	0
Terry, John (R)	+	0	+	0
Hanley, James (D)	+	0	−	0
Horton, Frank (R)	+	0	+	0
Conable, Barber (R)	0	0	−	0
Hastings, James (R)	+	0	−	0
Kemp, Jack (R)	+	0	−	0
Smith, Henry (R)	−	0	−	0
Dulski, Thaddeus (D)	0	+	−	+

North Carolina

	1	2	3	4
Jones, Walter (D)	0	0	+	0
Fountain, L. H. (D)	−	0	−	0
Henderson, David (D)	+	0	+	0
Galifianakis, Nick (D)	0	0	+	0
Mizell, Wilmer (R)	−	0	0	0
Preyer, Richardson (D)	+	0	−	0
Lennon, Alton (D)	−	0	+	0
Ruth, Earl (R)	−	0	−	0
Jonas, Chas. (R)	+	0	−	0
Broyhill, James (R)	−	0	−	0
Taylor, Roy (D)	−	0	−	0

North Dakota

	1	2	3	4
Andrews, Mark (R)	+	0	−	0
Link, Arthur (D)	0	0	+	0

Ohio

	1	2	3	4
Keating, Wm. (R)	+	0	−	0
Clancy, Donald (R)	+	0	+	0
Whalen, Chas. (R)	+	0	−	0
McCulloch, Wm. (R)	+	0	−	0
Latta, Delbert (R)	+	0	−	0
Harsha, Wm. (R)	+	0	−	0
Brown, Clarence (R)	−	0	−	0
Betts, Jackson (R)	−	0	−	0
Ashley, Thomas (D)	0	0	+	0
Miller, Clarence (R)	+	0	−	0
Stanton, Wm. (R)	−	0	−	0
Devine, Samuel (R)	+	0	+	0
Mosher, Chas. (R)	0	0	0	0
Seiberling, John (D)	+	0	+	+
Wylie, Chalmers (R)	+	0	−	0
Bow, Frank (R)	−	0	−	0
Ashbrook, John (R)	0	0	+	0
Hays, Wayne (D)	+	0	+	0
Carney, Chas. (D)	+	0	+	+
Stanton, James (D)	+	0	−	+
Stokes, Louis (D)	0	+	+	+
Vanik, Chas. (D)	+	+	+	+

	1	2	3	4
Minshall, Wm. (R)	+	O	—	O
Powell, Walter (R)	+	O	—	O

Oklahoma

	1	2	3	4
Belcher, Page (R)	—	O	—	O
Edmondson, E. (D)	—	O	O	O
Albert, Carl (D)	O	O	O	O
Steed, Tom (D)	O	O	—	O
Jarman, John (D)	+	O	—	O
Camp, John (R)	—	O	—	O

Oregon

	1	2	3	4
Wyatt, Wendell (R)	—	O	—	O
Ullman, Al (D)	—	O	—	O
Green, Edith (D)	—	O	—	O
Dellenback, John (R)	—	O	—	O

Pennsylvania

	1	2	3	4
Barrett, Wm. (D)	O	O	—	O
Nix, Robt. (D)	+	+	+	+
Byrne, James (D)	+	O	+	O
Eilberg, Joshua (D)	+	O	+	+
Green, Wm. (D)	+	+	+	O
Yatron, Gus (D)	+	O	+	+
Williams, Lawrence (R)	—	O	—	O
Biester, Edw. (R)	+	O	—	O
Ware, John (R)	—	O	—	O
McDade, Jos. (R)	+	O	O	O
Flood, Daniel (D)	—	O	+	O
Whalley, J. Irving (R)	O	O	—	O
Coughlin, R. L. (R)	—	O	—	O
Moorhead, Wm. (D)	O	+	—	+
Rooney, Fred (D)	+	O	—	O
Eshleman, Edwin (R)	+	O	—	O
Schneebeli, Herman (R)	—	O	O	O
Heinz, John H.* (R)	+	O	+	O
Goodling, Geo. (R)	O	O	+	O
Gaydos, Jos. (D)	+	O	+	O
Dent, John (D)	+	O	O	O
Saylor, John (R)	—	O	+	O
Johnson, Albert (R)	—	O	—	O

	1	2	3	4
Vigorito, Jos. (D)	O	O	+	O
Clark, Frank (D)	+	O	O	O
Morgan, Thomas (D)	+	O	—	O
Fulton, James# (R)	O	O	O	O
Conover, William* (R)	O	O	—	O

Rhode Island

	1	2	3	4
St. Germain, F. (D)	+	O	+	O
Tiernan, Robt. (D)	+	O	—	O

South Carolina

	1	2	3	4
Davis, Mendel* (D)	—	O	O	O
Spence, Floyd (R)	+	O	+	O
Dorn, W. J. B. (D)	—	O	—	O
Mann, James (D)	O	O	+	O
Gettys, Tom (D)	—	O	—	O
McMillan, John (D)	—	O	—	O

South Dakota

	1	2	3	4
Denholm, Frank (D)	+	O	+	O
Abourezk, Jas. (D)	+	O	O	+

Tennessee

	1	2	3	4
Quillen, James (R)	+	O	—	O
Duncan, John (R)	+	O	—	O
Baker, La Mar (R)	+	O	—	O
Evins, Joe (D)	+	O	O	O
Fulton, Richard (D)	—	O	O	O

LEGEND
1. Timber Bill
2. ADR Regulations
3. Closed Rule
4. Tax Reform Bill

SOURCE: *People and Taxes*, published by the Tax Reform Group, 1972.

+ Supported *People & Taxes* position

— Opposed *People & Taxes* position

O No action

\# Died or resigned during the session

* Elected to fill a vacancy during the session

	1	2	3	4
Anderson, Wm. (D)	+	o	o	+
Blanton, Ray (D)	−	o	o	o
Jones, Edw. (D)	−	o	+	o
Kuykendall, Dan (R)	−	o	−	o

Texas

	1	2	3	4
Patman, Wright (D)	−	o	+	o
Dowdy, John (D)	o	o	o	o
Collins, James (R)	+	o	−	o
Roberts, Ray (D)	o	o	−	o
Cabell, Earle (D)	o	o	−	o
Teague, Olin (D)	−	o	−	o
Archer, Bill (R)	+	o	−	o
Eckhardt, Bob (D)	+	o	+	o
Brooks, Jack (D)	−	o	−	o
Pickle, J. J. (D)	−	o	−	o
Poage, W. R. (D)	−	o	+	o
Wright, Jim (D)	o	o	−	o
Purcell, Graham (D)	o	o	−	o
Young, John (D)	−	o	−	o
de la Garza, Eligio (D)	+	o	−	o
White, Richard (D)	−	o	+	o
Burleson, Omar (D)	−	o	−	o
Price, Robt. (R)	−	o	−	o
Mahon, Geo. (D)	−	o	−	o
Gonzales, Henry (D)	−	o	+	o
Fisher, O. C. (D)	−	o	−	o
Casey, Bob (D)	−	o	−	o
Kazen, Abraham (D)	−	o	−	o

Utah

	1	2	3	4
McKay, K. Gunn (D)	o	o	+	o
Lloyd, Sherman (R)	−	o	−	o

Vermont

	1	2	3	4
Stafford, Robt.# (R)	o	o	o	o
Mallary, Richard* (R)	o	o	o	o

Virginia

	1	2	3	4
Downing, Thomas (D)	o	o	−	o
Whitehurst, G. Wm. (R)	+	o	−	o
Satterfield, David (D)	−	o	o	o
Abbitt, Watkins (D)	o	o	−	o
Daniel, W. D. (D)	+	o	−	o
Poff, Richard (R)	−	o	−	o
Robinson, J. K. (R)	−	o	−	o
Scott, Wm. (R)	−	o	−	o
Wampler, Wm. (R)	−	o	−	o
Broyhill, Joel (R)	−	o	−	o

Washington

	1	2	3	4
Pelly, Thomas (R)	o	o	−	o
Meeds, Lloyd (D)	+	o	+	+
Hansen, Julia (D)	−	o	+	o
McCormack, Mike (D)	+	o	+	o
Foley, Thomas (D)	−	o	+	o
Hicks, Floyd (D)	−	o	+	o
Adams, Brock (D)	−	+	+	o

West Virginia

	1	2	3	4
Mollohan, Robt. (D)	+	o	o	o
Staggers, Harley (D)	+	o	+	o
Slack, John (D)	−	o	+	o
Hechler, Ken (D)	+	+	+	+
Kee, James (D)	−	o	o	o

Wisconsin

	1	2	3	4
Aspin, Les (D)	+	+	+	+
Kastenmeier, Robt. (D)	+	+	+	+
Thomson, Vernon (R)	−	o	−	o
Zablocki, Clement (D)	−	o	+	o
Reuss, Henry (D)	+	+	+	+
Steiger, Wm. (R)	−	o	−	o
Obey, David (D)	+	o	+	+
Byrnes, John (R)	−	o	−	o
Davis, Glenn (R)	−	o	−	o
O'Konski, Alvin (R)	−	o	−	o

Wyoming

	1	2	3	4
Roncalio, Teno (D)	+	o	+	o

Members of the Finance and Ways and Means Committees

SENATE COMMITTEE ON FINANCE,
NINETY-SECOND CONGRESS

Majority:
Russell B. Long, Chm. (La.)
Clinton P. Anderson (N. Mex.)
Herman E. Talmadge (Ga.)
Vance Hartke (Ind.)
J. W. Fulbright (Ark.)
Abraham A. Ribicoff (Conn.)
Fred R. Harris (Okla.)
Harry F. Byrd, Jr. (Va.)
Gaylord Nelson (Wis.)

Minority:
Wallace F. Bennett (Utah)
Carl T. Curtis (Nebr.)
Jack Miller (Iowa)
Len B. Jordan (Idaho)
Paul J. Fannin (Ariz.)
Clifford P. Hansen (Wyo.)
Robert P. Griffin (Mich.)

SENATE COMMITTEE ON FINANCE, NINETY-THIRD CONGRESS

Majority:
Russell B. Long, Chm. (La.)
Herman E. Talmadge (Ga.)
Vance Hartke (Ind.)
J. W. Fulbright (Ark.)
Abraham A. Ribicoff (Conn.)
Harry F. Byrd, Jr. (Va.)
Gaylord Nelson (Wis.)
Walter F. Mondale (Minn.)
Mike Gravel (Alaska)
Lloyd Bentsen (Tex.)

Minority:
Wallace F. Bennett (Utah)
Carl T. Curtis (Nebr.)
Paul J. Fannin (Ariz.)
Clifford P. Hansen (Wyo.)
Robert Dole (Kans.)
Bob Packwood (Oreg.)
William V. Roth, Jr. (Del.)

Subcommittees

International Trade, Abraham Ribicoff, *Chairman*
Health, Herman E. Talmadge, *Chairman*
Private Pension Plans, Gaylord Nelson, *Chairman*
State Taxation of Interstate Commerce, Walter F. Mondale, *Chairman*
Foundations, Vance Hartke, *Chairman*
International Finance and Resources, Harry F. Byrd, Jr., *Chairman*

HOUSE COMMITTEE ON WAYS AND MEANS, NINETY-SECOND CONGRESS

Majority:
Wilbur D. Mills, Chm. (Ark.)
Al Ullman (Oreg.)
James A. Burke (Mass.)
Martha W. Griffiths (Mich.)
Dan Rostenkowski (Ill.)

Minority:
John W. Byrnes (Wis.)
Jackson F. Betts (Ohio)
Herman T. Schneebeli (Pa.)
Harold R. Collier (Ill.)
Joel T. Broyhill (Va.)

Majority:
Phil M. Landrum (Ga.)
Charles A. Vanik (Ohio)
Richard H. Fulton (Tenn.)
Omar Burleson (Tex.)
James C. Corman (Calif.)
William J. Green (Pa.)
Sam Gibbons (Fla.)
Hugh L. Carey (N. Y.)
Joe D. Waggoner (La.)
Joseph E. Karth (Minn.)

Minority:
Barber B. Conable, Jr. (N. Y.)
Charles E. Chamberlain
    (Mich.)
Jerry L. Pettis (Calif.)
John J. Duncan (Tenn.)
Donald G. Brotzman (Colo.)

HOUSE COMMITTEE ON WAYS AND MEANS, NINETY-THIRD CONGRESS

Majority:
Wilbur D. Mills, Chm. (Ark.)
Al Ullman (Oreg.)
James A. Burke (Mass.)
Martha W. Griffiths (Mich.)
Dan Rostenkowski (Ill.)
Phil M. Landrum (Ga.)
Charles A. Vanik (Ohio)
Richard H. Fulton (Tenn.)
Omar Burleson (Tex.)
James C. Corman (Calif.)
William J. Green (Pa.)
Sam Gibbons (Fla.)
Hugh L. Carey (N. Y.)
Joe D. Waggoner, Jr. (La.)
Joseph E. Karth (Minn.)

Minority:
Herman T. Schneebeli (Pa.)
Harold R. Collier (Ill.)
Joel T. Broyhill (Va.)
Barber B. Conable, Jr. (N. Y.)
Charles E. Chamberlain
    (Mich.)
Jerry L. Pettis (Calif.)
John J. Duncan (Tenn.)
Donald G. Brotzman (Colo.)
Donald D. Clancy (Ohio)
Bill Archer (Tex.)

II

THE HOUSE
AND SENATE
APPROPRIATIONS
COMMITTEES

6

A History of
the Process

The American Founding Fathers did not create our system of government out of whole cloth. Much of the debate on the Constitution centered on adaptation of the various European democratic models that then existed. The heart of all these systems was a balance of powers, and the framers of the Constitution spent hours delineating the relationships to be struck among the three branches of government.

One great power was handed to the legislative branch: the control of the nation's purse. James Madison would write in one of the *Federalist Papers* that "this power over the purse may, in fact, be regarded as the most complete and effective weapon with which any constitution can arm the immediate representatives of the people, for obtaining a redress of every grievance, and for carrying into effect every just and salutary measure."[1]

The writers of the Constitution clearly intended this power to be the major weapon in maintaining governmental balance, declaring flatly that "no money shall be drawn from the Treasury, but in Consequence of Appropriations made by Law. . . ."[2] It would be observed later that no other founders of a democratic nation had so definitively handed control of an executive budget to the legislative. Indeed, the original plan provided for a detailed review of executive budgets as well as revisions of them where necessary, to insure that financial control was appropriately related to the policies and programs of the executive agencies.

While reality often makes mockery of theory, Congress did— almost from the beginning—attempt to exert control over the budget. When they first convened in the spring of 1789, the legislators had only the bare outline given in the Constitution to work from in organizing their activities. A partisan debate broke out over the role the branch should play in budgetary matters. The Federalist administration of George Washington, particularly Secretary of the Treasury Alexander Hamilton, felt the Congress should merely pass on the budget as a whole. The legislators themselves were of two minds: first creating the original House Ways and Means Committee under non-Federalist Elbridge Gerry of Massachusetts and then turning around less than a month later to discharge the committee and turn over preparation of the budget to Hamilton.

What emerged from Hamilton's office just four days later was the first federal budget. From the modern view this appropriations request seems almost too small to be believed. It asked for only $639,000 to run the government for an entire year. Today that amount would not run the smallest agency in the bureaucracy for a month. Further, it asked for funds in only four areas: government pay, national defense, payment of debts incurred during the revolution, and disability payments to veterans.

For the next few years Hamilton continued to prepare the budget and Congress merely exercised approval rights. Party politics had not yet surfaced as such, but government opponents did take every opportunity to express their unhappiness with the state of the national treasury. Soon, one Hamilton enemy told his fellow House members, the Congress "would not be Representative of their constituents but of the Secretary." The leader of these attacks was Albert Gallatin, a Swiss-born Pennsylvanian who was first a senator (but removed on a straight party-line vote after his residency was challenged) and then a representative.

It was Gallatin and his fellow Republicans who deflected our system of government away from a more British model. In 1795 Hamilton resigned his post and the Republican majority in the House quickly established the second Ways and Means Committee. The committee was given power over both appropriations and taxes, another Gallatin proposal. Less than a week after this committee came into being, the executive put forward fiscal 1796 for its review, setting the pattern for future years.

There was one final battle between Hamilton and Gallatin. The Federalists, under Hamilton's direction, had submitted budgets of lump sums. Their requests asked for so much for defense, so much for this, so much for that, but made no breakdown of exactly what the monies would be used for. For over two years, Gallatin and Hamilton's successor, Oliver Wolcott, fought over how detailed the budget should be. In frustration, Wolcott wrote to Hamilton that "the management of the Treasury becomes more and more difficult. The Legislature will not pass laws in gross. Their appropriations are minute; Gallatin, to whom they yield, is evidently intending to break down this department by charging it with an impracticable detail."

This debate was not settled until Gallatin himself became Secretary of the Treasury under Thomas Jefferson. In his first message to the legislative branch, Jefferson—under pressure from Gallatin—urged that funds should be appropriated "in specific sums to every specific purpose susceptible to definition," that contingency funds be done away with, and that the transfer of funds from one purpose to another be prohibited. Hamilton quickly formulated a series of Federalist replies.

Professor Joseph Harris observes that "the views of Hamilton and Gallatin to some extent differed only in degree." Even Gallatin, he notes, would warn that the Congress could not foresee every need of the executive branch and that it would be wrong to totally handcuff the president on the expenditure of monies. In the end, Gallatin's view did win over Hamilton's, and Congress formalized the new relationship in 1802, when the House made Ways and Means a standing (permanent) committee (the Senate continued to use select—not permanent—committees for a while but eventually created its Finance Committee).

This formalization created new problems. Even in those times of low budgets (monies raised from customs duties alone could cover all necessary expenditures), the House Ways and Means Committee and the Senate Finance Committee had a heavy burden in trying to deal with both expenditures and income. This was especially true of the House group, where now—by a tradition long in force—all appropriations originated. In 1814 the House tried to lift part of the burden by creating a Committee on Public Expenditure. Although the committee nominally existed until 1880 it never really amounted to much of anything—in part because Ways and Means members were loath even then to give up any of their power.

More importantly in terms of the modern appropriations process, the executive agencies reacted to increased Congressional control by taking advantage of all the loopholes open to them in circumventing the required procedures. The transfer of funds from one project to another continued unabated and Congress did little to stop such violations of the appropriations laws. In addition, the number of requests for deficiency appropriations climbed rapidly. Agencies would simply go ahead and spend what money they felt they needed and then expect Congress to make it up. Legislators proved reluctant to deny such requests and "back-door spending" was born.

The period of American history covering both the Mexican-American War and the Civil War saw sharp changes in the appropriations process. During the Mexican War, 1846 to 1848, the annual cost of operating the United States government jumped from $27 million to $45 million.[3] The costs during the Civil War made those expenditures seem like chicken feed, however. By 1865, expenditures went past the billion dollar mark for the first time and the interest on the national debt rocketed to $100 million per year.[4] The Ways and Means and Finance committees were overworked to the point that, during the Civil War, Abraham Lincoln all but ignored the appropriations process and simply spent monies as he saw fit. There was almost no congressional opposition to this in a time of crisis but—even after Congress moved to reassert its authority in 1865—one major point had been made: the two congressional committees entrusted with both taxation and appropriations simply could no longer handle the burden.

Under normal circumstances both the Senate and the House committee would have fought to maintain their power over expenditures. Since 1802 they had dominated the Congress, and the chairmen of the committees had often challenged the power of the speaker of the House and other legislative leaders. The leader of House Ways and Means in 1865—Thaddeus Stevens—was, however, a man who declined to make such a fight. His objections were of the mildest nature, and on March 2, 1865, Ways and Means was stripped of one of its two major responsibilities and the first Appropriations Committee was created in the House. The Senate followed suit two years later.[5]

Within a decade the Appropriations committees managed to make themselves wildly unpopular with their legislative colleagues. Under a series of notably arrogant chairmen, the committees not only wielded their power like a club but managed to add a little heft by pushing through a rules change which allowed amendments dealing with substantive policy to be tacked on to appropriations bills. The effect was that the committees dominated both these areas of congressional concern.

The House finally revolted in 1877. First the committee was stripped of its power over rivers and harbors appropriations bills,[6] then as now *the* source of congressional "pork." In 1880 the appropriations for agriculture and forestry were assigned to other committees, and in 1885 Appropriations lost jurisdiction over foreign affairs, the Army, Indian affairs, the military academies, the Navy, and the post office. That left the House committee with only six of the fourteen funding bills.[7] The end result was chaos, which the Senate also managed to achieve by 1899.

With committees handling both the substantive legislation and the appropriations of most agencies, the bureaucrats moved to exploit the situation, building up more than cordial relations with the committees charged with overseeing their operations. The result was, one historian noted, "the one [committee] striving to surpass the other in securing greater recognition and more money for its special charge." No committee took notice of what the others did, and the agencies were free to submit their budgets directly to the Congress with no presidential overview.[8] To top it off, Appropriations still maintained control over deficiency requests of *all* agencies.

Throughout the better part of a thirty-year period neither the executive nor the legislative branch had any real control over the budget. Incredible monies, according to observers of the period, were wasted and the federal deficit continued to rise. Public outcry finally began to be listened to in 1909, when the Congress attached a rider to the sundry civil appropriations bill of that year directing the secretary of the Treasury to estimate the amount of revenue to be derived in the coming year. The secretary was to then advise the president of what monies would be available, the president in turn advising the Congress how expenditures could best be reduced to bring them within the estimated level of income.

Although the Congress clearly intended the rider to help in deflecting criticism toward the executive and not as any substantive change, this provision was the first step toward the modern budgetary system. Professor Harris has observed of the period before 1909 that the president's part in the process was especially remote. Thus in that year Congress handed to President William Howard Taft the means to begin presidential control of the budget, at least as it would appear when first presented to the legislative.

Taft seized the initiative. He not only had his Cabinet officers review the agencies' requests but looked over the requests himself. In 1910 he was able to push an appropriation through Congress giving him authority to hire staff to work on the budget. And in 1911 he created the Commission on Economy and Efficiency, the forerunner of the Bureau of Management and the Budget.

Taft's advances in this area made an issue out of the need for a unified national budget. In 1912 the Chamber of Commerce adopted the concept as a major part of its program. Both political parties had such a budget as part of their 1916 presidential platforms. Faced with this sort of pressure, Congress—ever last in action—finally set up a Select Committee on the Budget in 1919. The committee was charged with reviewing the entire financial system of the United States government and proposing legislation to untangle it.[9]

It took Congress almost two years to come up with a comprehensive plan. President Woodrow Wilson vetoed one in 1919 and the Senate and the House quarreled over key provisions in 1920.[10] The final system accepted by both branches called for the president to prepare an annual budget, bringing together the estimates of all agencies. The so-called Budget and Accounting Act of 1921 formalized Taft's commission, renaming it the Bureau of the Budget and placing it within the Treasury Department, and established the General Accounting Office, which was to be independent of the executive and serve as Congress' auditing arm. It was assumed by all concerned that both the House and the Senate would return to a single appropriations committee system. The House did so almost immediately, the Senate in 1922.

The thrust of the 1921 bill, the whole debate over the budget between 1909 and 1921, was to bring about a system whereby "national priorities" (to use a modern term) could be debated and an over-all budget would be produced without the fragmentation of previous years. What occurred, however, was fragmentation of a different sort. The president presented his budget as a whole. The Congress sent it to the Appropriations Committee as a whole. The committee promptly tore it apart and parceled out the pieces to its subcommittees. The budgetary plan was never put back together but, rather, each piece was voted upon separately.

This defect had little impact during the first ten years the system was in operation. Presidential cuts in agency requests seemed to intimidate the Congress and reductions were made in the over-all budgets for this period. There were even surpluses to aid in reducing the national debt, a whopping $738 million in 1930, for example.[11]

The modern problems of such a system began to surface during Franklin Roosevelt's New Deal. Between 1931 and 1940, expenditures rose from $4 billion to $9 billion. Back-door spending became prominent again and the congressional committees could, once again, barely keep ahead of executive requests. By the time Roosevelt and the Congress could cut down on domestic expenditures, World War II had begun and the military budget reached historic levels; modern spending levels had hit the United States. In less than two hundred years the Congress had gone from a budget of less than $700,000 to one of more than $250 billion.

This same Congress, however, still functions under a system that was set up in 1921. Warren Weaver can point out accurately that "the system is antiquated, slipshod, cumbersome and almost totally without organization or defensible rationale. It presents an open invitation to petty politicking and the grossest kind of irresponsible fiscal management. The operation is nothing short of a national disgrace. Congress likes it."[12]

Both Alexander Hamilton and Albert Gallatin would no doubt agree.

7

The Budget
Before Congress

Representative Louis Stokes (D., Ohio), a member of the House
Appropriations Committee, has spoken of the need to keep the
meetings and hearings of his committee closed: "From the view-
point of preventing a revolution in this country it might be
necessary. If the people out there knew what was going on in
there they might want to start a revolution."

Stokes was exercising his well-known sarcasm but his point is
well taken. The appropriations process of the United States is a
mess. As Warren Weaver has observed, if a corporation used the
national budget system, not only would the stockholders be outraged but the company would probably collapse.[1] "That is not
really stretching for an analogy," adds a Republican congressman
with a background in business:

> The voters are stockholders. They invest their money—
> through taxes—in the government and they want something
> back. We—the representatives and senators—are elected to

> oversee how the money is spent, like a board of directors.
> The President can be viewed as a chairman of the board.
> Frankly, if I was a leading stockholder in a company and
> the firm was run the way we run appropriations, I would
> fire the board, the chairman and everyone involved tomor-
> row. It is an outrage.*

The process of appropriations begins with the president's fiscal
arm, the Office of Management and the Budget. For six months
of any given year, OMB is really dealing with three budgets.
From January to July, it is preparing the budget for the fiscal
year two years hence, defending before Congress the budget for
the next fiscal year, and overseeing the actual spending of funds
for the current fiscal year. In January 1974, for example, OMB
was beginning to prepare the fiscal 1976 budget (the budget for
the year beginning July 1, 1975), defending the fiscal 1975
budget before Congress, and spending monies appropriated by
Congress for fiscal 1974. OMB staff members admit that it is
sometimes hard to keep all this straight.[2]

While President Richard Nixon was presenting his budget to
the Congress in January, the staff was doing the preliminary work
on the fiscal 1976 document. In the preliminary stage, budget
representatives of each agency are called in and go over possible
new programs or expenses with the staff, and projections of
federal income are made. In late spring or early summer, the
OMB director receives this material from his staff.

It is at this time, say, June 1974, that the president with his
OMB director and other White House staff makes decisions on
policy in terms of expenditures for the twelve months between
July 1975 and June 1976. Levels for each agency are set and
transmitted to agency heads. In mid-September the various
departments hand in the first drafts of their detailed budgets.

OMB reviews the requests in the fall, holding a series of
hearings in which department heads can justify and defend their

---

* Unidentified quotations are from confidential interviews with the Congress Project Staff.

budgets. The director goes over the requests himself in early December, taking into account both his staff's recommendations and the budgets themselves. The final changes and shape of the budget are then hashed out by the director and the president (and, in the Nixon administration, key staff aides) for a January delivery to Congress.

The document submitted by the president, and backed up with thousands of pages of facts and figures, is as close as we come to something that can be debated in terms of national priorities. In 1973, for example, Washington's Brookings Institution could review the Nixon budget for fiscal 1974 and conclude that "the federal government isn't going to have much extra money for domestic programs any time in President Nixon's second term unless there is a cutback in defense expenditures or some extensive tinkering with taxes."[3]

The Project on Budget Priorities, a Washington-based group of former government officials, could say that the Nixon budget was one aimed at the federal government's "withdrawing from a long-standing federal leadership role in programs to meet domestic human needs."[4] And Nixon himself could inform Congress that "the 1974 budget is clear evidence of the kind of change in direction demanded by the great majority of the American people. No longer will power flow inexorably to Washington. Instead the power to make many decisions and to help meet local needs will be returned to where it belongs—to the state and local officials."[5]

This kind of debate—no matter which side of the particular verbal conflict you happen to be on—is all to the good. It gets to the point that Senator J. William Fulbright was trying to make when he said that "a nation's budget is full of moral implications; it tells what a society cares about and what it does not care about; it tells what its values are."

The innate problem of a debate at this point is that it takes place *before* the appropriations process has begun. The Congress has yet to have its say, and what comes out of Capitol Hill months after the president's budget statement may bear little resemblance to what he had in mind. "It is a very curious system," a House reporter said. "We give the budget message a lot of coverage even though we who cover the Congress know things are just beginning. Then we tend to go off and ignore the real nitty-gritty of the situation except for taking note of a particularly nasty battle or two."

Although this book deals with the appropriations process within the Congress, it is important to take note of some problems inherent in the whole budget process. First, the president often uses some fancy hocus-pocus in presenting his budget. In 1971, for example, Senator Mark O. Hatfield (R., Oreg.), had his staff go over a Nixon budget which seemed to indicate that more federal spending would go for domestic needs than military needs for the first time in years. The Nixon figures had domestic monies for the fiscal year at 41 percent of all spending, defense at 36 percent.

The Hatfield staff discovered considerable distortion. Much of the so-called "human resource budget" consisted of fixed expenditures over which Congress had no immediate control: social security, railroad retirement payments, and so forth. Nixon had also thrust such items as veterans' benefits and the operations of the Selective Service System into "human resources." By the time the staff had rearranged the figures to more accurately reflect just where the national dollars were being spent, the percentages came out to military costs, 48.4 percent; costs from past wars, 16.4 percent; domestic services and programs, 17 percent; and other expenditures, 18.2 percent.[6]

Nor is the deception limited to broad categories. The Pentagon has long had a tradition of doing some fancy figuring on its various weapons systems. In the fiscal 1973 budget the Navy received $299 million for a new atomic aircraft carrier, the CVN-70. There is no mention of the eventual cost of this ship. In the fiscal 1974 budget the CVN-70 was funded for another $657 million. The Navy will need, according to military experts, at least another $16 million to finish the ship—at a total of $1 billion.

There is more, though. The carrier will have room for one hundred aircraft and is designed for the new F-14 fighter-bomber. Aircraft procurement for the ship will cost an initial $1 billion. Four times during the ship's lifetime these aircraft will have to be replaced. The CVN-70 also needs four escort ships, all nuclear-powered. That will cost another $1 billion. And the cost to operate this ship during its lifetime will come to a total of $4.3 billion. In this military version of Topsy the Congress had committed the taxpayer to an expenditure in excess of $10.3 billion for one ship.[7]

When I mentioned the figures to a moderate member of the House Armed Services Committee, the congressman seemed honestly upset. He said, "The goddamn Navy didn't tell us the thing was going to cost *that* much!"

Beyond this managerial magic there are what Louis Fisher has called "the dark corners in the budget." Fisher estimates that "upward of $10 billion to $15 billion [are] obscured in the budget because of confidential funds, secret funds or poorly justified budget presentations."[8]

In the fiscal 1973 budget, for example, there was one item labeled "Operation and Maintenance, Defense Agencies." These funds, totaling $4.3 million, are to be used for "emergencies and extraordinary expenses, to be expended on the approval or authority of the Secretary of Defense, and payment may be made on his certificate of necessity for confidential military purposes, and his determination shall be final and conclusive upon the accounting officers of the Government." All the bureaucratic mumbo jumbo boils down to: the Secretary of Defense can spend these millions without telling anyone what he spends it for.

There are countless such "contingency" funds strewn throughout the budget. The Coast Guard ($15,000), the Chief of Police of the District of Columbia ($200,000), the State Department ($2.1 million), the Atomic Energy Commission ($100,000) all have such funds. More predictable (and perhaps more defensible) monies in this area are given to the Federal Bureau of Investigation and the Bureau of Narcotics and Dangerous Drugs. The so-called "Plumbers Operations" of 1971 and 1972 were apparently funded out of a $1.5 million Special Projects fund in the White House. No one is really sure, since the administration refused to release that information.[9]

The largest invisible expenditure in the budget is for the United States intelligence community. In 1971, *Newsweek* estimated the total cost of our spying both at home and abroad at about $6 billion. Senator William Proxmire (D., Wis.), used the same figure in a 1973 debate. The senator suggested that $2.8 billion went for Air Force intelligence, $1 billion for the National Security Agency, $775 million each for Army and Navy intelligence, $750 million for the Central Intelligence Agency, and smaller amounts for other agencies. It should be pointed out that Congress has no one to blame but itself for this vast invisible expenditure. The authorizing legislation which set up the CIA in 1947 allows the agency to simply siphon off funds from other departments (normally the Pentagon) to fund its operation. This leads to a great deal of frustration among members of Congress who do not put the CIA on the same level with God, country, and motherhood. "Since we do not know what the over-all figure for the CIA is," complained Senator Alan Cranston of California, "every other figure in the defense budget is open to suspicion as to its over-all accuracy."

In addition to these restrictions on debate, there remains an even larger problem with the budget: back-door spending. The Senate Committee on Government recently noted that "in its final report of April 18, 1973, the Joint Study Committee on Budget Control identified four types of back-door spending: (1) borrowing authority under which a Federal agency is authorized to borrow money from the Treasury or from the public for certain purposes; (2) contract authority which allows agencies to incur obligations in advance of appropriations; (3) permanent appropriations which become available without any current action of Congress; and (4) mandatory entitlements in which the Federal government, again in advance of appropriations, is obligated to pay benefits established by law."[10]

To make this concept of "back-door spending" somewhat more comprehensible, some examples are in order. Veterans' benefits have long been set at a certain level by law. These are benefits which the government is obligated to pay. The program which under surplus agricultural commodities are removed is financed by an amount equal to 30 percent of all yearly tariff receipts. The Agriculture Department does not have to return to the Congress for funding each year.[11]

So often are these funding devices used that "only 44 percent of the 1974 budget will go through the regular appropriations process." The Senate Government Operations Committee goes on in its report to point out that "over the past five years, Congress has cut appropriations bills by $30 billion but added $30 billion in back-door spending. The actual impact of these back-door actions is even greater if one considers that they often impose a permanent and continuing obligation upon the federal government and that authority added through the back door often compels higher outlays in future years."[12]

The overall point is that, when the president hands his budget to the Congress, he really hands over for review only a fraction of the monies to be spent in the fiscal year. Through various means, which include allowing the executive to get away with shady figures and authorizing different types of back-door spending—Capitol Hill has given up more than half of its responsibility over the budget. When multiyear appropriations are added, an astonishing 75 percent of the budget can be described by both the Senate Government Operations Committee and OMB as expenditures which "cannot be directly controlled" by the Congress.[13]

What remains of the presidential presentation is turned over to either the House Appropriations Committee (where authorization for new programs is not needed) or to the various "substantive" committees of the House and Senate. Eventually all the appropriation requests end up in House Appropriations. Here, by tradition, the process begins.

8

The Men Who
Serve in the House

The Congress is more than just a thing, a piece of governmental machinery which can be treated in the abstract. The Congress is men and women—some good, some bad, many mediocre—who, for any number of reasons, have been elected to the House and Senate to represent their fellow citizens. The clash over the direction this country's appropriations process should take was as much a personal clash between Hamilton and Gallatin as it was between divergent ideas. "One reason that this place seems so irrational at times," a House member once said, "is because it is made up of people. And normal men and women are not always rational."

When the president turns over his budget to the Congress, he turns it over initially to the fifty-five men and women who make up the House Appropriations Committee. For no particularly good reason, other than tradition, this committee acts first on all spending bills. "The House committee," observes Professor

Richard Fenno, perhaps the leading authority on the congressional appropriations process, "is not only the first legislative body to act, but the most important one as well."[1] It is within the small hearing rooms and offices of the committee that the budget comes as close to sharp congressional scrutiny as it will anywhere in the process. The Appropriations members spend months on the various spending bills and are granted an aura of expertise by other members. The whole committee rarely challenges the reports of subcommittees. The whole House rarely challenges the reports of the committee. "Everyone here says this is a powerful committee and sometimes complains about it," comments a Democratic newcomer to Appropriations, "but no one ever challenges our preeminence. The other House members don't have the time to dig into what we're doing. Hell, I don't have time to dig in to what the other subcommittees are doing. And we keep it that way by making information generally unavailable. That's the reason we're even more powerful than Ways and Means. A member can always track down some information on taxes. He just doesn't have time to track down information on what we do. We just run the whole show."

To be part of that show is something to be coveted. The importance of other committees comes and goes with events beyond the control of Congress. Appropriations (and Ways and Means, despite the committee member's comment) maintains its importance no matter what.

It is the personalities and politics of the committee members, then, which determine to a great degree how the money is spent within the federal government. Fenno contends that the Appropriations Committee reflects the mood of the House at any given time.[2] "As a practical matter," he has written, "the House expects the Committee to do the bulk of all appropriations decision-making. What the House wants, however, is some assurance that the Committee's decision is likely to command wide-spread support in and out of the chamber."[3]

The current (1974) chairman of the committee is Texan George H. Mahon. Like his predecessors, he attained his position of power by outliving his rivals for the post. Like his predecessors, he has numerous powers at his command. He can sit as a voting ex officio member of any subcommittee. He can influence the naming of members to the committee, although this is nominally done by the Democratic members of the House Ways and Means Committee and beginning in 1975 was done by the House Democratic Caucus. He can name the chairmen of all subcommittees and the members of those sub-groups. He can even decide just how many subcommittees there will be and what areas they will cover. But, like his predecessors, he is supposed to make the Appropriations process as smooth as possible and not create unnecessary political storms.

Originally elected to the House in 1934, Mahon is now an alert seventy-three and entering his eleventh year as committee chairman. He comes out of the arid flatlands of west Texas and the rough-and-tumble politics of that region. He frankly seems too gentle to have survived that sort of infighting. Sitting amidst the splendor of his Capitol office, he looks more the southern gentleman than a man from the political frontier.

Mahon has a reputation that matches appearances. Richard Bolling has termed the Texan "an honorable conservative, a very able man."[4] Former Republican Congressman Frank Bow, until 1972 Appropriations' ranking minority member, was often critical of the chairman but not as a person. "He is one of the finest gentlemen I've ever known," says Bow.[5]

Although he is one of the powers in the House, Mahon receives little press coverage. Peg Simpson, an Associated Press reporter, admits that "really, nobody [at AP] covers him on a regional basis" and adds that "he rarely puts out news releases."[6] Fred Zimmerman of the *Wall Street Journal*, which has come to be recognized in recent years as one of the country's leading newspapers, seems almost perplexed by the lack of the coverage when he says that "we've done no major pieces on Mahon in a long time and I don't know why . . . he is very accessible."[7]

Part of it is certainly that, as Samuel Shaffer of *Newsweek* notes, "the nation seldom knows about committee chairmen even if they should."[8] Mahon, though, runs his committee in such a way that he does not fit easily into one of the roles set up by the press for politicians. He is not a hero, he is not a villain. Zimmerman makes the same point when he notes that "our coverage of Appropriations is spotty, erratic and eccentric and one reason is that Mahon is not a big wheeler-dealer . . . he doesn't see himself as a power broker like Wilbur Mills does."[9]

Mahon is simply not a Clarence Cannon running the appropriations process single-handedly. He is not one of the "petty barons" which congressional observers from Woodrow Wilson on have railed about in print.[10] He does seem open and quite even-handed. Committee member David Obey (D., Wis.), far to the left of the conservative Mahon, maintains that, while Appropriations would occasionally benefit from Mahon's being a tougher chairman, "there would have been less freedom and openness."[11]

A House liberal who often fought Cannon during the early 1960s says that Mahon "simply allows more to happen in terms of debate on issues. He does not attempt to impose his will at every turn and does not take it personally when someone opposes his position on an issue. Just take a look at the votes which took place in the full committee during his time as chairman. Now a lot of those open meetings—the SST, Boland's end-the-war amendment—would have never been allowed to take place under Cannon."

Some House members suggest that Mahon is just smarter in some ways politically than Cannon. Toward the end, they say, Cannon was forced into floor fights more and more often. "He wasn't aware that the House make-up was changing," says one congressman. Mahon, on the other hand, has allowed more debate, taken on a number of traditional liberals as members and generally shown an excellent ability to juggle around committee procedures so as to avoid major conflicts on the floor.

He has not, however, seriously disrupted the traditions of the committee. "I have a rather straightforward philosophy about federal spending," he says. "Except in time of war or deep emergency, why not restrict public spending to the revenues in hand or in sight?"[12] This philosophy has kept him in the mainstream of committee thinking for over three decades: cut as much as possible. It is an approach that is far more consistent in theory than in reality, as will be noted later.

Additionally, Mahon has done little to change the subcommittee system and, in fact, allows the subcommittee chairmen more leeway than did Cannon. Chairmen like Jamie Whitten of Agriculture and Bob Sikes of Military Construction are allowed to use their power like a club. Only once did Mahon move to hinder a subcommittee chairman. Shortly after he took the chair in 1964, he moved four pro-foreign-aid members onto Otto Passman's Foreign Operations subcommittee. He did so partly to assert his power and partly at the request of fellow Texan Lyndon Johnson, whose foreign aid programs were being tied up by Passman.

An Appropriations committee chairman, it has been observed, "is not expected to be arbitrary or vindictive to attempt to aggrandize his personal position at the expense of others. His surveillance over and participation in subcommittee work is expected to be minimal. He is expected to support subcommittee autonomy and display confidence in their decisions. He is expected, in all his actions, to be an exemplar of the Committee's style—a model for the imitation of others. He is expected, therefore, to work as hard as, if not harder than, any member of the committee. He is expected to be as well informed as, if not better informed than, any member of the Committee about the subject matter and the technicalities of the appropriations process. He is expected to work harmoniously with others and compromise in case of differences."[13]

Although this observation was made during the time of Clarence Cannon, George Mahon fits it more closely than did Cannon. He uses the power he has very seldom, allowing the other members of the committee—particularly subcommittee chairmen—to do the work as they see fit.

Within this context, where the chairman does not dominate the committee as he might, it is more important to take note of the kind of member chosen to sit on Appropriations. One general point can be made. Under Clarence Cannon, the committee was quite unbalanced. Southern conservative Democrats dominated Appropriations while other areas and ideologies went unrepresented or underrepresented.[14]

This has not entirely changed. The southern Democrats now have a proportional share of the membership. They represent 31 percent of all Democrats in the House and have 32 percent of the seats on Appropriations. Eastern Democrats are still somewhat underrepresented, with 24 percent of the total Democratic membership and only 15 percent of the committee's seats. Border state and Midwest Democrats are overrepresented slightly while those of the Far West are slightly underrepresented.[15]

Southern Democrats continue to hold the ranking spots among their party's Appropriations leadership. Of the top ten members in terms of service, half are southerners and another comes from a southern border state, Kentucky. The thirteen subcommittees are chaired by six southerners, two border-staters, three easterners and two westerners. Not a single Democrat from the Midwest chairs a subcommittee.

This is still a far cry, however, from the Cannon era, when the southerners had a wildly disproportionate share of the seats, so dominating the committee that of all the years of service Democrats put into Appropriations between 1947 and 1964 the southerners had over 41 percent.[16] And there seems to have been a decided shift in terms of regional representation under Mahon. Of the twelve most recent committee members named under Mahon, only three have been southerners.[17]

The Republicans tend to overrepresent in a different direction. Forty-one percent of all their seats are held by Midwesterners. This group makes up 34 percent of all House Republicans. The East is slightly underrepresented (25 percent versus 27 percent) as is the South (14 percent versus 18 percent). The border states, which elect few Republicans, have no GOP seats. Western

Republicans are the only single group which has Appropriations representation exactly equal to its representation on the floor: 18 percent.

This is basically the same pattern followed in the Cannon years when midwestern Republicans put in nearly half the total years of service the GOP put into Appropriations between 1947 and 1964.[18] The major differences are an increase in southern seats and a decrease in eastern seats. This reflects changes in the GOP electoral strength in those areas fairly accurately.

While the regional membership does seem to more accurately reflect the makeup of the House than in the past, there remains the question of whether the attitudes of the men and women named to Appropriations have substantively changed.

Jamie Whitten (D., Miss.), is perhaps the best known of all the committee members. During the 1960s, he used his Agriculture Subcommittee to block numerous pieces of legislation aimed at relieving the suffering of the poor. It was once written of him that he has "anesthetized his soul to human misery and indignity."[19]

Whitten's own district was one of those that could have used such programs as food stamps, breakfast programs and other projects aimed at curbing malnutrition. In 1962 Whitten blocked a program which would have trained rural poor to drive tractors. He has consistently used his power to block a minimum wage for farm workers. In 1967 he eliminated the funding sought for a breakfast program. His explanation on the latter was that if the federal government "started doing everything for citizens, you may end up with a certain class of people doing nothing to help themselves."[20]

Whitten maintains that many of these cuts are also aimed at carrying out a mandate given all Appropriations members by the House: to cut the budget as much as possible. The cuts Whitten makes or supports are frequently of a nature that suggests he does so on substantive rather than economic grounds. He has consistently supported agricultural subsidies, a program which forks over 63 percent of its funds to the richest 7 percent of the farms in the country while the poorest 50 percent get only 9.1 percent.[21] Whitten also gives major consideration to the Agricultural Conservation Program. This program subsidizes the fertilizer industry to the tune of $225 million in fiscal year 1973.[22] Every president since Eisenhower has attempted to eliminate the ACP; each one has failed.

Beyond the jurisdiction of his committee, Whitten's fiscal stance is not much of a challenge to the most wasteful of all government agencies, the Pentagon. He has voted against every major cut in defense spending in recent years including ABM, the B-1 bomber, and the F-14 fighter. He has, however, voted to eliminate Model Cities (1967), rat control (1967), legal services and child care for the poor (1971) and unemployment compensation for farm workers (1970). Whitten voted to subsidize the SST (1971) and the Lockheed Aircraft Corporation (1971), two expenditures which would cost the American taxpayer a total of $308.5 million.

It is difficult, however, to fault Whitten in some areas. He works hard, putting in sixteen hours a day during the hearings on his appropriations area. Dr. Spencer Smith, a Capitol Hill lobbyist for the Citizens Committee on Natural Resources, says that Whitten's subcommittee hearings are "damn well-conducted" and that the group's reports are "well-documented and pretty impressive."[23] Harrison Wellford, formerly a consultant to the Washington-based Center for Study of Responsive Law and a long-time Whitten watcher, considers Whitten "very able. He's a very hard worker. He's always been briefed. He believes that what he's doing is right."[24]

Massachusetts Democrat Ed Boland is a man who has carved out a different career for himself. Boland is a New Deal liberal out of the classic mold. Not well known outside of his home state, he is a quiet, hard-working representative who rarely gets press coverage even in the state's largest newspaper, the Boston *Globe*.

Boland is very much part of a Democratic machine which has dominated the state's politics since before the Depression. He is close to the Kennedy family, having headed JFK's 1960 presidential campaign in Ohio and having nominated Ted Kennedy for the United States Senate in 1962. Boland's best friend and long-time roommate in Washington is House Majority Leader Thomas P. "Tip" O'Neill of Massachusetts. It is an indication of Boland's standing within the party hierarchy that it was almost he, rather than O'Neill, who received the blessing of House Speaker Carl Albert for the majority leader slot.

The Massachusetts Democrat went onto Appropriations shortly after entering the Congress. He was put on to fill a slot normally held by a New Englander but only with considerable assistance from the then Majority Leader John McCormack, another Massachusetts representative. In the mid-1960s, he moved up to chairmanship of the HUD, Space and Science Subcommittee which covers the FCC, NASA, the SEC, and the Veterans Administration among other agencies.

Boland is very careful to balance his liberal district's interests with the desires of the men and women he works with on Appropriations and in the House leadership. He has consistently refused to join in efforts to do away with the seniority system, noting that "the system works, the problem rests with the persons involved."[25] He says he defers to other subcommittee chairmen on their bills, rarely moving for an amendment. When Appropriations decided on whether to open up their committee and subcommittee sessions to the public, Boland was in the majority that voted down such a move.

On the floor his votes also tend to be balanced. Boland has consistently voted against the Vietnam War since 1968—often taking an active role in those efforts—but has voted against major cuts in the defense budget including deletion of the B-1 bomber and the F-14 fighter. He voted against the loan to Lockheed but voted for the SST.

Ed Boland is generally viewed by other House members as a "friendly," hard-working, knowledgeable representative. Members of his subcommittee say he is very fair in such areas as allocating time for questions. Other Appropriations members consider him

astute in his subcommittee's areas and tend to follow his judgments. A southerner who admitted he actively disliked many
northern liberals termed Boland "one of the best we got. He just
works and works and never makes too much of a mess."

Frank Evans has Barry Goldwater to thank for being in the
Congress at all. First elected during the Johnson landslide of
1964, Evans knocked off an incumbent representative in a Republican district. He has had to tread carefully ever since although
his margins have increased with each passing election.

A congressman from any district where his party is outnumbered has to be somewhat unique. Evans manages by keeping on
top of his district's problems and by working hard within the
House structure. While profiling the congressman for the Congress Project, Karen Winkler found him "friendly, relaxed and
conscientious. . . . Having gained the support of a variety of
interest groups," she observed, "he is constantly weighing priorities, attempting to strike a balance. Neither flamboyant nor
consistently outspoken, he is not the sort of politician who stirs
up controversy or rocks his own party's boat."[26]

It is this ability to keep up with all the pressures a representative must face while not alienating anyone that helped Evans
attain a seat on the Appropriations Committee. Like Boland he
sought a seat that had traditionally been held by a representative
from his area. Like Boland he had the support of party leaders.
Unlike Boland, it is said that he sought it to help in his reelection
campaign.

Evans has not been particularly outspoken on that committee.
Part of the reason may be that he devotes much of his time to
Jamie Whitten's subcommittee on agriculture. Until 1975 that
group oversaw consumer agencies as well, and Evans was usually
the lonely voice of the consumer on the committee. "He never
really challenges the chairman, though," says an Appropriations
staff member. "Maybe it's because it's a losing cause. I think that
it's just that he knows things don't get done that way."

On the floor, Evans' votes have become more traditionally
liberal with each passing year. He has consistently voted against

the Indochina war and increased defense spending and supported domestic programs for the poor. Within the committee, he has voted against some other subcommittee reports and supported the move to open Appropriations sessions to the public.

Elford Cederberg of Michigan is another Appropriations member who is hardly a household word. Yet the Republican holds a unique and powerful position on the committee. He is now the ranking minority member, which gives him great input on what GOP members join the committee and the power to decide on what subcommittees they will sit. By tradition, he—as well as the chairman—can sit as voting ex officio member of all subcommittees.

Cederberg's basic belief is that "it is essential that Congress cooperate in holding the line in spending"; he terms the entire Kennedy-Johnson domestic program as "fiscal irresponsibility."[27] He views his committee's role as being one of cutting each potential expenditure as much as possible.

Like Whitten, Cederberg tends to vote for cuts in some limited areas. His record on defense spending is solid pro-Pentagon. In defending the ABM system, Cederberg stated that "I have heard testimony from the head of the Central Intelligence Agency, the Secretary of Defense, and others. I have concluded, in light of the information available to me regarding activities in the missile field by potential enemies, that I must, in the interest of our country, support President Nixon's ABM program."[28] He did not think it was in the interest of the country to control rats, maintain the Office of Economic Opportunity, or increase federal support of higher education.

Yet even the liberals like Cederberg. Don Riegle, the liberal Democrat from Michigan, has written that "although our voting records differ sharply, I like Cedie, respect his straightforward manner, and we are cordial to each other."[29] Another liberal observes that "it's hard to dislike a guy who works as hard as he does and who actually believes he's doing something right."

Another House Republican who sits on Appropriations, Silvio Conte of Massachusetts, manages to get along with others in his party despite votes that often send them up a wall. Conte is aligned with the liberal wing of the GOP in the House and has frequently gone against the leadership's line on key issues.

Conte came to Appropriations through a fluke. In 1958, the aging Republican leader Joe Martin of Massachusetts lost to Indiana's Charlie Halleck in a particularly bitter struggle for the minority leader's post. Halleck had his own choice for Appropriations but Martin decided to put up Conte. The ousted leader still had enough votes to surprise Halleck and Appropriations' ranking minority member, John Taber, and thrust Conte into the slot. So unexpected was his triumph that Chairman Clarence Cannon came over to inquire whether he was a liberal or a conservative. The Massachusetts congressman replied, "An American." Conte himself says he "got away with it"[30] but he was kept off his first choice for subcommittee—Health, Education and Welfare—until 1971 by Taber and his successors, Ben Jensen and Frank Bow.

Conte regularly infuriates his party leadership by voting against some defense projects and for domestic programs. He has dueled with Jamie Whitten for years over farm subsidies, building up his minority each year. In the past few years, Whitten has become concerned enough to trade his help in the passage of such programs as food stamps for liberal votes against Conte. In 1972 it was two liberals, James Scheuer of New York and Andrew Jacobs of Indiana, who caused Conte to lose in a 191-191 tie. One voted no and one voted present, both waiting until after the first call of the roll. Conte's comments on these liberals, and others, are unprintable.

Conte still, however, manages to keep the respect of most members. He is very likable for one thing. And he works hard and well on his duties. Most members would agree with reporter Sal Micciche of the *Boston Globe*, who observes that "he does his work. When he gets up to condemn or extol, people know he's looked into the statistical or historical background."[31]

It would seem that these five representatives have relatively little in common as a group. Whitten and Conte are sworn enemies on a major issue. Conte and Evans tend to vote a liberal line. Boland is middle-of-the-road. Whitten and Cederberg are what, under congressional definitions, can be termed conservative. Yet, like any political system, there must be some pattern to their appointments to Appropriations.

One point is rather obvious. These men all work hard. None is looking to go on to bigger and better things such as the Senate. Conte, for one, has turned down his party's nomination for higher office at least once. They are happy in the House and put time and effort into its processes.

This seems to weigh heavily when it comes to choosing members. "We want to know whether he has the ability and whether he will work and attend the meetings," says a member of the House Ways and Means Committee whose Democratic members choose committee members. "There's a lot of detail work. . . . It's a laborious job, so diligence is one thing."[32]

Additionally, all of them (and this would include Mahon as well) are frequently defined by their colleagues as "likable," "friendly," "nice guys." A Democratic party leader pointed out that, while his party can take divergent opinions on the issues in Appropriations members, they will never choose someone who is consistently at odds with his fellow party members or with the other party, or who puts his objections forward too vehemently. "Liberals like Bella Abzug would never get on Appropriations," he says, "but neither would reactionaries like Joe Waggoner. We are not so much looking for middle-of-the-roaders as we are for people who know when to keep their mouths shut and when to go along."

This same representative uses Ohio's black congressman, Louis Stokes, as an example of a liberal whose presence on Appropriations might seem unusual. "Stokes has to do part of his talking to keep his constituents happy," he notes. "We know that. He got on because he knows how to work and what the score is. He's no problem to work with."

The Republicans seem to be somewhat more concerned with party line on spending issues. "We don't want people in there who will just spend," says a party leader. "Right now the Democrats seem to liberalize the committee so we want to put people on who will balance things. If we didn't we would be run over."

This leader and others in the GOP admit, though, that they also stress the qualities of people who can go along and not make waves. Totally rock-ribbed conservatives who are outspoken in their beliefs are not chosen to fill slots on Appropriations.

Both parties also tend to look for representatives who plan to stay in the Congress for considerable periods of time. Conte, Boland, Cederberg, and Whitten all win with at least 60 percent of the vote each time they come up for election. Frequently they are unopposed. Evans is somewhat different. He was apparently put on the committee to bolster his reelection chances. This is a somewhat new drift in Appropriations selection process. Several other recent additions have been put on to help them with the voters.

Finally, both Democrats and Republicans maintain that they still look for men and women who will guard the public purse. On the face of it, this is inconsistent. Whitten and Cederberg (and Boland, to a degree) regularly go along with funding questionable military projects. Rarely do any of the five members challenge pork projects which flow out of Appropriations to the representatives' districts. Only Conte's consistent challenge to farm subsidies stands out.

"It is sort of crazy," muses a House liberal. "We want them to cut but we still want those pet projects. I guess, in that regard, we want them to create illusions: cut as much as possible without endangering our little projects. The conservatives want them to cut domestic spending and keep up national defense. The liberals want them to cut the military and build up domestic. I think it's only an indication of House sentiment still that they cut domestic and keep up the military."

A more moderate member adds that "we really do want them to keep up appearances only. The government has now reached the point where it can't run without big influxes of money."

Actual budget cutting, then, is not something of prime concern for representatives choosing the Appropriations membership. Far more important are a member's ability to work and get along with committee members and other congressmen. A somewhat academic view of the ideal Appropriations member made over thirteen years ago seems to have held up: the House leadership of both parties wants responsible legislators on the committee and "a responsible legislator is one whose ability, attitudes and relationships with his colleagues serve to enhance the prestige of the House of Representatives. He is one who has a basic and fundamental respect for the legislative process and who understands and appreciates its formal and informal rules."

The Appropriations member is the representative who can get by, by going along—at least most of the time.

9

The House Subcommittee System

At one time, all House committees could deal with their problems in full committee. As the workload got heavier, the committees had to split up into subcommittees. Now, only three committees —Rules, Internal Security, and Ways and Means—have no subcommittees.* The Foreign Affairs Committee has ten subcommittees but nearly all the major bills are really decided in the full committee.[1]

The Appropriations Committee has had a complex subcommittee structure almost since its inception. The nature has fluctuated with time, necessity and, occasionally, the whims of its chairmen, who have had the power to change the makeup as they see fit.

There are now thirteen Appropriations subcommittees (see Appendix 3). It is within these smaller groups that the real

---

* In 1975 the Ways and Means Committee formed subcommittees, and the Internal Security Committee was abolished.

work of the committee is done, and the power of the subcommittees cannot be overrated. "Occasionally, a subcommittee will become so powerful that its influence will exceed that of a full committee." In describing the impact of certain of these groups, one legislator points out that: "The reports of the Appropriations subcommittees are more important than statute law because these are the bibles of the operating agencies for the coming year." The reason for this sort of clout is the same reason Appropriations is ranked as one of the powerful committees: money.

The number of members assigned to each subcommittee varies from group to group. Most have eleven seats: seven Democrats and four Republicans. The Defense Subcommittee has twelve, however, and five other subcommittees have only eight. There seems to be no particular reason for the size of a subcommittee. The Legislative Subcommittee, which handles a relatively small segment of the budget, has eleven members while Military Construction and Public Works, which handle much of the giant federal pork barrel, both have only eight.

The size of a subcommittee is one power the chairman has over the smaller groups. Another is whether a subcommittee exists at all. A regularly used power is the chairman's right to determine what each subcommittee will handle.

In 1970, George Mahon apparently became disenchanted with the large sums other subcommittees were granting environmental programs and agencies which oversaw consumer rights. He was also unhappy when the administration succumbed to environmentalists' pressure and moved pesticide regulation programs from the Agriculture Department to the Environmental Protection Agency.

At the start of the next session, the Appropriations chairman surprised just about everyone by shifting all environmental and consumer protection programs to Jamie Whitten's Agriculture Subcommittee. Joe Browder of the Friends of the Earth environmental group exclaimed, upon hearing the news of the switch, "Oh, my God! I'm almost overcome. . . . They would have to look very hard to find anyone less sensitive to environmental problems

than Representative Whitten."[2] Other environmental and consumer groups were equally overcome, no doubt remembering
Whitten's horrendous voting record on their issues.

Mahon was unmoved. Asked to defend the move, he quietly
said that "I just decided that since the environment is becoming
so increasingly important, and so much of it has to do with
agriculture—food stamps, soil conservation, pesticides, meat
inspection—that it would be a logical move."[3] He would not hear
of moving the areas to more responsive subcommittees despite
the pleas of some of his own committee members.

The other great power the chairman has over the subcommittees is his right to name the majority members of each group.
Since he can also change the size of a committee, a chairman can
literally alter the makeup of a subcommittee overnight. In the
early 1960s, for example, Clarence Cannon kept John Fogarty's
HEW Subcommittee—the committee's most liberal—at a level of
four Democrats and three Republicans. On crucial votes, he and
ranking minority member John Taber, who shared Cannon's
conservative outlook, could exercise their ex officio voting rights
and, with the three Republicans, outvote Fogarty five-to-four.

George Mahon rarely uses that particular method, but he has
wielded his clout to shift balances on at least two subcommittees
since he took over. His classic confrontation with a subcommittee
chairman came shortly after he replaced Cannon in 1964. Otto
Passman of Louisiana had been chairman of the Foreign Operations Subcommittee since 1955. He had been placed in that
position by Cannon, who found Passman's aversion to foreign aid
to his liking. The southerner confused and annoyed at least two
presidents trying to figure out how to force them to deal more
charitably with their measures. Dwight Eisenhower once told an
aide after a Passman visit to the White House, "Remind me never
to invite that fellow down here again."[4] John Kennedy once complained to a House leader, "What am I going to do about Otto
Passman?" Kennedy did not take the leader's suggestion and
Passman is still alive and well.[5]

Lyndon Johnson had watched Passman tie up his fiscal 1964

foreign aid measure for most of 1964. Johnson, the master of Capitol Hill wheeling and dealing, decided to call in Mahon to see if something could be done about the Louisianian. The President had two cards—his tie to Mahon as a Texan and Mahon's desire to assert himself. A reporter observed at the time that "the timing of Mahon's ascension to the committee chairmanship was important; the aid bill was the last regular measure that had to be passed by the House. It was now on this issue that Mahon had to show whether he was going to be in effective control of the committee. Reluctant as he was to begin by taking on a powerful subcommittee chief, Mahon chose to stand by his fellow Texan."[6] Johnson and Mahon defeated Passman on the floor.

At the start of the next session, Mahon moved to insure that there would be no repeat of the battle. When three vacancies came up on the Democratic side of the subcommittee, Mahon filled them with Julia Butler Hansen of Washington, Jeffrey Cohelan of California, and Clarence Long of Maryland—all supporters of foreign aid. This gave the group some balance, limiting Passman's ability to single-handedly hold up a multimillion dollar program.

Two years later, Mahon moved to reshape the Labor, Health, Education and Welfare Subcommittee. The chairman changed the size of the group. He then named conservatives William Natcher of Kentucky, Neal Smith of Iowa, W. R. Hull of Michigan, and Bob Casey of Texas as new members.

Mahon handles the naming of subcommittee members somewhat differently from past chairmen. Cannon's theory on the appointment of subcommittee chairmen was that, "No member of the Committee should be obligated by his supporters to a certain appropriation. He should be able to take a judicial point of view of appropriations, a neutral view."[7] Cannon did not always adhere to this rule—Jamie Whitten of Agriculture is perhaps the outstanding example—but it was a general practice.

Mahon and his Republican counterpart, ranking minority member Cederberg, do not hold to this. For the first time in years, a majority of members of the Interior Subcommittee are from states directly affected by that department. The chairwoman is Julia Butler Hansen of Washington, a state which received the second highest total of Interior monies among all the states in 1972: $190 million. Hansen's own district received some $14 million from Interior.[8] This shift is more in line with the thinking on most committees.

It does, however, cut two ways. While representatives are more likely to put time and energy into areas of concern to their constituents, they are also more likely to dip deeply into the pork barrel when they have this opportunity. In 1960, the Military Construction Subcommittee had three of five Democratic members who had only minor defense spending in their districts and no major Pentagon installations.[9] The current membership does quite a bit better. Of the eight members, five had over the national average in 1972 defense expenditures in their districts.[10] Chairman Robert Sikes of Florida saw $540.2 million flow into his district which all manages to maintain a whopping fourteen military installations within its boundaries.[11] Republican Burt Talcott of California helped to obtain $374 million in military monies for his district, which has three defense sites.[12] Other figures for the subcommittee range from $381.4 million (K. Gunn McKay, D., Utah) to only $10.8 million (David Obey, D., Wis.).[13]

These men were named to the subcommittee although the chairman knew they would have a vested interest in maintaining high military expenditures and construction. Although Sikes has been a force in Pentagon decisions to locate many installations in his district, a number of them were there before he entered the House. Fort Ord Army Base, the biggest site in Talcott's district, was a major base before he was elected.

This particular conflict—the interest of representatives in certain areas versus pork-barreling—has been a problem for Congress since the eighteenth century. There is no clear resolution for it. On substantive matters, such as foreign affairs, it leads to black and white decisions—the pendulum between proponent and opponent swinging back and forth as the times change. On appropriation matters, there is a clear need for representatives to be on committees which deal in areas of interest to their constituents. That is a political fact of life under the current system. The idea is to be reelected and, by way of example, Colorado voters interested in Interior Department decisions will not be impressed by a sound record on the Judiciary Committee.

On the Appropriations Committee, each member sits on at least two and sometimes three subcommittees. One obvious problem is that a member has to spread himself very thin. The demands on a representative's time (and his staff's) from constituents are significant enough without having to keep up with all the activities of three subcommittees. Normally, this leads to a member choosing just one subcommittee on which to concentrate his efforts. Jamie Whitten, for example, sits on Defense and Public Works as well as Agriculture. He is rarely seen at sessions held by Defense and Public Works. David Obey sits on both Military Construction and Labor and HEW, but concentrates on the latter since it is of more interest to his constituents.[14]

This leads to the great problem of the Appropriations subcommittees: the dominance of the chairmen. When a member is forced to decide among two or three committees as to which he will concentrate on, he is forced into having to ignore the work of the other one or two. He cannot, then, walk into a subcommittee session and make a great impact on material he has not concentrated on.

The chairmen have other advantages as well. They have been on the committee the longest. They know the material inside and out or, at the very least, think they know the material inside out. They have a great deal of control over the flow of information within the committee. Although the Appropriations chairman names all committee staff members, most are attached to one subcommittee and tend to stay there for an extended period. This tends to insure that staff members are primarily responsible to the chairman. "He is always very nice to me," says a subcommittee member of the staff member attached to his group. "He'll answer my questions to a point. That point tends to be when I start to disagree with the tack the chairman is taking in the hearings. Then he clams up."

Another Appropriations aide admits that he approaches other subcommittees the same way. "Look, I've worked with my chairman a lot of years and I like the job," he says. "I know I should probably help out the other members more but the guy is my boss. Besides, most of the time I tend to agree with him so why help out the other side."

Former Appropriations member Don Riegle of Michigan summed it up with: ". . . each subcommittee has from one to three staff members [five for Defense] who work for its Democratic chairman and, while these people are non-partisan, they have little time to assist the other members of the subcommittee. On Foreign Ops [Operations], for example, we have one staff member for nine subcommittee members. Even if I could have one ninth of his time available to me directly, I couldn't scratch the surface of the budget our subcommittee is considering . . . I could use five full-time assistants on my Appropriations Committee work alone."[15]

"You get more access to the staff and their work the longer you stay around," adds a Republican member. "The chairman gets most of the time and most of the information. Then the ranking Republican—if he and the subcommittee chairman aren't feuding or something. What little time is left goes to the other Democrats. If you're a low-ranking Republican, you may never see a staff member."

The aides are generally responsible for most of the questions asked by the chairman during sessions. "The rest of us have to pore through all the material a department gives you or have a staff guy expend valuable time and energy doing it," comments a midwestern Democrat. "The chairman has the staff man put his questions together. I took a look at the list of questions once. All the bright ones were the staff's. God, without them, the chairman would sound like a perfect fool all of the time instead of part of it."

The chairman controls the flow of the meeting. Under rules adopted by the House, the chairman gets the first five minutes of questioning, then other members each get five minutes, and the chairman then gets to cross-examine. He can use up all the remaining time if he desires.[16]

Riegle recalls one run-in he had with the chairman of Foreign Operations, Otto Passman. It took place during the height of the Indochina war and the witness was Secretary of State William Rogers.

> I hurried back to the subcommittee but found our session with Secretary Rogers an empty exercise. The House has long since abandoned its responsibility to dig into policies of the executive branch. While he can be a scrooge on specific items in the budget, Otto Passman makes it clear he has little interest in pursuing "policy" questions, and today he used the "reform" rules to effectively squelch any penetrating cross-examination of the Secretary. . . . Once the five-minute periods were exhausted, Otto used all the remaining time.
>
> Rogers is . . . ring-wise on subcommittee appearances and for him a House Foreign Ops session is a piece of cake—compared, for example, to the hostile questioning of a Senate Foreign Relations Committee meeting. . . . So Rogers was relaxed and agreeable. He let Otto do most of the talking. He nodded and smiled for nearly two hours and offered us generalities that provided us less insight than this morning's Washington *Post*.[17]

When Riegle finally had an opportunity to examine Rogers, he began to push him on some past inconsistencies in American Cambodian policies. Passman first cut in and defended the Secretary of State. Riegle continued to press and Rogers began to fidget in the witness chair. Passman then interrupted to say, "The gentleman from Michigan has now consumed *seven* minutes." The antiwar member did not have another chance to question Rogers.[18]

"The way we elicit information is a disgrace," says a current member. He points out that chairmen like Passman and Bob Sikes of Military Construction tend to run roughshod over the other members. Others, like Whitten and Ed Boland of HUD, Space and Science, try to be fair. Still, he says, the questioning is never very pointed. "We are very picky. We focus in on one project, a line item here, something there. We never really try to deal with questions like, 'Should we be spending this much for that when we need this?' We never go to the heart of the matter on any of the subcommittees I have been on."

This congressman uses as an example the manner in which John Rooney runs his State, Justice, Commerce and Judiciary subcommittee. Rooney is regularly faced with long lists of payroll employees and contract employees. The aging Brooklyn Democrat, who had been asked to step down in 1974 by the machine which runs the politics of his area of New York, never questions the department witnesses as to the broad areas in which these employees will be used. Instead he goes down a list, picks off a name here and a name there and ask what they do and what their records are. "That sure is a hell of a way to learn something, isn't it?"

Rooney (and other chairmen) also like to cross-examine witnesses on small and unimportant parts of programs that somehow attract their attention. During a recent hearing on the State Department budget, Rooney launched into a dialogue with the department's witness on the removal of "security risks" from the State Department; Rooney spent considerable time running through a list and questioning whether the individuals were men, women, alcoholics, or homosexuals.

When the hearings are finally concluded, work begins on the subcommittee report. Normally, the subcommittee chairman and the chief staff member do the bulk of the writing. "I have an area that I'm pretty good in so the chairman comes to me before he writes it up," says a Democratic member. "The rest of the time I just get left out."

Another congressman says he does not even get that courtesy. "My chairman just ignores me," he complains. "I get the bill as he wants it at the markup session. [A markup session is the subcommittee hearing at which a bill is discussed and finalized before presentation to the full committee.] He just drops it in my lap.

"When I first got here, I couldn't even keep up. He would just rattle off the figures and, even if there was a project that I wanted input on, we'd be by it before I knew it. Now, at least, I can keep up but he still is mighty quick and you have to be sharp to make your points."

Former member Riegle recalls that, frequently, Passman would just ignore the other members. After Passman had breezed past part of the AID budget during one markup session, another member asked that discussion be reopened. "Otto brushed off that request. 'We've buried it,' he said, 'and put flowers on the grave. Let's not dig it up now.' "[19]

The chairman is expected to meet two goals, however. First, he is expected to keep dissent within his own ranks down to an absolute minimum. Majority members are not generally expected to challenge their own chairman. To achieve this, some chairmen go to extreme ends. Pennsylvania's Dan Flood, the dapper ex-Shakespearean actor who chairs the Labor and HEW Subcommittee, is said to run his markup sessions like an auction. If a member objects to some item, Flood will break in and say, "Now, wait a minute, can't we do something here? . . . There's no need to argue. . . . How about this hospital? We can move that into your district, it's right next door now."

It is also expected that partisanship will be minimized. A good chairman is expected to confer with the ranking minority on each bill. If there is a major disagreement, it is expected it will be ironed out before the markup session. "It's a marvel to sit back and watch my chairman and the ranking Republican do their act," says a subcommittee Democrat. "No one else gets a word in. They've gone over everything beforehand and they work hand-in-glove. If you attack a proposal, you attack both of them."

While markup sessions can be quick affairs, auctions, or love feasts between the parties, one thing does get careful attention:

the pork barrel. Obviously, all subcommittees do not govern areas that contain pork. It is hard to ring dough for the district out of budgets covered by the Legislative and Foreign Operations subcommittees. The other subcommittees handle a lot of it, though, and the very idea of pork barreling runs counter to what has traditionally been the underlying attitude of Appropriations: cut where possible.

"Look, pork exists," says a subcommittee chairman, "that is a political fact of life. What we try to do is balance things out. If a guy is facing a tough fight for reelection, we try to give him what we can to help him along. We sometimes ask a guy to postpone a project for a year if he can. We really do try to cut."

Not every chairman even tries, especially on his own projects. The Agriculture Department poured over $89.6 million into Jamie Whitten's district in 1972.[20] As previously noted, the Pentagon spent $540.2 million in Military Construction chairman Bob Sikes's Florida district in 1972. The military also seems to feel the district is an ideal spot for Army and Air Force bases. Fourteen are now located there, employing some 44,000 district residents—nearly ten percent of the district's entire population.[21]

Tennessee's Joe Evins, chairman of the Public Works and AEC Subcommittee, manages to outdo even the best in getting federal funds. In 1971 he helped get in excess of $655.5 million for his district, including some $6.2 million in public works funds which had not been included in the administration budget and an unbudgeted $4.1 million in improvements for the Atomic Energy Commission (AEC) facility at Oak Ridge, Tennessee.[22] In 1972, this figure dropped off to $401.5 million—still a tidy sum for one district.[23]

Once a subcommittee makes these decisions on pork and other matters, that is usually that. Members of the full committee rarely challenge a subcommittee report. There seem to be two reasons for this. One is a quid pro quo rationale: you scratch my back, I'll scratch yours. "A guy who gets up and challenges some part of a subcommittee bill can expect to see some of his pet projects killed," says a committee member. "You just don't doubt the wisdom or honesty of another subcommittee. It just isn't done except in extreme circumstances."

Beyond the quid pro quo, members of the full committee normally receive a subcommittee report at the same time they sit down to the committee table to discuss it. "They drop these tomes —thousands of pages—in front of you and they're off and running before you get past page one," observes a Republican member. "You can't even read the documents they give you in the time allotted. Unless you're looking for something very specific, you just might as well sit back and not even listen."

Riegle describes what a typical committee vote is like:

> The full Appropriations met . . . to consider the HUD–Veterans Hospitals–NASA bill. When I arrived, twenty minutes late, subcommittee chairman Eddie Boland, a Democrat from Massachusetts, was explaining what the bill contained . . . .
>
> Boland spoke rapidly and knowledgeably about our HUD appropriation. In the ensuing discussion, Ed Patten, a white-haired, ham-fisted, former high-school teacher from New Jersey, took the floor. Standing five feet ten and weighing at least two hundred and fifty pounds, he resembles the stereotype of an effusive, cigar-chewing U.S. congressman. Drawing on what he called "personal experience," he gave an impassioned description of the virtue of public housing programs.
>
> When he finished, Boland said, "Love that boy from Perth Amboy." Friendly laughter rippled across the room.
>
> Doc Long [Clarence Long, D., Md.] raised a question about the treatment of drug addicts in veterans' hospitals. Chairman George Mahon . . . was hunched over talking to Jamie Whitten. At the appropriate point, I sought recognition to ask about the funds that the subcommittee had considered to finance home-ownership counseling services for low-income families. Boland said the money was in the bill.
>
> Charlie Jonas from North Carolina, the ranking Republican on the subcommittee, rose to present figures showing that the various federal housing programs have created obligations forty years into the future. He pointed out that with

this bill we were further obligating the government to pay some $80 billion over the next forty years. His facts were sobering.

Boland completed his explanation of this very complicated bill. Mahon led the applause and there was general table-thumping. Then came a moment of conflict. Del Clawson, a conservative Republican from California, rose to offer an amendment that would strike out the money for home-ownership counseling services. His staff had uncovered a booklet describing an endless number of existing counseling services. Why, he asked, do we need another one?

Boland disputed Clawson but not too energetically so I sought recognition and urged the committee to keep the money in the bill. Counseling funds, I said, are vital to the success of the program, and I cited the difficulties we've had with the low-income housing program in my own district.

Mahon called for a show of hands. Clawson's amendment passed, 20-to-18. Sid Yates, a Democrat from Illinois, de-manded a record vote and the roll call began. Most Repub-licans voted the way they had informally, but now that the results were going to be on the record, some of the Demo-crats switched. On this second go-round, we defeated the amendment 22-to-19. Burt Talcott challenged the tally, but it was accurate. George Andrews [an Alabama Democrat no longer in the House] moved the bill for adoption by the committee; it passed and members got up to leave, having approved an expenditure in the next fiscal year of another $18 billion.[24]

The House generally tends to treat these subcommittee reports, as approved by the full committee, with benign neglect. Tradi-tionally, the reports are rarely challenged. "About the only time is on something like the SST," observes a northern Republican. "When the committee itself splits on an issue, then there is usually a fight. Most of the time, though, they come in here united and we just approve what they've done."

Another House member contends that the reports might be more often challenged if there was an opportunity to study the bill and the back-up material. "Appropriations is the most secretive goddamn committee in the House," he says. "They put out their reports on Thursday for action on the next Tuesday. That gets them around the three-day rule but a lot of members go home Thursday and don't come back until early Tuesday so they really don't get a chance to see the bills. It's ridiculous."

Although other members express similar discontent, no one has really moved to do much about it. "We just sit back," observed one, "and let those guys on Appropriations run the show."

10

The Senate System

To say that the House and the Senate work differently is an understatement. The two chambers are worlds apart in tone, working procedures, traditions, and attitudes. To walk from the House side of the Hill to the Senate side is to walk from a workingman's bar to the high-priced bar in another section of town.

In 1967 when the late Robert Kennedy, then a senator from New York, concluded a scathing denunciation of Senator Robert Byrd of West Virginia with "I thought I was dealing with *men*," it was considered "the fiercest personal attack within recent Senate memory." In the House, that remark would have gone almost unnoticed. One House member, the tart-tongued Wayne Hays of Ohio, often makes worse comments about his colleagues, although he later strikes many from the record.

The differences between the chambers extend far beyond floor commentary and general demeanor. A senator must be responsive to an entire state which takes in rural, suburban, and urban areas. Most congressmen represent districts which do not have this kind of mix. All states have an array of businesses for which tax and trade decisions are of great importance—oil, liquor, tobacco, sugar, textiles, minerals, chemicals, and insurance are among them. Although no one would describe the exchange between the decisions that are helpful to these special interests and forthcoming campaign contributions as a direct ratio, enough has been written about it to make the inference clear.

A senator simply faces a greater array of special interests than the House member. A representative may have one or two major interest groups with which he or she will have to deal regularly to insure reelection. A senator must face large state-wide organizations in a variety of areas. Taking the 1972 elections as an example, it can be honestly said that House members face far less trouble getting reelected. Only 12 percent of the House were newcomers in 1972. More than half came to Capitol Hill because the incumbents had died, retired, or resigned to run for other political offices. Of the 330 incumbents who did seek reelection, only ten—3 percent—were defeated.[1]

In that same year, thirty-three senators were up for reelection.[2] Five Senate seats had been vacated by retiring incumbents. Of the remaining twenty-eight, eight were taken by challengers to the incumbent, a turnover of around 29 percent. Seven incumbents were, additionally, involved in close races which resulted in the seven (Lee Metcalf of Montana, Bob Griffin of Michigan, John McClellan of Arkansas, Carl Curtis of Nebraska, Mark Hatfield of Oregon, Claiborne Pell of Rhode Island, and John Tower of Texas) receiving less than 55 percent of the votes cast.

Under ordinary circumstances, it costs a great deal to run for the United States Senate. Senator Edward Brooke of Massachusetts raised close to one million dollars in campaign monies for his 1972 reelection bid despite the fact that he was facing a "political nobody." Tower of Texas, faced with major competition in the general election, spent in the millions. It was not until recently that House races began to break the $100,000 mark in spending by an individual candidate. Most lower chamber contests still are relatively cheap affairs—at least in comparison to the Senate contests.[3]

No matter how you view these spiraling costs of elections, there is one basic point: senators must appeal to a far wider variety of special interests and voters than House members.

Recognition of this fact by senators tends to make them feel somewhat superior to House members. The upper chamber sees decisions and decision-making in the House as a parochial affair. "All those other guys care about is their little dinky districts," complained one senator to me during a debate on busing. "I have to worry about a whole state. They can usually look around and see how their little bunch of voters wants them to vote. I have to balance ten different views of the same situation from ten different sets of voters who will try to retire me if I don't vote their way. The House has it easy."

A representative from that senator's own state sees it differently. "The Senate has it easy," he said. "We work down here while they play statesman. They have more staff and their staff doesn't have to spend half the time on constituent problems we do. Their committees are a farce. We do all the work and they get all the TV and print coverage. I'm lucky if I get to go back to my district once every two weeks. He [the senator] is back there all the time. There are times I really resent the other side."

The representative's point about committees reflects a major difference between the two chambers. A House member's best bet for influence within his own chamber is to work hard on his committee and hope that the voters will keep him in long enough so that he can rise to chairmanship of his group or, at least, a key subcommittee. On the floor itself, he is simply one of 435 votes—his vote is not important in itself, but his committee position can be.

A senator, on the other hand, is one of only one hundred votes. In an era when the long-dominant conservative coalition of southern Democrats and Republicans is closely checked by a liberal coalition, a single vote can be crucial. Power is right there on the floor. Further, each senator normally sits on two full committees. A House member will sit on only one. A senator simply cannot pay the same attention to a single committee that the House member can. "Senate committees are important as arenas in which decisions are made," notes one observer, "but they are not especially important as sources of individual member influence—not when compared to House committees."

This whole attitude toward committees has a major impact on the appropriations process. By tradition, the House committee handles all bills first. Senate Appropriations simply sits and waits for the House to act on the measures. The House committee honestly does put a great deal more work into each of their bills. Senate Appropriations works from the House documents and projections.

Further—given the nature of their political existence—the members of the Senate Appropriations Committee are more likely to experience pressure to rescue projects cut or reduced by the House. Senators are more likely to take a broad view of any given appropriation.

Two generalities about the Senate position in the appropriations process have evolved from these differences in approach. One has become the foundation of a House joke: the Senate is called the Upper Chamber because it "ups" everything the House sends over there. The other is a view of the Senate Appropriations Committee as a sort of appeals court where cuts by the House can be appealed by the Executive and special interest groups.

The Senate Appropriations Committee currently has twenty-six members: fifteen Democrats and eleven Republicans. While this is the official number of members, the actual number is much larger. Senate rules allow three members of substantive committees involved to serve ex officio on Appropriations when their area is being discussed. (The rules also stipulate that one of the three be assigned to the conference with the House on the bill.) By the time all the outsiders have become involved, nearly one half of the Senate will sit on Appropriations at one time or another during a session.[4]

A quick glance at some of the members of the committee is instructive. The chairman is John McClellan, the thirty-two-year veteran from Arkansas. McClellan has held the post for only a few years. In the summer of 1972 he succeeded the late Allen Ellender of Mississippi, who had succeeded the long-time chairman, Carl Hayden of Arizona, just a few years before that.

Despite the fact that he is seventy-eight years old, McClellan leads a Senate existence that is almost hard to believe. In addition to chairing Appropriations, he is the second ranking majority member on both the Government Operations and Judiciary committees. He chairs two of the latter's subcommittees: Criminal Laws and Procedures and Patents, Trademarks and Copyrights. In all, he serves on fourteen of these two committees' sub-groups as well as putting in time on joint study committees on Budget Control and Federal Expenditures.[5]

Within Appropriations, McClellan chairs the subcommittees on Defense and Intelligence Operations (actually a subcommittee of the Defense Sub) and sits on Foreign Operations, Interior, Public Works, and State, Justice, Commerce, the Judiciary, and Related Agencies.[6] The size of this workload seems to bear out the most commonly expressed opinion of McClellan: hard-working and tough.

McClellan made his reputation outside the Senate through his toughness. In 1954, Senator Joe McCarthy began what would become known as the Army-McCarthy hearings. McClellan was a member of the Government Operations Subcommittee holding the sessions. While avoiding an outright confrontation with McCarthy, the Arkansas Democrat managed to score heavy points by his challenges to both the Wisconsin Republican and the Army. At one point in the hearings, McCarthy's aide, Roy Cohn, was testifying about a piece of paper allegedly written by a former Communist which had supposedly led McCarthy into his probe of the Army:

> "Point of Order," McClellan suddenly growled. "I want to know if it is a complete document." Cohn, stunned, looked toward McCarthy and blurted, "Pardon me?"

"I'm asking you, not Senator McCarthy," said Senator McClellan. Cohn vaguely replied, "The document was submitted to the staff, sir, and I submitted it to the chairman." McCarthy and Cohn now took a twenty-minute recess to work out their answer. But when they returned McClellan had another, more broad and more important question: "You keep talking about Communists that you want to investigate, and I haven't been able to get the name of one of them yet."[7]

McClellan went on to conduct his own series of investigations as chairman of that same subcommittee, further solidifying his reputation as a hard-nosed investigator. While he has slipped in recent years—often allowing his interrogations to go off on tangents—he can still focus in on a witness as sharply and persistently as any questioner in Congress.

The Appropriations chairman can also still wheel and deal. In 1972, McClellan managed to thwart the will of most of the Senate and kill off the most important piece of consumer legislation to come before that session: establishment of an independent Consumer Protection Agency which would serve as the purchasers' advocate before the various regulatory agencies. The bill was sponsored by a bipartisan group led by Abraham Ribicoff (D., Conn.), Charles Percy (R., Ill.), and Jacob Javits (R., N.Y.).

McClellan began his maneuvers to scuttle the bill by persuading Ribicoff, chairman of the Government Operations Subcommittee on Executive Reorganization, to postpone his group's action on the bill until after the Arkansas primary. (McClellan was facing a tough challenge from Representative David Pryor.) Ribicoff did not want to offend the chairman and postponed action until after the primary, and again when a June run-off was required to decide the McClellan-Pryor race.

As soon as the incumbent won his run-off, Ribicoff reported the CPA measure to the full committee. McClellan not only began to delay full committee consideration of the bill but used the Government Operations staff director, James Calloway, to coordinate an opposition which included the White House and major business interests. The chief McClellan tactic was to have bill opponents not attend committee sessions when the measure was under discussion. The chairman would then insist that a quorum had to be present before action could be taken—something he had done only rarely in the past on other bills. When supporters could rally a quorum, opponents would hustle from their hiding places to offer an endless stream of weakening amendments.

The tactics resulted in the CPA bill being tied up until late September—over three months. When a floor vote finally loomed, McClellan and other opponents began a filibuster against the measure. Twice, supporters moved for cloture (which would have shut off the filibuster) and twice they failed to get the necessary two-thirds vote—out-fought by McClellan. The measure died.[8]

On most issues, the Appropriations chairman votes a very conservative line. "I've always been called a conservative and I've never resented it," he has said. "I did not become a senator to transfer the United States into a socialistic, paternalistic state."[9] He is very much part of the Senate's inner circle—an exclusive club within the exclusive club—although it has been noted that "in a body where cordiality and the easy joke ingratiate one to the other, McClellan is dour . . . brusque. Respected, at times feared, usually little known by his colleagues, he slaps no backs, indulges in no more than handshakes, keeps his own counsel and goes his own way."[10]

If McClellan is a bit brusque for a senator, he at least looks the role. Another Appropriations Democrat, Warren Magnuson of Washington, looks like a leftover from New York's Boss Tweed mob. Magnuson moves through the Senate in a wardrobe that other members insist he mugged a wino to obtain. A thick black cigar is usually thrusting out of his mouth. His body resembles a sack of potatoes. Watching Magnuson work a floor vote is not at all unlike watching Richard Daley work a Chicago City Council meeting: a smile, a slap on the back, a joke.

And, like Daley, Magnuson wins. This strangely anachronistic man is one of the Senate's most powerful members, perhaps the most powerful. "If a Senate poll were taken to pick that clubby group's half-dozen most popular, most influential and most anonymous members," one reporter has suggested, "chances are that on all three lists would appear one name: Maggie."[11] Others have put it more bluntly: "What Maggie Wants, Maggie Gets."[12]

Magnuson is only seventy, yet he has been on Capitol Hill longer than all but two senators and four representatives.[13] He was first elected to the House in 1937 and moved up to the Senate in 1944. Through his long service he has accumulated a considerable amount of seniority. He is chairman of the Commerce Committee and sits on the Aviation Subcommittee which has so much to do with the well-being of Washington's biggest industry: Boeing. Additionally, he is second-ranking majority member on the Aeronautical and Space Sciences (another plus for Boeing) and the Select Committee on Equal Educational Opportunity.

On Appropriations, he ranks second to McClellan. The Washington Democrat chairs the committee's sub-group on Labor and HEW as well as sitting on three other subcommittees: Defense; Public Works and AEC; and State, Justice, Commerce, the Judiciary and Related Agencies.

By all accounts, Magnuson is one of the most likable men in the Senate. The senator was a hit in Washington social circles from his arrival on Capitol Hill and his drinking bouts and zest for women often made for delicious rumor. Magnuson played poker at the White House with Franklin Roosevelt while most young New Deal politicians just yearned to be seen with the President. "Whenever the President would lose, he paid us in checks. He'd knew we'd never cash them," Magnuson recalls.[14]

Through the years, the senator would also go fishing with Harry Truman, hold regular drunks with House Speaker Sam Rayburn and swim with John Kennedy. He maintained a strong friendship with Lyndon Johnson. It is quite a unique rise in Senate history. Most men, as they accumulate power, manage to alienate at least some people. Magnuson has managed to avoid that. "He doesn't have any enemy on either side of the aisle," claims Majority Leader Mike Mansfield of Montana, and that does seem to be the case.

Yet Magnuson manages to get things done. His Commerce Committee has churned out much of the truly substantial consumer legislation in recent years, such as Federal Trade Commission warranty legislation and hazardous materials regulations. One indicator of both the tone of his legislation and his success may be that Magnuson was the most vetoed senator during the Nixon years.

Despite occasional lapses—such as the SST and his sponsorship of a bill which would have overturned four Supreme Court antitrust decisions against the El Paso Natural Gas Company—Magnuson has built up an enviable record of progressive legislation while gradually increasing his personal clout within the upper chamber. John Kennedy once said of the senator that

> most members of the Senate, as you can already judge, have developed the art of speaking with precision and clarity and force. The secret of Senator Magnuson's meteoric Senate career has been the reverse . . . he speaks in the Senate so quietly that few can hear him. He looks down at his desk. He comes into the Senate late in the afternoon. He is very hesitant about interrupting other members of the Senate. When he rises to speak most members of the Senate have left. He sends his messages up to the Senate; everyone says, "What is it?" and Senator Magnuson says, "Well, it's nothing important," and the Grand Coulee Dam is built.[15]

No one tells those kinds of stories about Republican Milton Young of North Dakota. No one tells any stories about Milton Young of North Dakota. He could conceivably be the most colorless man in the United States Senate. Yet Young has accumulated enough seniority and worked hard enough to have gained considerable power within the upper chamber.

As befits a senator from a predominantly rural state, Young gives much of his attention to the Agriculture and Forestry Committee where he sits on the Agricultural Research and General Legislation, and Agricultural Marketing and Stabilization of

Prices subcommittees. He is ranking minority member on the latter.

On Appropriations, Young is the ranking minority member. He sits on the Defense and Intelligence Operations subcommittees as the Republican leader as well as holding seats on the subcommittees of Agriculture, Environment and Consumer Protection, Interior, and Public Works.

Young is a very basic conservative. He has voted to cut many domestic programs but not in a totally reactionary manner. Other senators say he weighs decisions and can be persuaded to vote for some measures, particularly self-help programs. He rarely votes against military expenditures but has voted, for example, to reduce American troops in Europe.

The senator seems to pay careful attention to his Appropriations work. When the Senate passed a rule limiting minority party members to holding only one spot as a ranking member, Young chose to stay on Appropriations rather than Agriculture. He chose the former "because it is a much more powerful and important committee."[16] When asked what he felt would be the most important reforms the Senate could make in its processes, Young suggested a rule that "no member serving on the Appropriations Committee could serve on any other standing committee," as well as some rules to increase committee attendance.[17]

The Senate Appropriations Committee is made up of men like McClellan, Magnuson, and Young. The membership has been made up, traditionally, of the chamber's inner circle. The three mentioned previously are examples. Montana's Mike Mansfield, the majority leader, has a seat on the committee, as does majority whip Robert Byrd of West Virginia. Four committee chairmen hold seats: Magnuson (Commerce), Mississippi's John Stennis (Armed Services), Thomas Eagleton (District of Columbia), and Gale McGee (Post Office and Civil Service). Of the other Democratic members, only William Proxmire of Wisconsin and Birch Bayh of Indiana can be said to be outside the "establishment." And Proxmire was kept off the committee for years.

The Republican side shows much the same tendency. While

no floor leaders are on the committee, Young was the ranking member of Agriculture while Roman Hruska of Nebraska, Norris Cotton of New Hampshire, Hiram Fong of Hawaii, and Charles Mathias of Maryland all hold ranking positions on key committees.

With this sort of politically high-priced talent around, the chairman is not nearly as important as in the House. "There's no way you can compare Mahon and McClellan," says a senator who has served in both chambers. "If Mahon wants to do something, he just does it. If McClellan tried he would have to face Magnuson and Mansfield and Byrd and those other guys that are just as powerful as he is."

Subcommittee chairmen are not nearly as powerful either, at least not in the same way the House subcommittee chairmen are. In the House, the power of the subcommittee chairmen conflicts with that of those who chair substantive committees. George Mahon and Armed Services Chairman F. Edward Hébert of Louisiana, for example, both have a great deal of power over the military and the Pentagon must pay heed to both. In the Senate, McClellan chairs the Appropriations Subcommittee on Defense but the Armed Services chairman, John Stennis, is also on the subcommittee. Magnuson chairs the Commerce Committee and sits on the Appropriations subcommittee in that area. Alan Bible of Nevada chairs the Appropriations Subcommittee on the Interior and also sits on the Interior Committee.

There is a substantial overlap between Appropriations and other committees in the Senate. This is far different from the House where the Appropriations group is isolated from the rest of the committees. The result is what might be expected. "We decide what projects ought to be funded on one committee and then turn around and make sure they are funded on the other," says one Appropriations member. "You have to remember that even if there was not so much overlap that this would happen. So many senators are involved and so many have their pet projects and pet agencies that we would increase appropriations anyway. There is a certain code in the Senate that you don't mess with other people's projects. Look what happened to Bill Proxmire when he tried it." (Proxmire, when he first entered the Senate, happened to cut out some pet projects. Appropriations cut out projects earmarked for Wisconsin instead.)

The House assessment that the Senate consistently ups their allocations seems accurate. One recent survey showed the average increase by the Senate over the House allocation was nearly 10 percent during the years 1968 to 1972. Fenno found that, during another period, the Senate Appropriations added funds to the executive's budget estimates 18.9 percent of the time and met the estimates 18.4 percent. During the same period, the House committee added only 7 percent of the time and met the estimates 15.8 percent.[18] Perhaps more importantly, the Senate committee added monies to the House figures over half the time (56.2) while decreasing less than 10 percent.[19]

Nor do the same restrictions which seem to apply to challenges to the Appropriations Committee on the House floor seem to apply here. One estimate is that three times as many amendments are offered to the Senate Appropriations bill as there are to the House bill and that this tendency is increasing, partly as a result of disenchantment among the senators with the military and its spending.[20] A review of one period showed that the Senate amended the Appropriations bills over 11 percent of the time, generally increases. The House bills were changed about 6 percent of the time, generally decreases.[21]

Overall, it can be said that the Senate Appropriations Committee plays a lesser role in the appropriations process than does the House but the whole Senate plays a greater role than the whole House. The Senate provides some balance in giving the congressional portion of this process more of an interview since the senators must take into account the requirements and demands of a far greater segment of the population. The Senate committee and the Senate as a whole does tend to act as an appeals court for the executive agencies whose budgets have been cut in the House, as will be noted more fully later.

Finally there does seem to be an even more crucial change in the relative positions of the House and the Senate. The House has long had a tendency to cut domestic programs and spare the military. For some time, the Senate has defended domestic spending but has not challenged the House decisions on the Pentagon. In recent years the Senate has seemed more willing to challenge expensive defense projects, particularly on the floor. This could prove to be a key change in the appropriations process.

11

The Conference
Committee

One of the most controversial of all congressional procedures is the conference committee. Rarely do the Senate and House agree on a bill. If the Senate amends a bill initiated in the House and the lower chamber refuses to concur in those amendments, the measure goes to the conference committee where differences will, presumably, be ironed out.

More than a few representatives, senators and outside observers see the conference committee more as a third branch of Congress than as an offshoot of the two chambers. The late Senator George Norris (R., Nebr.) once raked the whole concept by saying,

> The members of this "house" are not elected by the people. The people have no voice as to who these members shall be. . . . This Conference Committee is many times, in very important matters of legislation, the most important branch of our legislature. There is no record kept of the workings of the Conference Committee. Its work is performed, in the

main, in secret. No constituent has any definitive knowledge as to how members of this Conference Committee vote, and there is no record to prove the attitude of any member of the Conference Committee. . . . As a practical proposition, we have legislation, then, not by the voice of the members of the Senate, not by the members of the House of Representatives, but we have legislation by the voice of five or six men. And for practical purposes, in most cases, it is impossible to defeat the legislation proposed by this Conference Committee. Every experienced legislator knows that it is the hardest thing in the world to defeat a conference report.[1]

Despite decades of controversy and despite at least one major attempt to reform its procedures in 1946 and another in 1970,[2] the conference committee remains one of Capitol Hill's most undemocratic institutions. The key reason is the manner in which conferees are chosen. Nominally, the list is drawn up by the vice-president in the Senate and by the speaker in the House. The names are then approved by the full chambers.

What actually happens is that the presiding officers simply accept the names submitted to them by the chairman of the committee involved and the whole House and Senate unquestioningly support the choices. In the House, the chairman usually picks three or four senior majority members—including himself, if he likes—from his committee and two or three members from the minority, normally including the ranking member. The Senate chairman does the same but—in the case of an appropriations bill—must include at least one member of the substantive committee involved. The Appropriations chairman must, for example, include a member of the Armed Services Committee when his committee confers on the Pentagon budget.

This gives the chairman incredible power over the stance his group will take vis-à-vis the position of the other chamber. Senate Appropriations chairman John McClellan chairs the Defense Subcommittee. When the Pentagon budget is sent to conference committee, he normally picks a group that includes himself, Armed Services chairman John Stennis, who sits on the Defense

Subcommittee of Appropriations, another Armed Services Committee member—Henry Jackson of Washington, say—and another Defense Subcommittee member such as Gale McGee of Wyoming as majority members. As minority members, he would pick ranking subcommittee member Roman Hruska of Nebraska and, perhaps, Norris Cotton of New Hampshire, another subcommittee member. In recent years, the Senate has frequently attached such antiwar amendments as the Mansfield amendment and others to this bill or substantially cut the appropriations for weapon systems. McClellan can pick a group, however, that is made up of men who voted against the amendments and the cuts. The fate of these determinations by the full Senate in conference committee is predictable.

One of the more recent and outrageous examples of this sort of conference committee loading took place in 1970. At issue was the funding of a supersonic transport plane, the SST. The House had approved $290 million in federal monies to aid private companies in developing the aircraft. Under heavy pressure from environmentalists, the Senate, by a narrow margin, deleted the money from their version of the bill.

The Appropriations subcommittee chairman involved was Warren Magnuson. Magnuson, as has been noted, has an enviable record in many legislative areas but the Washington senator represents a state dominated by the Boeing Aircraft Company. He had not only voted for the SST money but had led the floor fight for it. Magnuson ended up heading the Senate conferees. In fact, four of the seven Senate conferees were members who had voted *for* the funding.

The conference committee, as might be expected, recommended that the SST be funded for $210 million. The House, which had voted for it, thought this was a nice compromise. A majority of the Senate, however, was outraged. One journalist has observed that "Magnuson insisted on the floor that he had fought like a tiger for the Senate position, but, with no record to sustain him, the SST opponents were understandably skeptical." Perhaps because the whole affair was just a little too blatant the Senate ignored a time-honored tradition and refused to concur in the conference report. The SST vote was held over to the next session as a result of this impasse and, the next year, the plane was voted down by a majority of both houses. "But, in the interim," an observer has noted, "the conference system had come perilously close to enacting a program that half of the Congress had flatly refused to authorize."

One point is clear. Since the committee chairmen have control over the makeup of the conference group, they can overturn a decision of their chamber or sustain a position their house has not taken. Conference committees have even managed to include legislation which did not appear in either house's version of the bill. In 1970, for example, a conference group wrote a clause in a federal salary bill giving the president certain powers over government employee pay hikes. Not only did the clause not appear in either the House or Senate version but it had never even come up during the committee hearings on the measure.

In 1965, the Senate and the House became deadlocked over some key provisions of that year's agriculture appropriations bill. The impasse lasted for two months. In an effort to break the log jam, the Senate representatives decided to resort to that time-honored tradition, the quid pro quo. In return for their support on some items, the House conferees were given a little pork. The top item was $100,000 to begin work on a $1 million laboratory in Oxford, Mississippi. Oxford happens to be in Agriculture Subcommittee chairman Jamie Whitten's district. The deadlock was broken and, despite some opposition in the Senate, the conference report was approved.

In fairness, there is a flip side to this sort of legislative hanky-panky. The conference committee also has proven a buffer against some very blatant pork-barreling and some very dubious law. Frequently, the House or the Senate will pass a measure or include a provision in a measure that the members know will never make it past the conference.

This can take place with either substantive legislation or with appropriations. A House member will plead with Appropriations to include a project for his district in the House bill even if it is struck out by the Senate. When the conference report comes back and the dam, hospital, or HEW facility is not included, the representative can then plead with his constituents that he tried mightily to fund this project and did so well that the all-knowing House Appropriations Committee made it part of their bill. And then, to his great outrage, a group of nameless, nasty senators conspired to keep this worthy venture from the voters. It works beautifully time after time.

On the substantive level, House members or senators are frequently released from restraints in supporting a certain measure through the knowledge that the other chamber will wipe it out in conference. In recent years, representatives from anti-busing districts who might not on a real vote find it in their conscience to vote against busing have been freed of that particular political problem by the Senate majority's refusal to go along with anti-busing measures. These members can vote for such a clause and know it will be knocked out. And House liberals do not have to make a major effort on the House floor. Everyone goes home happy. It may be lousy procedure, but it does periodically save the nation from inane laws.

Still the conference committee stands as a unique problem in the appropriations process. The committee, under even noncontroversial or usual circumstances, does create entirely new legislation, based upon what the House and Senate have approved—but new legislation nevertheless. With each passing year, the power of a conference becomes more and more pronounced. Both houses have all but become unable to meet the deadline for passage of a new fiscal year budget. This creates a great pressure to get the appropriations bill through as quickly as possible as the deadline approaches or has passed. Normally, it is at this point that the bill is in conference. When the conference report finally hits the floor for a vote, it is rare that the Senate or House will turn it down—even if it does not come close to upholding the chamber's position.

While the committee chairmen can juggle their house's representatives so that they do not actually reflect the will of the full house, it is far more normal that the group will hold the position taken by their fellow representatives or senators. As a result, the ill feelings that often dominate House-Senate relationships surface. One long-time senator recalls that during one conference a brawl almost broke out.

> I remember one time when McKellar was chairman of Senate Appropriations, and we were having a conference—on civil appropriations. The thing went on about six or eight weeks. We'd come back every two weeks, disagree, and come back again. [House Chairman Clarence] Cannon was saying, "I'll do this," and "I'll do that." Of course he had met with his conferees before, but he was doing all the talking. McKellar finally said, "How do the other House conferees feel about it?" And McKellar started to poll the House conferees. Cannon got so mad they almost had a fight—and they would have too. McKellar was going to hit him with a cane. Oh, those conferences can get tough sometimes.[3]

At one point, the animosity between the two houses became so intense that the appropriations process ground to a halt for six months. In December 1961, the House and Senate conferees finally worked out a compromise on a supplemental appropriations bill that included several controversial items. The report was considered highly favorable to the House position and there was some doubt that the Senate would approve the measure. The lower chamber pulled a fast one: it passed the report and then promptly adjourned for the session. The Senate had no choice but to approve the bill.

At the beginning of the next session, the House passed a resolution demanding the House be the scene of one-half of all conference committee meetings, ending a tradition under which the Senate hosted all such sessions. The resolution went on to criticize the Senate for always increasing the appropriations as passed by the House. The upper chamber was outraged. It bipartisanly attacked the House proposal. Mike Mansfield, normally a mild-mannered man, took the floor to exclaim that "we have taken a 'shellacking' and I think it is outrageous."[4] The late Everett Dirksen, then minority leader, cried that "an outrage is being perpetrated on the Senate."[5] The Senate, in response, promptly passed a resolution calling for half the appropriations bills each year to originate on their side of the Capitol, ending another long tradition.

From the middle of January to late July, both houses flatly refused to move into conference on any appropriations bills, even bills funding agencies to keep them going until the dispute was settled. Several almost ran out of money. Finally, under public pressure, the Congress decided to set up a committee to mediate the differences. This committee decided to set up a permanent committee to find permanent answers to the problems posed by the conflicts between the House and the Senate. By mutual consent, the two houses ended the 1962 quarrel, but the underlying animosity was undiminished.[6]

While no similar outbreak of hostility has taken place in recent years, there is still no love lost between the two bodies. Representative Riegle of Michigan once recalled a conference committee session he attended while he was on Appropriations:

> Eight House members and four senators were present. There were several items of disagreement, most of them in areas where the Senate had added money to the House-passed bill. We yielded on most of them. Our chairman was Tom Steed, from Oklahoma. Theirs was Joe Montoya, a Democrat from New Mexico. He had a plane to catch and was curt, abrasive, demanding. I resented his rudeness and, at the first opportunity, challenged one of his assertions. We battled to a draw. One by one, the twenty or so items of disagreement were resolved. Finally we reached agreement.[7]

"It really is surprising we get things done in those conferences at times," says a Senate Democrat. "That's especially true of the money bills. We—the Senate and the House—always disagree on something."

This senator says one of the big problems originates from his house. "We have this thing about protecting every other senator's pet project. It doesn't make any difference who the senator is or whether the project is worth a good goddamn but we fight like hell to keep it in. The House is right about that. We do care about keeping in individual projects more than they do."

This senator and others feel that there are two main reasons for this division. First, the House members can always say the Senate kept them from getting the project through. "That won't work for us. Voters say, 'Hell, you outrank 'em. You shoulda' done something.'" Second, there is that time-honored Senate tradition: the filibuster. "I don't know how often a senator has threatened to filibuster an appropriations measure to death if we didn't keep his project in."

Reporter Warren Weaver calls this "polite blackmail." "As recently as 1962, the Senate added $2 million to the House-passed Public Works Appropriation bill to begin work on Bruces Eddy Dam in Idaho. While the conferees met, Senator Frank Church of that state promised, 'If they strike out Bruces Eddy, I shall hold the Senate floor as long as God gives me strength to stand.' Apparently more impressed by the senator's power supply than by his previous opposition to the filibuster, the committee yielded."[8]

Most of the time differences are settled in conference by simple horse-trading. "Sometimes we sit down and we'll trade items one, two and ten for items three, eleven and fifteen from the Senate side," observes one representative. "Other times we split the difference. Say the House has appropriated $4 million for a program and the Senate has funded it for $6 million. Well, sometimes we settle at $4.5 million or $4.8 million or $5 million. I think most of the time we—the House—win in that kind of trading. We just know more about the appropriations than the Senate does."

A senator agrees that the individual House member may know more than the individual senator in a conference. "But we have more staff. They can counteract the expertise of the House committee. Most of the time we just sit across the table from each other and see who blinks first. It is the most incredible way to deal with the nation's money. We don't debate the differences, we just sit there like kids and play fiscal chicken. It's stupid."

Statistics show that the Senate wins in conference far more often than does the House. One review shows that, of 331 conference decisions, the Senate "won" 187, the House 101 and on 43 occasions the difference was evenly split.[9] Yet this is less important than the "substantiveless" way such conferences are run. The conferees do not care so much if their decisions are financially sound or if they reflect some sort of balancing of priorities as whether they have upheld the honor of their chamber: either by keeping in pet projects or "winning" by having the report figure come out closer to their house's than the other's.

And this is all done out of public sight. Only very rarely are conferences open to other members of Congress, let alone the public. There are no votes taken nor are any records kept except for the final conference report. Frequently the conferees do not even represent their own house's position on key issues. It is, as the one senator suggested, an insane system.

12

Some Reforms
for the System

There is little or no question that, at this time in history, the Congress is in a position inferior to that of the Executive. The past three Presidents—Kennedy, Johnson, and Nixon—have extended the power of the Oval Office to levels undreamed of by the Founding Fathers. Some of the men who formulated the Constitution certainly had nightmares about this kind of presidential control of the government but the blueprint they devised seemed ideal for balancing the powers of the executive with the powers of the other branches.

Despite the downfall of the Nixon administration, the Congress has still not regained its position in the Founding Fathers' scheme of things. This is particularly true of the appropriations process. On one level, the legislative branch has all but given up on its oversight functions over the federal budget. Through lack of staff and a refusal to use the General Accounting Office as it was originally intended, the Appropriations committees of the House and the Senate do no real digging into the use of federal funds or cost overruns which now seem a way of bureaucratic life.

On a second level, the Congress faces a major constitutional challenge to its spending prerogatives from the Oval Office. This has taken the form of impoundment of funds by the President, funds that the Congress had legally appropriated and the President had refused to veto. Both at this level and at the oversight level, Congress is failing.

Any reform of the congressional appropriations system is going to be difficult. Both senators and representatives seem inordinately enamored of the status quo. Any major changes are viewed as direct challenges to the power of Congress as a whole or one or the other chamber or one of the Appropriations committees. Reforms have been tried in the past and, by and large, they have either failed to pass or, once passed, have been roundly ignored.

Yet the Congress cannot go on with the current process for much longer. By 1976 at the latest, the budget will top the $300 billion mark. That size budget can simply not be dealt with through rules and traditions set up when the budget had barely topped $300 *million*.

Overall Recommendations

One reform which has been suggested repeatedly in recent years is a change in the fiscal year. Currently, the fiscal year runs from June 30 to July 1. Congress therefore has from only January 1 to June 30 to enact a budget before the fiscal year begins. This short period has resulted in chaos. Neither the House nor the Senate has the time to truly dig into the president's requests, resulting in sloppy cuts or rubber-stamping. When a dispute does arise, it will frequently carry beyond the June 30 deadline and the Congress must then pass measures to allow agencies to keep spending at the previous year's level.

It would seem only rational to change the fiscal year to a January 1 to December 31 cycle, matching Congress' year. Authorizing committees could then have from, say, January 1 (or when the president's budget is submitted in January) until June 1 to consider legislation on new budget authority. During this same period, the Appropriations committees could hold sessions on the spending of the previous year's authorization by various agencies. From late June—giving Congress some time to clean up business —until October 1, Appropriations would consider new funding. The months of November and December would be set aside for consideration of the overall budget by both houses.

Another reform which has been suggested, and actually tried before, would seem to fit in here. An omnibus appropriations bill, wherein all appropriations were considered as one bill rather than as thirteen or fourteen separate ones, was tried in 1950. It seemed to work fairly well although some senators and representatives complained that there was not sufficient time to study the measure. With some safeguards, the omnibus bill could serve as the ideal vehicle for the much-needed debate on national priorities.

As under the current system, the Appropriations committees would review funding through their subcommittees. There seems to be no way to logically avoid this fragmentation at the committee level. Instead of reporting out each subcommittee's report as it came through, Appropriations would hold all such reports until an overall document could be put together. This would apply to both the House and the Senate committees, ending the system whereby the House considers funding first. These reports would have to be reported to both houses by October 1—a not unreasonable limit given the change in the fiscal year.

Both houses would then have one month to consider their separate bills. No vote could be taken until the last week in October, insuring at least two weeks of debate. It would be hoped that the members of both chambers would devote more time under this system to mulling over national priorities than fighting over pork.

During November and December, the two most fragmented months of the congressional year due to the Thanksgiving and Christmas recesses, the House and Senate conferees will try to reconcile the differences between the two bills. The conference committee would have until December 10 to report out a compromise. This would give the two houses sufficient time to debate that report.

This proposal obviously runs counter to the most prominent reform now being considered on Capitol Hill: the Ervin-Percy bill. This measure would set up a budget committee in each house with representations from both Appropriations and revenue committees. These committees would set limits on spending in each area of the budget. This would seem a needlessly elaborate scheme and would not truly solve the problem of a few men, particularly on the House side, dominating the appropriations process. Even if limits were set, the Appropriations committees could ignore them.

It would obviously be to the benefit of the broad approach to the budget if the House Ways and Means Committee and the Senate Finance Committee could finish their work prior to consideration of new spending. At the moment, there is almost no real contact between the revenue and the Appropriations committees.

Committee Procedures

One of the most difficult problems to deal with on the committee level is whether representatives and senators whose districts and states are heavily affected by a certain department or agency should have seats on the Appropriations subcommittees governing those areas. The obvious response would seem to be that they should not. Yet, during Clarence Cannon's era, this was tried. Two trends resulted. First, a great deal of logrolling took place among the members of the various subcommittees. An easterner on agriculture would trade off his vote on a project for a midwesterner's district in return for, say, a health laboratory in his home district. Second, domestic spending programs seem to sustain the bulk of the cut.

It seems a questionable reform to set up some sort of limitation on the subcommittee seats a member can hold. Logrolling makes it just that much more difficult for the member on the floor and the public to understand just what is going on in the committee. Some areas of the budget might, however, be more severely cut than others under such rules.

One substantial reform which can be undertaken is the opening of all committee and subcommittee sessions to the public and press. Most House committees now have open meetings and do not find it an impediment to work. This rule should be extended, in particular, to markup sessions where the real decisions are made. While not all these meetings and hearings will be particularly well attended at the beginning, this is no excuse for not allowing the press and public access to these most important of congressional gatherings.

Some other procedures of the committees might well be democratized. One change that might be considered is to allow the full committee to vote on the membership of the subcommittees instead of having those groups handpicked by the chairman. The subcommittees, in turn, would have the right to pick their own chairman and ranking minority leader. Obviously this would initially present problems in the House, given the rather conservative makeup of that committee. Yet it seems a logical step which could have greater benefits in the long run than it would have deficits in the short run.

Additionally, subcommittee reports should be made available to the full committee membership one full week prior to a vote. Currently most subcommittee reports are not available until the day of the vote and an intelligent debate and vote are next to impossible. The concept should logically be extended to the full House and Senate and would be under the time schedule suggested previously.

Both the House and Senate should consider a modified version of the Senate system whereby representatives of the substantive committee involved in a given area of appropriations are allowed to sit in on committee debates on bills affecting their areas. A possible system would allow one member of the authorizing committee or committees (chosen by the committee membership and not the chairman) to sit in on the subcommittee markup sessions in their area. Three committee members, two members of the majority and one from the minority, could sit in on the full committee consideration of the bill. These representatives would not be allowed to vote but could participate in the debate.

Conference Committee

Since it is impossible to totally avoid conference committees, some changes have to be made in the current structure if one small group of men is not to continue dominating the appropriations process at this point. The first shift would come in the selection of the conferees from each house. The list of potential members of the group, as chosen by the committee chairman, should be made available to other members of the house at least twenty-four hours prior to a vote on the list. Members would have the right to move for amendment of the list by striking out names and replacing them with others. This would open the possibility of conferees being more reflective of the entire house's position, particularly on controversial issues.

Another important step would be to open up the conference committee process. Not only should these meetings be open to the public and press but records should be kept of votes and transcripts of debates made available to the members before a vote. These documents should be made available to the full houses at least four working days prior to a vote so that the members can better debate the compromise.

Oversight

One problem mentioned by nearly every representative and senator was the lack of hard information on how the money allocated was being spent by the agencies involved. Further, some complained of a lack of staff to do hard digging on new programs.

Congress needs no new authority to deal with this problem. Appropriations can now hire as much staff as it needs to accomplish its task. This authority should be exercised to hire perhaps three times the hundred or so staffers now working for the committees. Further, the Congress should make far greater use of the General Accounting Office, which was set up to give Capitol Hill an accounting arm similar to the executive's Office of Management and Budget. The Appropriations committees have, for a variety of reasons, not seen fit to adequately fund the GAO, so that the agency is largely incapable of undertaking major investigations as it should. This funding should be forthcoming and the committees should make major use of the GAO while dealing with past use of appropriations and cost overruns.

The new fiscal schedule proposed would allow Appropriations some time to review this past spending. During the first few months of each year, the committees could deal with nothing but investigations of whether monies appropriated by Congress were being spent as the legislative intended. This might be facilitated by extending the current trend of funding programs for two or three years rather than just one. Such a move would give the Appropriations committees even more time to tend to their oversight responsibilities.

It is eminently clear that all or most of these reforms must be undertaken, and quickly. It is no longer a question of just making the appropriations process more responsive to the needs of the people but one of actually keeping the money processes of the United States on an even keel. Congress has largely failed to act as a major partner in government in the appropriations process by refusing to modernize their procedures. The executive now has an inordinate control over key aspects of federal budget-making simply by the refusal of Congress to act. Both the House and the Senate seem more concerned about retaining the status quo, retaining their parochial powers and traditions and retaining pork for their states and districts than making a good budget.

Appendices

Ideology: Senate Appropriations Committee

	ADA	COPE	LCV	NAB	NSI
Democrats (by rank)					
John McClellan (Ark.)	10	0	0	60	90
Warren Magnuson (Wash.)	60	100	42	40	50
John Stennis (Miss.)	0	0	0	55	100
John Pastore (R.I.)	75	90	49	40	33
Alan Bible (Nev.)	35	60	16	64	80
Robert Byrd (W. Va.)	35	70	20	46	60
Gale McGee (Wyo.)	35	83	24	14	80
Mike Mansfield (Mont.)	80	88	63	0	10
William Proxmire (Wis.)	75	70	90	67	0
Joseph Montoya (N.M.)	45	90	42	40	60
Daniel Inouye (Hawaii)	65	100	33	0	22
Ernest Hollings (S.C.)	25	40	42	30	67
Birch Bayh (Indiana)	80	88	52	10	10
Thomas Eagleton (Mo.)	70	90	75	50	0
Lawton Chiles (Fla.)	35	11	50	40	50
Republicans (by rank)					
Milton Young (N.D.)	5	10	7	64	80
Roman Hruska (Nebr.)	5	0	4	91	100
Norris Cotton (N.H.)	0	0	0	88	100

Clifford Case (N.J.)	80	100	95	36	22
Hiram Fong (Hawaii)	10	10	20	55	100
Edward Brooke (Mass.)	80	90	77	33	33
Mark Hatfield (Oreg.)	55	50	47	33	0
Theodore Stevens (Alaska)	35	86	32	36	80
Charles McC. Mathias (Md.)	60	80	57	60	38
Richard Schweiker (Pa.)	60	100	79	42	70
Henry Bellmon (Okla.)	10	22	19	38	100

ADA: Americans for Democratic Action, a generally liberal group which opposed the war in Indochina and has been strong in the civil rights movement. A high rating indicates support for liberal issues.

COPE: Committee on Political Education, the lobbying arm of the AFL-CIO. High vote indicates pro-union stance.

LCV: League of Conservation Voters. High rating indicates support for environmentalist positions.

NAB: National Association of Businessmen. Generally supports cuts in spending but also acts on business issues. A high rating indicates support of cuts and business community.

NSI: The National Security Index of the American Security Council. The group opposes all cuts in military spending. High rating indicates a strong pro-Pentagon stance.

All ratings are for 1972.

APPENDIX 2.

Ideology: House Appropriations Committee

	ADA	COPE	LCV	NAB	NSI
Democrats (by rank)					
George Mahon (Tex.)	6	30	7	80	100
Jamie Whitten (Miss.)	6	30	6	78	100
John Rooney (N.Y.)	25	100	4	38	100
Robert Sikes (Fla.)	13	20	6	82	100
Otto Passman (La.)	6	43	7	86	100
Joseph Evins (Tenn.)	19	50	15	33	100
Edward Boland (Mass.)	69	91	60	17	22
William Natcher (Ky.)	31	64	13	25	60
Daniel Flood (Pa.)	44	91	27	25	100
Thomas Steed (Okla.)	19	73	11	40	100
George Shipley (Ill.)	25	67	25	30	67
John Slack (W. Va.)	25	70	11	27	100
John Flynt (Ga.)	6	10	17	86	86

	ADA	COPE	LCV	NAB	NSI
Neal Smith (Iowa)	50	90	27	17	44
Robert Giaimo (Conn.)	31	70	47	40	20
Sidney Yates (Ill.)	94	100	80	8	0
Julia Butler Hansen (Wash.)	50	100	24	13	62
Joseph Addabbo (N.Y.)	94	91	73	18	10
John McFall (Calif.)	44	91	0	9	100
Edward Patten (N.J.)	81	82	47	25	56
Clarence Long (Md.)	56	82	0	27	22
Robert Casey (Tex.)	6	27	7	60	100
Frank Evans (Colo.)	75	82	40	33	22
David Obey (Wis.)	100	100	91	0	0
Edward Roybal (Calif.)	100	100	79	9	0
J. Edward Roush (Ind.)	50	91	64	17	40
Louis Stokes (Ohio)	100	90	83	10	0
K. Gunn McKay (Utah)	31	89	21	30	80
Tom Bevill (Ala.)	19	82	5	46	100
Edith Green (Oreg.)	25	64	61	22	67
Robert Tiernan (R.I.)	75	91	63	9	13
Bill Chappell (Fla.)	0	10	0	75	100
Bill Burlison (Mo.)	44	72	27	18	60

Republicans (by rank)

	ADA	COPE	LCV	NAB	NSI
Elford Cederberg (Mich.)	0	18	20	92	100
John Rhodes (Ariz.)	6	30	25	89	100
William Minshall (Ohio)	13	44	49	88	100
Robert Michel (Ill.)	6	30	15	89	100
Silvio Conte (Mass.)	63	60	93	33	44
Glenn Davis (Wis.)	0	13	25	100	100
Howard Robison (N.Y.)	50	9	47	83	50
Garner Shriver (Kans.)	0	18	33	83	100
Joseph McDade (Pa.)	38	56	32	42	100
Mark Andrews (N.D.)	6	36	47	67	88
Louis Wyman (N.H.)	0	27	33	92	100
Burt Talcott (Calif.)	0	33	40	89	100
Wendell Wyatt (Oreg.)	25	60	20	58	100
W. Jack Edwards (Ala.)	0	10	18	88	100
William Scherel (Iowa)	0	10	27	82	100
Robert McEwen (N.Y.)	0	22	27	89	100
John Myers (Ind.)	0	27	20	73	100
J. Kenneth Robinson (Va.)	0	9	7	92	100
Clarence Miller (Ohio)	6	0	60	100	90
Earl Ruth (N.C.)	0	0	20	83	100
Victor Veysey (Calif.)	6	44	36	88	100
R. Lawrence Coughlin (Pa.)	38	36	86	67	75

ADA: Americans for Democratic Action, a generally liberal group which opposed the war in Indochina and has been strong in the civil rights movement. A high rating indicates support for liberal issues.

COPE: Committee on Political Education, the lobbying arm of the AFL-CIO. High vote indicates pro-union stance.

LCV: League of Conservation Voters. High rating indicates support for environmentalist positions.

NAB: National Association of Businessmen. Generally supports cuts in spending but also acts on business issues. A high rating indicates support of cuts and business community.

NSI: The National Security Index of the American Security Council. The group opposes all cuts in military spending. High rating indicates a strong pro-Pentagon stance.

All ratings are for 1972.

APPENDIX 3.
Monies Voted on in Fiscal 1973

HOUSE APPROPRIATIONS SUBCOMMITTEES

AGRICULTURE-ENVIRONMENTAL AND CONSUMER PROTECTION:

Covers the Agriculture Department, the Environmental Protection Agency and nearly all other related agencies. Voted on in excess of $11 billion.

DEFENSE:

Covers all military spending except for construction. Voted on in excess of $70 billion.

DISTRICT OF COLUMBIA:

Covers all spending for the District of Columbia.

FOREIGN OPERATIONS:

Covers all foreign aid but not State Department budget. Voted on in excess of $10 billion.

HUD—SPACE—SCIENCE—VETERANS:

Covers the National Aeronautics and Space Administration, Housing and Urban Development, the Veterans Administration and certain science projects. Voted on in excess of $18 billion.

INTERIOR:

Covers the Interior Department. Voted on in excess of $2.2 billion.

LABOR—HEALTH, EDUCATION, AND WELFARE:
> Covers both the Labor Department and HEW. Voted on in excess of $90 billion.

LEGISLATIVE:
> Covers expenditures for legislative branch. Voted on in excess of $540 million.

MILITARY CONSTRUCTION:
> Covers all military construction. Voted on in excess of $10 billion.

PUBLIC WORKS—AEC:
> Covers all public works projects and the Atomic Energy Commission. Voted on in excess of $12 billion.

STATE, JUSTICE, COMMERCE, AND JUDICIARY:
> Covers State, Justice and Commerce Departments and expenditures for the judicial branch. Voted on in excess of $3.5 million.

TRANSPORTATION:
> Covers Transportation Department. Voted on in excess of $8.1 billion.

TREASURY—POSTAL SERVICE—GENERAL GOVERNMENT:
> Covers Treasury Department, independent agencies and Executive branch. Voted on in excess of $40 billion.

SENATE SUBCOMMITTEES

> Senate subcommittees cover approximately the same areas as the House subcommittees.

APPENDIX 4.
Budgets

(all figures in millions)	1973[1]	1974[2]	1975[3]
Legislative Branch	540	658	734
The Judiciary	183	213	310
Executive Office of President	49	112	121
Funds appropriated to President	3,733	4,603	4,414

Agriculture	10,028	9,311	9,184
Commerce	1,368	1,519	1,712
Defense—military	73,297	78,400	84,600
Defense—civil	1,703	1,621	1,712
Health, Education and Welfare	82,040	96,768	110,959
Housing and Urban Development	3,592	4,983	5,550
Interior	2,253	3,774	2,657
Justice	1,531	1,938	2,106
Labor	8,639	8,590	10,043
State	591	743	793
Transportation	8,183	8,444	9,059
Treasury	30,960	35,849	37,633
Atomic Energy Commission	2,393	2,328	2,886
Environmental Protection Agency	1,114	2,559	3,991
General Services Administration	468	306	883
NASA (space administration)	3,311	3,177	3,272
Veterans Administration	11,968	13,241	13,594
Other independent agencies	11,449	13,343	14,528
Allowances for contingencies and civilian pay increase		300	1,561
Intragovernmental transactions[4]	− 8,400	− 10,000	− 10,700
TOTAL OUTLAYS	246,526	274,660	304,445

[1] Actual spending for year ending June 30, 1973.

[2] Estimated spending for year ending June 30, 1974.

[3] President's budget for year ending June 30, 1975.

[4] Transfer of funds between agencies that appear as spending in other figures.

Members of the Appropriations Committees

Majority:

Allen J. Ellender, Chm. (La.)
John L. McClellan (Ark.)
Warren G. Magnuson (Wash.)
John C. Stennis (Miss.)
John O. Pastore (R.I.)
Alan Bible (Nev.)
Robert C. Byrd (W. Va.)
Gale W. McGee (Wyo.)
Mike Mansfield (Mont.)
William Proxmire (Wis.)
Joseph M. Montoya (N.M.)
Daniel K. Inouye (Hawaii)
Ernest F. Hollings (S.C.)

Minority:

Milton R. Young (N. Dak.)
Karl E. Mundt (S. Dak.)
Margaret Chase Smith (Maine)
Roman L. Hruska (Nebr.)
Gordon Allott (Colo.)
Norris Cotton (N.H.)
Clifford P. Case (N.J.)
Hiram L. Fong (Hawaii)
J. Caleb Boggs (Del.)
Charles H. Percy (Ill.)
Edward W. Brooke (Mass.)
Mark O. Hatfield (Oreg.)
Ted Stevens (Alaska)

Subcommittee on Agriculture, Environmental and Consumer Protection

Majority:	*Minority:*
McGee, Chm.	Hruska
Stennis	Young
Proxmire	Fong
Byrd	Boggs
Mansfield	Hatfield
Inouye	

Subcommittee on Defense

Majority:	*Minority:*
Ellender, Chm.	Young
McClellan	Smith
Stennis	Allott
Pastore	Hruska
Magnuson	Cotton
Mansfield	Case
Bible	

Subcommittee on the District of Columbia

Majority:	*Minority:*
Inouye, Chm.	Hatfield
Montoya	Stevens
Hollings	

Subcommittee on Foreign Operations

Majority:	*Minority:*
Proxmire, Chm.	Fong
McGee	Brooke
Ellender	Hatfield
McClellan	

Subcommittee on Housing and Urban Development; Space; and Science

Majority:	*Minority:*
Pastore, Chm.	Allott
Magnuson	Smith
Ellender	Hruska
Stennis	Case
Mansfield	Fong
McGee	

Subcommittee on Interior

Majority:	*Minority:*
Bible, Chm.	Stevens
McClellan	Young
Byrd	Boggs
McGee	Hruska
Montoya	Hatfield
Inouye	

Subcommittee on Labor; Health, Education, and Welfare

Majority:	*Minority:*
Magnuson, Chm.	Cotton
Stennis	Case
Bible	Fong
Byrd	Boggs
Proxmire	Brooke
Montoya	Stevens
Hollings	

Subcommittee on Legislation

Majority:	*Minority:*
Hollings, Chm.	Cotton
Ellender	Brooke
Inouye	

Subcommittee on Military Construction

Majority:	*Minority:*
Mansfield, Chm.	Brooke
Proxmire	Boggs
Montoya	Stevens
Hollings	

Subcommittee on Public Works

Majority:	*Minority:*
Stennis, Chm.	Hatfield
Ellender	Young
McClellan	Hruska
Magnuson	Smith
Bible	Allott
Byrd	Case
Pastore	Cotton
McGee	

Subcommittee on State Justice Commerce, and Judiciary

Majority:	*Minority:*
McClellan, Chm.	Smith
Ellender	Hruska
Pastore	Fong
Mansfield	Brooke
Hollings	

Subcommittee on Transportation

Majority:	*Minority:*
Byrd, Chm.	Case
Stennis	Smith
Magnuson	Allott
Pastore	Cotton
Bible	Stevens
Proxmire	

Subcommittee on Treasury; U.S. Postal Services; General Government

Majority:
Montoya, Chm.
Ellender
Inouye

Minority:
Boggs
Allott

SENATE COMMITTEE ON APPROPRIATIONS, NINETY-THIRD CONGRESS

Majority:
John L. McClellan, Chm. (Ark.)
Warren G. Magnuson (Wash.)
John C. Stennis (Miss.)
John O. Pastore (R.I.)
Alan Bible (Nev.)
Robert C. Byrd (W. Va.)
Gale W. McGee (Wyo.)
Mike Mansfield (Mont.)
William Proxmire (Wis.)
Joseph M. Montoya (N. Mex.)
Daniel K. Inouye (Hawaii)
Ernest F. Hollings (S.C.)
Birch Bayh (Ind.)
Thomas F. Eagleton (Mo.)
Lawton Chiles (Fla.)

Minority:
Milton R. Young (N. Dak.)
Roman L. Hruska (Nebr.)
Norris Cotton (N.H.)
Clifford P. Case (N.J.)
Hiram L. Fong (Hawaii)
Edward W. Brooke (Mass.)
Mark O. Hatfield (Oreg.)
Ted Stevens (Alaska)
Charles McC. Mathias, Jr. (Md.)
Richard S. Schweiker (Pa.)
Henry Bellmon (Okla.)

Subcommittee on Agriculture, Environmental and Consumer Protection

Majority:
McGee, Chm.
Stennis

Minority:
Fong
Hruska

Majority:
Proxmire
Byrd
Inouye
Bayh
Hollings
Eagleton

Minority:
Young
Hatfield
Bellmon

Subcommittee on Defense

Majority:
McClellan, Chm.
Stennis
Pastore
Magnuson
Mansfield
Bible
McGee

Minority:
Young
Hruska
Cotton
Case
Fong
Brooke

Subcommittee on Intelligence Operations

Majority:
McClellan, Chm.
Stennis
Pastore

Minority:
Young
Hruska

Subcommittee on the District of Columbia

Majority:
Bayh, Chm.
Inouye
Chiles

Minority:
Mathias
Bellmon

Subcommittee on Foreign Operations

Majority:	*Minority:*
Inouye, Chm.	Brooke
Proxmire	Hatfield
McGee	Mathias
McClellan	
Chiles	

Subcommittee on Housing and Urban Development; Space; Science; and Veterans

Majority:	*Minority:*
Proxmire, Chm.	Mathias
Pastore	Case
Stennis	Fong
Mansfield	Brooke
Inouye	Stevens
Bayh	
Chiles	

Subcommittee on Interior

Majority:	*Minority:*
Bible, Chm.	Stevens
McClellan	Young
Byrd	Hruska
McGee	Hatfield
Montoya	Bellmon
Inouye	
Chiles	

Subcommittee on Labor; Health, Education, and Welfare

Majority:	*Minority:*
Magnuson, Chm.	Cotton
Stennis	Case

Majority:	*Minority:*
Bible	Fong
Byrd	Brooke
Proxmire	Stevens
Montoya	Schweiker
Hollings	
Eagleton	

Subcommittee on Legislation

Majority:	*Minority:*
Hollings, Chm.	Cotton
Bayh	Schweiker
Eagleton	

Subcommittee on **Military Construction**

Majority:	*Minority:*
Mansfield, Chm.	Schweiker
Proxmire	Mathias
Montoya	Bellmon
Hollings	

Subcommittee on **Public Works**; Atomic Energy Commission

Majority:	*Minority:*
Stennis, Chm.	Hatfield
McClellan	Young
Magnuson	Hruska
Bible	Case
Byrd	Stevens
Pastore	Schweiker
McGee	Bellmon
Montoya	

Subcommittee on State Justice Commerce, and Judiciary

Majority:	*Minority:*
Pastore, Chm.	Hruska
McClellan	Fong
Mansfield	Brooke
Hollings	Cotton
Magnuson	
Eagleton	

Subcommittee on Transportation

Majority:	*Minority:*
Byrd, Chm.	Case
Stennis	Cotton
Magnuson	Stevens
Pastore	Mathias
Bible	Schweiker
Mansfield	

Subcommittee on Treasury; U.S. Postal Services; General Government

Majority:	*Minority:*
Montoya, Chm.	Bellmon
Bayh	Hatfield
Eagleton	
Chiles	

HOUSE COMMITTEE ON APPROPRIATIONS, NINETY-SECOND CONGRESS

Majority:	*Minority:*
George H. Mahon, Chm. (Tex.)	Frank T. Bow (Ohio)
Jamie L. Whitten (Miss.)	Charles R. Jonas (N.C.)
George W. Andrews (Ala.)	Elford A. Cederberg (Mich.)
John J. Rooney (N.Y.)	John J. Rhodes (Ariz.)
Robert L. F. Sikes (Fla.)	William E. Minshall (Ohio)

Majority:

Otto E. Passman (La.)
Joe L. Evins (Tenn.)
Edward P. Boland (Mass.)
William H. Natcher (Ky.)
Daniel J. Flood (Pa.)
Tom Steed (Okla.)
George E. Shipley (Ill.)
John M. Slack (W. Va.)
John J. Flynt, Jr. (Ga.)
Neal Smith (Iowa)
Robert N. Giaimo (Conn.)
Julia Butler Hansen (Wash.)
Joseph P. Addabbo (N.Y.)
John J. McFall (Calif.)
W. R. Hull, Jr. (Mo.)
Edward J. Patten (N.J.)
Clarence D. Long (Md.)
Sidney R. Yates (Ill.)
Bob Casey (Tex.)
David Pryor (Ark.)
Frank E. Evans (Colo.)
David R. Obey (Wis.)
Edward R. Roybal (Calif.)
William D. Hathaway (**Maine**)
Nick Galifianakis (N.C.)
Louis Stokes (Ohio)
J. Edward Roush (Ind.)
K. Gunn McKay (Utah)

Minority:

Robert H. Michel (Ill.)
Silvio O. Conte (Mass.)
Glenn R. Davis (Wis.)
Howard W. Robison (N.Y.)
Garner E. Shriver (Kans.)
Joseph M. McDade (Pa.)
Mark Andrews (N. Dak.)
Louis C. Wyman (N.H.)
Burt L. Talcott (Calif.)
Donald W. Riegle, Jr. (Mich.)
Wendell Wyatt (Oreg.)
Jack Edwards (Ala.)
Del Clawson (Calif.)
William J. Scherle (Iowa)
Robert C. McEwen (N.Y.)
John T. Myers (Ind.)
J. Kenneth Robinson (Va.)

Subcommittee on Agriculture, Environmental and Consumer
Protection

Majority:

Whitten, Chm.
Natcher
Hull
Shipley
Evans

Minority:

Andrews (N. Dak.)
Michel
Scherle

Subcommittee on Defense

Majority:	*Minority:*
Mahon, Chm.	Minshall
Sikes	Rhodes
Whitten	Davis
Flood	Wyman
Addabbo	
McFall	
Flynt	

Subcommittee on the District of Columbia

Majority:	*Minority:*
Natcher, Chm.	Davis
Giaimo	Scherle
Pryor	McEwen
Obey	Myers
Stokes	
McKay	

Subcommittee on Foreign Operations

Majority:	*Minority:*
Passman, Chm.	Shriver
Rooney	Riegle
Long	McEwen
Roybal	Robinson
Hathaway	
Galifianakis	

Subcommittee on HUD; Space; Science; and Veterans

Majority:	*Minority:*
Boland, Chm.	Jonas
Evins	Talcott
Shipley	McDade
Giaimo	Clawson
Pryor	
Roush	

Subcommittee on Interior and Related Agencies

Majority:	*Minority:*
Hansen, Chm.	McDade
Obey	Wyatt
Yates	Clawson
Galifianakis	

Subcommittee on Labor; Health, Education,and Welfare

Majority:	*Minority:*
Flood, Chm.	Michel
Natcher	Shriver
Smith	Conte
Hull	Robinson
Casey	
Patten	

Subcommittee on Legislation

Majority:	*Minority:*
Casey, Chm.	Bow
Evans	Cederberg
Hathaway	Rhodes
Roush	Wyatt
Bevill	

Subcommittee on Military Construction

Majority:	*Minority:*
Sikes, Chm.	Cederberg
Patten	Jonas
Long	Talcott
Hansen	
McKay	

Subcommittee on Public Works; Atomic Energy Commission

Majority: *Minority:*
Evins, Chm.   Rhodes
Boland   Davis
Whitten   Robison
Slack
Passman

Subcommittee on State, Justice, Commerce, and Judiciary

Majority: *Minority:*
Rooney, Chm.   Bow
Sikes   Cederberg
Slack   Andrews (N. Dak.)
Smith
Flynt

Subcommittee on Transportation

Majority: *Minority:*
McFall, Chm.   Conte
Boland   Minshall
Yates   Edwards
Steed

Subcommittee on Treasury; U.S. Postal Services; General Government

Majority: *Minority:*
Steed, Chm.   Robison
Addabbo   Edwards
Roybal   Riegle
Stokes   Myers
Bevill

HOUSE COMMITTEE ON APPROPRIATIONS, NINETY-THIRD CONGRESS

Majority:

George H. Mahon, Chm. (Tex.)
Jamie L. Whitten (Miss.)
John J. Rooney (N.Y.)
Robert L. F. Sikes (Fla.)
Otto E. Passman (La.)
Joe L. Evins (Tenn.)
Edward P. Boland (Mass.)
William H. Natcher (Ky.)
Daniel J. Flood (Pa.)
Tom Steed (Okla.)
George E. Shipley (Ill.)
John M. Slack (W. Va.)
John J. Flynt, Jr. (Ga.)
Neal Smith (Iowa)
Robert N. Giaimo (Conn.)
Julia Butler Hansen (Wash.)
Joseph P. Addabbo (N.Y.)
John J. McFall (Calif.)
Edward J. Patten (N.J.)
Clarence D. Long (Md.)
Sidney R. Yates (Ill.)
Bob Casey (Tex.)
Frank E. Evans (Colo.)
David R. Obey (Wis.)
Edward R. Roybal (Calif.)
Louis Stokes (Ohio)
J. Edward Roush (Ind.)
Gunn McKay (Utah)
Tom Bevill (Ala.)
Edith Green (Oreg.)
Robert O. Tiernan (R.I.)
Bill Chappell, Jr. (Fla.)
Bill D. Burlison (Mo.)

Minority:

Elford A. Cederberg (Mich.)
William H. Minshall (Ohio)
Robert H. Michel (Ill.)
Silvio O. Conte (Mass.)
Glenn R. Davis (Wisc.)
Howard W. Robison (N.Y.)
Garner E. Shriver (Kans.)
Joseph M. McDade (Pa.)
Mark Andrews (N. Dak.)
Louis C. Wyman (N.H.)
Burt L. Talcott (Calif.)
Wendell Wyatt (Oreg.)
Jack Edwards (Ala.)
William J. Scherle (Iowa)
Robert C. McEwen (N.Y.)
John T. Myers (Ind.)
J. Kenneth Robinson (Va.)
Clarence E. Miller (Ohio)
Earl B. Ruth (N.C.)
Victor V. Veysey (Calif.)
Lawrence Coughlin (Pa.)
C. W. Young (Fla.)

Subcommittee on Agriculture, Environmental and Consumer Protection

Majority:
Whitten, Chm.
Shipley
Evans (Colo.)
Burlison
Natcher
Smith (Iowa)
Casey

Minority:
Andrews
Michel
Scherle
Robinson

Subcommittee on Defense

Majority:
Mahon, Chm.
Sikes
Flood
Addabbo
McFall
Flynt
Giaimo
Whitten

Minority:
Minshall
Davis
Wyman
Edwards

Subcommittee on the District of Columbia

Majority:
Natcher, Chm.
Stokes
Tiernan
Chappell
Burlison
McKay
Roush

Minority:
Myers
McEwen
Coughlin
Young

Subcommittee on Foreign Operations

Majority:	*Minority:*
Passman, Chm.	Shriver
Rooney	Miller
Long	Conte
Roybal	Coughlin
Bevill	
Roush	
Yates	

Subcommittee on HUD; Space; Science; and Veterans

Majority:	*Minority:*
Boland, Chm.	Talcott
Evins	McDade
Shipley	Scherle
Roush	Ruth
Tiernan	
Chappell	
Giaimo	

Subcommittee on Interior

Majority:	*Minority:*
Hansen, Chm.	Wyatt
Yates	Veysey
McKay	
Long	
Evans	
McDade	

Subcommittee on Labor; Health, Education and Welfare

Majority:	*Minority:*
Flood, Chm.	Michel
Natcher	Shriver

Majority:	*Minority:*
Smith	Conte
Casey	Robinson
Patten	
Obey	
Green	

Subcommittee on Legislation

Majority:	*Minority:*
Casey, Chm.	Wyman
Evans	Cederberg
Giaimo	Ruth
Green	Coughlin
Flynt	
Roybal	
Stokes	

Subcommittee on Military Construction

Majority:	*Minority:*
Sikes, Chm.	McEwen
Patten	Davis
Long	Talcott
Obey	
McKay	

Subcommittee on Public Works; Atomic Energy Commission

Majority:	*Minority:*
Evins, Chm.	Rhodes
Boland	Davis
Whitten	Robison
Slack	Myers
Passman	

Subcommittee on State, Justice, Commerce, and Judiciary

Majority:
Rooney, Chm.
Slack
Smith
Flynt
Sikes

Minority:
Cederberg
Andrews
Wyatt

Subcommittee on Transportation

Majority:
McFall, Chm.
Yates
Steed
Hansen
Boland

Minority:
Conte
Minshall
Edwards

Subcommittee on Treasury; U.S. Postal Services; General Government

Majority:
Steed, Chm.
Addabbo
Roybal
Stokes
Bevill
Shipley
Slack

Minority:
Robison
Miller
Veysey
Young

Notes

CHAPTER 1. FILLING THE COFFERS:
THE REVENUE COMMITTEES

1. Randall B. Ripley, *Party Leaders in the House of Representatives* (Washington, D.C.: The Brookings Institution, 1967), pp. 22 and 56.
2. *National Journal*, April 10, 1971, p. 784.
3. Udall and Tacheron, *The Job of the Congressman* (Indianapolis: Bobbs-Merrill Company, 2nd ed., 1970), p. 163.
4. *Citizens Look at Congress*, profile of Representative Dan Rostenkowski, Ralph Nader Congress Project (Washington: Grossman, 1972), p. 2.
5. Ways and Means Committee Report to accompany H.R. 14370, April 26, 1972, pp. 88–125.
6. Ibid.
7. *Congressional Record*, June 21, 1972, p. H.5868.
8. Ibid., pp. H.5869–70.
9. Ibid., pp. H.5871–2.
10. Barber Conable, member of House Ways and Means Committee, Hearings on *Tax Credits for Non-Public Education* (Aug. 14, 1972), *Part 1*, p. 40.
11. Ibid.
12. *Congressional Record*, Vol. 118, No. 125, pp. 7290–7300.
13. *Citizens Look at Congress*, profile of Senator Abraham Ribicoff, Ralph Nader Congress Project (Washington: Grossman, 1972), p. 6.
14. *New York Times*, November 27, 1972, p. 35.
15. *Congressional Record*, November 17, 1969, Vol. 115, p. 22552.
16. Laurence Woodworth, "Procedure Followed by Congress in Enacting

Tax Legislation and the Role of the Joint Committee Staff in that Process," reprinted from *Proceedings of the University of Southern California Law Center, Eighteenth Tax Institute*, 1966, p. 28.

17. *Congressional Record*, August 7, 1972, Vol. 118, p. 7299.
18. John F. Manley, *The Politics of Finance: The House Committee on Ways and Means* (Boston: Little, Brown, 1970), p. 310.
19. Laurence Woodworth, "Where Tax Bills Run the Gauntlet," *Business Week*, June 11, 1966, p. 106.
20. Woodworth, "Procedure Followed by Congress," pp. 27–28.
21. Manley, *The Politics of Finance*, p. 310.
22. Woodworth, "Procedure Followed by Congress," p. 26.
23. Stanley S. Surrey, "The Congress and the Tax Lobbyist—How Special Tax Provisions Get Enacted," in Frank E. A. Sander and David Westfall, eds., *Readings in Federal Taxation* (Mineola, New York: The Foundation Press, Inc., 1970), p. 25.
24. Frank Fowlkes, "House Turns to Protectionism Despite Arm-Twisting by Nixon Trade Experts," *National Journal*, August 22, 1970, pp. 1820–21.

CHAPTER 2.   INSIDE THE COMMITTEES:
RULES, HEARINGS, AND CONFERENCES

1. Hearings of Ways and Means Committee on Tax Reform, March 9, 1973, p. 2658 of "unrevised stenographic minutes." (N.B.: Stamped "duplication or quotation strictly forbidden." Published copy not available as of 5/1/73.)
2. Ibid., p. 2653.
3. Ibid., p. 2655.
4. Thomas Stanton, "Jousting with Wilbur Mills & Co.," *ADA World*, February 1973, p. 4.
5. Statement of the Reverend William L. Matheus to the House Ways and Means Committee, March 7, 1973.
6. Letter from John M. Martin, Jr., to Mary Ann Fiske, February 23, 1973.
7. Hearings of Ways and Means Committee on Tax Proposals Contained in the President's New Economic Policy, Part 4, September 17, 1971, p. 1174.
8. *Congressional Quarterly Weekly Reports*, February 12, 1972, pp. 301ff.
9. Stanton, "Jousting with Wilbur Mills & Co.," p. 4.
10. *Congressional Record*, February 7, 1973, Volume 119, No. 36, p. H.1429.
11. Ibid., p. H.1435.
12. Ibid., p. H.1436.
13. Ibid., p. H.1435.

14. Ibid., p. H.1435.
15. Ibid., p. H.1443.
16. Ibid., p. H.1447–48.
17. Ibid., p. H.1437.
18. Ibid., p. H.1441.
19. *Congressional Record*, June 21, 1972, Vol. 118, No. 101, pp. H.5864–65.
20. *Congressional Record*, June 22, 1972, Vol. 118, No. 102, p. H.5965.
21. *Congressional Record*, November 18, 1970, Vol. 116, Part 28, p. 37825.
22. *Congressional Record*, Vol. 115, Part 17, p. 22552.
23. *Congressional Record*, October 5, 1971, Vol. 117, No. 147.
24. *Congressional Record*, February 9, 1972, p. H.980.
25. *Congressional Record*, November 18, 1970, Vol. 116, Part 28, p. 37837.
26. Ibid., pp. 37824–25.
27. Ibid., p. 37826.
28. Ibid., p. 37838.
29. Ibid., p. 37827.
30. Ibid., p. 37839.
31. Ibid., pp. 37839–40.
32. Ibid., pp. 37841–42.
33. *Congressional Record*, November 19, 1970, Vol. 116, Part 28, p. 38228.
34. *Congressional Record*, June 21, 1972, Vol. 118, No. 101, p. H.5866.
35. Ibid., p. H.5871.
36. Ibid., p. H.5876.
37. Elizabeth Drew, "Washington," *Atlantic Monthly*, June 1972, p. 18.
38. *Congressional Record*, March 15, 1973, Vol. 119, No. 41, p. H.1830.

CHAPTER 3.   HOW THE COMMITTEES AVOID OVERSIGHT

1. *Congressional Record*, June 30, 1972, pp. S.10980–85.
2. Rita Richard Campbell, *Economics of Health and Public Policy* (Washington: American Enterprise Institute, 1971), p. 27.
3. U.S., Congress, Senate, Committee on Finance, Hearings on *Medicare and Medicaid: Issues, Programs and Answers*, 91st Cong., 2nd sess. (1970), p. 117.
4. Ibid., p. 22.
5. U.S., Congress, Senate, Committee on Finance, Hearings on *Medicare and Medicaid: Issues, Programs and Answers*, 91st Cong., 2nd sess. (1970).
6. Ibid.

7. Stanley S. Surrey, "Tax Incentives as a Device for Implementing Government Policy: A Comparison with Direct Government Expenditures," 83 *Harvard Law Review* 705, 722 (1970).

8. Erickson and Millsaps, "Taxes, Goals, and Efficiency: Petroleum and Defense," in Joint Economic Committee Print, *The Economics of Federal Subsidy Programs, Part 3, Tax Subsidies*, pp. 286, 300 (1972).

9. Stanley S. Surrey, "Tax Subsidies as a Device for Implementing Government Policy: A Comparison with Direct Government Expenditures," in Joint Economic Committee, *The Economics of Federal Subsidy Programs, Part 1—General Study Papers*, pp. 74, 94 (1972).

10. Blum, "The Effects of Special Provisions in the Income Tax on Taxpayer Morale," in Joint Committee on the Economy Report, *Federal Tax Policy for Economic Growth and Stability*, 84th Cong., 1st sess. (1955), pp. 251–252.

11. Walter Heller, "Some Observations on the Role and Reform of the Federal Income Tax," in House Committee on Ways and Means, *Tax Revision Compendium*, 96th Cong., 1st sess. (1959), pp. 181, 190.

12. President Lyndon B. Johnson, 1966 Economic Report, p. 18.

13. Stanley S. Surrey, "The United States Income Tax System—The Need for a Full Accounting," in *Annual Report of the Secretary of the Treasury, 1968*, p. 326.

14. *Congressional Record*, December 13, 1967, p. H.16890.

15. Surrey, mimeographed copy of statement.

16. President Richard Nixon, Message to Congress, April 21, 1969.

17. Surrey, "Tax Subsidies," p. 94, footnote 17.

18. Ibid., p. 75.

19. *Congressional Record*, October 13, 1969, p. S.12371.

20. Surrey, "Tax Incentives," p. 728, footnote 32.

21. S.3968, introduced June 16, 1970.

22. Joint Economic Committee, minority report on the President's February 1971 Economic Report, p. 135.

23. Taubman and Rasche, "Subsidies, Tax Law, and Real Estate Investment," Joint Economic Committee Print, *The Economics of Federal Subsidy Programs, Part 3, Tax Subsidies*.

24. Ott and Ott, "The Tax Subsidy Through Exemption of State and Local Bond Interest." Ibid., p. 305.

25. Erickson and Millsaps, "Taxes, Goals, and Efficiency." Ibid., pp. 296, 300.

26. Sunley, "The Federal Tax Subsidy of the Timber Industry." Ibid., p. 317.

27. McLure, "The Income Tax Treatment of Interest Earned on Savings in Life Insurance." Ibid., p. 370.

28. *Congressional Record*, May 11, 1971, p. S.6611.

29. *Congressional Record*, November 16, 1971, p. S.18766.

30. Ibid., pp. S.18767–68.

31. *Congressional Record*, November 20, 1971, p. S.18765.

32. Tax Institute of America, *Tax Incentives: A Symposium* (Lexington, Mass.: Heath Lexington Books, 1971).

CHAPTER 4.   MONEY TALKS

1. Louis Eisenstein, *The Ideologies of Taxation* (New York: Ronald Press, 1961), pp. 3–4.
2. Roy Blough, *The Federal Taxing Process* (Englewood Cliffs, N.J.: Prentice-Hall, 1952), p. 41.
3. *Congressional Record,* October 13, 1972, p. S.18047.
4. Paul Douglas, *In the Fullness of Time* (New York: Harcourt Brace Jovanovich, 1972), pp. 446–47.
5. Fowlkes and Lenhart, "Two Money Committees Wield Power Differently," *National Journal,* April 10, 1971, p. 780.
6. John F. Manley, *The Politics of Finance: The House Committee on Ways and Means* (Boston: Little, Brown, 1970), p. 81.
7. Eileen Shanahan, "House Tax Panel Eases Rule on Foundation Spending," *New York Times,* October 14, 1971, p. 35.
8. *Congressional Record,* February 29, 1972, p. H.1497ff.
9. *Washington Star,* September 13, 1972.
10. Confidential Memorandum to Members of the Committee on Ways and Means, from John M. Martin, Jr., Chief Counsel, September 13, 1972.
11. David J. Stern, *The Rape of the Taxpayer* (New York: Random House, 1973), p. 42.
12. Ibid., p. 46.
13. "The Day Congress Played Santa: A Look at the Christmas Tree Bill," *Washington Post,* December 25, 1966, pp. A–1, A–10.
14. Ibid.
15. Ibid.
16. Joseph Spear, "Speak Up, I've Got a Lobbyist in My Ear," *Washington Monthly,* v. 21:2, April 1972, p. 18.
17. Ibid.
18. Secretary of Treasury Douglas Dillon, *Tax Hearings before the Committee on Ways and Means,* 87th Cong., 1st sess. (1961), p. 38.
19. Robert Metz, "Study May Lead to Tax Changes," *New York Times,* January 9, 1961, p. 85.
20. U.S., Congress, Senate, Committee on Finance, *Hearings on Nominations,* 87th Cong., 1st sess. (March 22-23, 1961), pp. 7–43, 45–77.
21. David J. Stern, "Congress, Politics, and Taxes: A Case Study of the Revenue Act of 1962" (Ph.D. dissertation, Claremont Graduate School, 1965), pp. 42–43.
22. Ibid., p. 253.
23. "Meet Your Executive Committee: It Serves a Vital Leadership Role," *Convention Daily,* U.S. Savings and Loan League, November 5, 1962, p. 5.
24. Douglas, *In the Fullness of Time,* p. 432.
25. Stern, *The Rape of the Taxpayer,* p. 299.

26. Douglas, *In the Fullness of Time*, pp. 434–36.

27. Young, "Savings and Loan: the 4.75 percent Bonanza," *The Nation*, December 8, 1962, p. 397.

28. Douglas, *In the Fullness of Time*, p. 436.

29. Stern, *The Rape of the Taxpayer*, p. 303.

30. *Congressional Quarterly Almanac*, 1969, p. 605.

31. U.S., Congress, House, Committee on Ways and Means, *Hearings on the Subject of Tax Reform*, 91st Cong., 1st sess., part 9, p. 3181ff, especially p. 3186ff.

32. Ibid., p. 3187.

33. Ibid., p. 3255.

34. Ibid., pp. 3258, 3261, 3273, 3277–78, 3282, 3291, 3320ff.

35. U.S., Congress, Senate, Committee on Finance, *Hearings on the Tax Reform Act of 1969*, 91st Cong., 1st sess., part 5, especially pp. 4484–4554, 4493.

36. *See, e.g.*, Field, "The Tax Treatment of Oil," in JEC, *Oil Prices and Phase II, Hearings before the JEC*, 92nd Cong., 1st sess. (1972), p. 34; Remarks of Senator William Proxmire, *Congressional Record*, October 27, 1971.

37. "Oil Expert Says IRS Section Favors Industry," *Washington Post*, January 11, 1971, p. A–4.

38. Joseph Pechman, *Federal Tax Policy* (New York: Norton, 1971), p. 32.

39. Internal Revenue Code of 1954, S7805.

40. *New York Times*, January 5, 1971.

41. "Business Gets U.S. Tax Help," *Washington Post*, January 12, 1971, p. 1.

42. The Budget of the United States Government, Fiscal Year 1972 (Washington, D.C.: Government Printing Office, 1971), pp. 374–382, 412.

43. Report of the President's Task Force on Business Taxation (September 1970), p. 29.

44. "Treasury Issues Liberalized Rules on Depreciation," *Wall Street Journal*, January 12, 1971, p. 2.

45. Presidential news conference, March 2, 1971; see *New York Times*, May 3, 1971, p. 66.

46. "Treasury Now Says Law Doesn't Require Depreciation Hearing," *Wall Street Journal*, January 14, 1971, p. 6.

47. "Hearing Assured on Depreciation," *New York Times*, January 26, 1971, p. 16.

48. Ibid., p. 16.

49. Ibid., p. 16.

50. Don Oberdorfer, "A Curious Kind of Tax Break," *Washington Post*, April 7, 1971, p. A17.

51. Common Cause press release, 1971.

52. "Heller Joins Critics of Tax Break Plans," *Sacramento Bee*, April 13, 1971.

53. *Congressional Record*, April 26, 1971.

54. "Depreciation Plan Criticized," *Washington Post*, April 5, 1971, p. D-11.
55. *Congressional Record*, April 23, 1971, p. E.3401.
56. *Congressional Record*, April 27, 1971, p. E.3507.
57. "Heller Joins Critics of Tax Break Plans," *Sacramento Bee*.
58. "Backers Say Plan of White House Is Needed," *New York Times*, November 13, 1971, p. 24.
59. "Treasury Hearings on Guidelines for Department Begin," *Wall Street Journal*, May 4, 1971, p. 18.
60. "Connally Says Politics Inspire Critics of Tax Cut for Business," *New York Times*, July 8, 1971, p. 1.
61. *Los Angeles Times*, May 7, 1971, section J, p. 2.
62. *Kiplinger Tax Letter*, April 23, 1971.
63. "Five-Pronged Attack Poses Serious Threat to ADR System and Multimillion Dollar Bonanza," *Tax Planning Ideas*, May 1, 1971, p. 3.
64. *Congressional Record*, October 5, 1971, p. H.9158.
65. Ibid., p. H.9169.
66. *Congressional Record*, November 12, 1971, p. S.18381.
67. Ibid.
68. Ibid., p. S.18410.
69. Ibid., p. S.18411.
70. Statement of Under Secretary of Treasury for Monetary Affairs Paul O. Volcker, *Finance Committee Hearing on Trade Act of 1970*, October 9, 1970 (mimeographed copy).
71. "Nixon Tax-Incentive Talk Begins to Bear Fruit," *Christian Science Monitor*, August 8, 1970, p. 12.
72. Written Statements and Other Materials Submitted by Administration Witnesses to the Committee on Ways and Means During Hearings on the Subject of Foreign Trade and Tariffs, May 12, 1970, pp. 31–50.
73. Stanley S. Surrey, "DISC: A Billion-Dollar Tax Loophole Hidden in New Economic Policy," *Congressional Record*, November 20, 1971, p. S.19204.
74. Frank Fowlkes, "House Turns to Protectionism Despite Arm-Twisting by Trade Experts," *National Journal*, August 22, 1970, p. 1819.
75. *Trade Act of 1970*, H.R. 91–1435, to accompany H.R. 18970, 91st Cong., 2nd sess., pp. 178–180.
76. Ibid., p. 190.
77. U.S., Congress, House, Committee on Ways and Means, *Hearings on Tariff and Trade Proposals*, 91st Cong., 2nd sess., part 9, p. 2609.
78. *Analysis of Treasury Domestic International Sales Corporation Proposal* (confidential committee print prepared for the Committee of Ways and Means by the staff of the JCIRT), July 13, 1970, p. 15.
79. "Nader Hits Tax Break to Exporters," *Washington Post*, November 1, 1970, p. A5.
80. Tom Field, statement before Committee on Finance hearing on Trade Act of 1970, October 9, 1970.
81. *Congressional Record*, October 9, 1970, p. 36058.

82. "DISC: Boon to Trade or Loophole?" *Wall Street Journal*, December 3, 1970, p. 2.
83. Report, Embassy of the United States of America, The Hague, Office of the Ambassador, July 15, 1971.
84. U.S., Congress, House, Committee on Ways and Means, *Hearings on Tax Proposals Contained in the President's New Economic Policy*, 92nd Cong., 2nd sess., pp. 7, 16, 99.
85. *New York Times*, October 6, 1971.
86. Reprinted in *Congressional Record*, November 20, 1971, p. S.19204.
87. U.S., Congress, Senate, Hearings on H.R. 10947, *The Revenue Act of 1971*, 92nd Cong., 1st sess., p. 16.
88. Ibid., p. 32.
89. Ibid., p. 722.
90. Ibid., p. 737.
91. Ibid., p. 16.
92. *Congressional Record*, November 20, 1971, p. S.19206.
93. Surrey, "DISC: A Billion-Dollar Tax Loophole."
94. *Congressional Record*, November 20, 1971, p. S.19200.
95. *Congressional Record*, November 22, 1971, p. S.19363.
96. *Congressional Record*, December 9, 1971, p. H.12116.
97. Ibid.
98. Ibid., p. H.12133.
99. Ibid., p. 21095.
100. Roy Blough, *The Federal Taxing Process*.
101. Eisenstein, *The Ideologies of Taxation*.
102. Ferdinand Lundberg, *The Rich and the Super Rich* (New York: Bantam Books, 1969), p. 323.

II. The House and Senate Appropriations Committees

CHAPTER 6.   A HISTORY OF THE PROCESS

1. James Madison, *Federalist Papers*, 1788.
2. *United States Constitution*, Article 1, Section 9, Clause 7.
3. *Historical Statistics of the United States—Colonial Times to 1957* (Washington: U.S. Department of Commerce, 1960), p. 711.
4. Ibid.
5. *Congressional Quarterly Guide to the Congress of the United States* (Washington, 1971), p. 151.
6. Ibid., p. 186.
7. Ibid.
8. Warren Weaver, Jr., *Both Your Houses—The Truth About Congress* (New York: Praeger, 1973), p. 252.

9. Ibid., p. 252.
10. Ibid.
11. *Historical Statistics,* Department of Commerce, p. 711.
12. Weaver, *Both Your Houses,* p. 248.

CHAPTER 7.   THE BUDGET BEFORE CONGRESS

1. Warren Weaver, Jr., *Both Your Houses—The Truth About Congress* (New York: Praeger, 1973), pp. 247–248.
2. Ibid., p. 253.
3. Peter Milius, "Brookings Grim on Domestic Budget," *Washington Post,* July 19, 1973, p. A21.
4. "Program and Objectives" (Washington: Project on Budget Priorities).
5. Walter Pincus, "The Budget: What's Up," *The New Republic,* Vol. 168, p. 15.
6. Sanford Gottlieb, "State Within a State," *Dissent,* October 1971, Reprint, page 8.
7. *Setting National Priorities—The 1973 Budget* (Washington: The Brookings Institution, 1973).
8. Louis Fisher, *Working Papers,* June 1973.
9. U.S., Congress, Senate, Select Committee on Presidential Campaign Activities (Watergate Committee): *Hearings,* 93rd Cong., 1st sess., 1973.
10. U.S., Congress, Senate, Joint Study Committee on Budget Control, *Report,* 93rd Cong., 1st sess., April 18, 1973.
11. Ibid.
12. Ibid.
13. Ibid.

CHAPTER 8.   THE MEN WHO SERVE
IN THE HOUSE

1. Richard F. Fenno, Jr., *The Power of the Purse* (Boston: Little, Brown, 1966), p. 1.
2. Ibid., pp. 414–503.
3. Ibid.
4. Interview with Representative Richard Bolling (D., Mo.) by Congress Project researchers, July 20, 1972; *Citizens Look at Congress,* profile of George Mahon, Ralph Nader Congress Project (Washington: Grossman, 1972), p. 2.
5. Interview with Representative Frank Bow (R., Ohio) by Congress Proj-

ect researchers, July 19, 1972; *Citizens Look at Congress*, profile of George Mahon, p. 2.

6. Interview with Peg Simpson by Congress Project researcher, July 6, 1972; *Citizens Look at Congress*, profile of George Mahon, p. 10.

7. Interview with Fred Zimmerman by Congress Project researcher, July 6, 1972; *Citizens Look at Congress*, profile of George Mahon, p. 10.

8. Interview with Samuel Shaffer by Congress Project researcher, July 25, 1972; *Citizens Look at Congress*, profile of George Mahon, p. 12.

9. Interview with Fred Zimmerman, Congress Project.

10. *Citizens Look at Congress*, profile of George Mahon, p. 14.

11. Interview with Representative David Obey (D., Wis.) by Congress Project researcher; *Citizens Look at Congress*, profile of George Mahon, p. 21.

12. George H. Mahon, "We're Spending Our Way to Disaster," *Nation's Business*, April 1972.

13. Fenno, *The Power of the Purse*, p. 137.

14. Ibid., p. 59.

15. *Congressional Directory—1974.*

16. Fenno, *The Power of the Purse*, p. 59.

17. See for recent years, *Congressional Directory*.

18. Fenno, *The Power of the Purse*, p. 59.

19. Nick Kotz, *Let Them Eat Promises* (Englewood Cliffs, N.J.: Prentice-Hall, 1969), p. 101.

20. Ibid., p. 97.

21. *Congressional Quarterly Almanac—1972*, p. 346.

22. Interview with Nick Kotz by Congress Project researcher, May 1972; *Citizens Look at Congress*, profile of Jamie Whitten (D., Miss.), p. 10.

23. Interview with Dr. Spencer Smith by Congress Project researcher, 1972; *Citizens Look at Congress*, profile of Jamie Whitten (D., Miss.), 1972, p. 16.

24. Interview with Harrison Wellford by Congress Project researcher, 1972; *Citizens Look at Congress*, profile of Jamie Whitten, p. 16.

25. Interview with Edward Boland (D., Mass.), June 15, 1972; *Citizens Look at Congress*, profile of Edward Boland, p. 10.

26. *Citizens Look at Congress*, profile of Frank Evans (D., Colo.), 1972.

27. Representative Elford A. Cederberg (R., Mich.), "Congressman Cederberg Reports," undated, House of Representatives, Washington.

28. Cederberg Legislative Report, June 27, 1969; *Citizens Look at Congress*, profile of Elford A. Cederberg (R., Mich.), p. 10.

29. Donald Riegle, *O Congress* (Garden City, N.Y.: Doubleday, 1972).

30. Interview with Representative Silvio O. Conte (R., Mass.) by Congress Project researcher, June 26, 1972; *Citizens Look at Congress*, profile of Silvio O. Conte, 1972, p. 17.

31. Interview with Sal Micciche, reporter for the *Boston Globe*, by Congress Project researcher, July 1972; *Citizens Look at Congress*, profile of Representative Silvio O. Conte (R., Mass.), 1972, p. 22.

32. Fenno, *The Power of the Purse*, pp. 25–26.

CHAPTER 9.   THE HOUSE SUBCOMMITTEE SYSTEM

1. Richard F. Fenno, Jr., *Congressmen in Committees* (Boston: Little, Brown, 1973), pp. 107–108.
2. Joe Browder, Friends of the Earth, 620 C Street, S.E., Washington, D.C. 20003.
3. Interview with Representative George Mahon (D., Tex.) by Congress Project researcher, July 13, 1972; *Citizens Look at Congress*, profile of Representative George Mahon, 1972, p. 15.
4. "The Master Chef," *Time* magazine, Sept. 28, 1972, p. 20.
5. Roland Evans, Jr., "The Scrooge of Foreign Aid," *Harper's*, January 1962, pp. 78–83.
6. Elizabeth Drew, "Mr. Passman Meets His Match," *The Reporter*, Nov. 18, 1964, pp. 40–43.
7. Fenno, *Congressmen in Committees,* p. 126.
8. Michael Barone, Grant Ujifusa, Douglas Matthews, *The Almanac of American Politics,* 1974 ed. (Boston: Gambit), p. 1066.
9. Richard F. Fenno, Jr., *The Power of the Purse* (Boston: Little, Brown, 1966), p. 143.
10. Barone, et al., *The Almanac of American Politics,* 1974 ed.
11. Ibid., p. 190.
12. Ibid., p. 82.
13. Ibid., pp. 1023, 1110.
14. Fenno, *The Power of the Purse,* pp. 161–162.
15. Donald Riegle, *O Congress* (Garden City, N.Y.: Doubleday, 1972), pp. 174–175.
16. Ibid., p. 105.
17. Ibid., pp. 104–105.
18. Ibid., pp. 105–106.
19. Ibid., p. 267.
20. Barone, et al., *The Almanac of American Politics,* 1974 ed., p. 539.
21. Ibid., p. 190; Barone, et al., *The Almanac of American Politics,* 1972 ed., pp. 142–143.
22. Office of Economic Opportunity, *Federal Outlays, Fiscal Year 1971, Tennessee,* Springfield, Virginia, National Technical Information Service, pp. 13-207530-43, February 1972.
23. Barone, et al., *The Almanac of American Politics,* 1974 ed., p. 948.
24. Riegle, *O Congress,* p. 98.

CHAPTER 10.   THE SENATE SYSTEM

1. *1972 Congressional Vote Statistics—93rd Congress,* National Republican Committee, Washington, 1972, p. 2.

2. *Congressional Directory, 1971.*
3. See *1972 Congressional Campaign Finances* (ten volumes), Campaign Finance Monitoring Project, Common Cause, 1974.
4. *Standing Rules of the United States Senate and Provisions of the Legislative Reorganization Acts of 1946 and 1970 Relating to Operation of the Senate,* Jan. 18, 1972, Committee on Rules and Administration, United States Senate, p. 19–20 (section 6).
5. Charles B. Brownson, *1973 Congressional Staff Directory,* Washington, 1973.
6. Ibid.
7. "The Game," *Time* magazine, June 7, 1954, p. 18.
8. *Congressional Record,* Oct. 3 and 5, 1972.
9. Allan Drury, "The Man Who Replaced McCarthy," *New York Times Magazine,* February 20, 1955, pp. 15, 34.
10. Ibid.
11. Dan Cordetz, "The Senate's 'Maggie'," *Dun's,* April 1972.
12. "What Maggie Wants, Maggie Gets," *Dun's,* April 1972.
13. *Congressional Directory, 1974,* pp. 241, 244.
14. William Prochnau, interview with Senator Warren G. Magnuson, KVOS-TV, December 1971.
15. President John F. Kennedy, speech at Olympia Hotel, Seattle, Washington, November 1961.
16. Interview with Senator Milton Young (R., N.Dak.) by Congress Project researcher, July 1972; Ralph Nader Congress Project, *Citizens Look at Congress* (Washington: Grossman, 1972), profile of Senator Milton Young, 1972, p. 3.
17. Ibid., p. 9.
18. Fenno, *The Power of the Purse,* pp. 357, 573.
19. Ibid., p. 575.
20. Ibid.
21. Ibid.

CHAPTER 11. THE CONFERENCE COMMITTEE

1. George W. Norris, "The Model Legislature," address at Lincoln, Nebraska, Feb. 22, 1934, reprinted in *Congressional Record,* Feb. 27, 1934.
2. Legislative Reorganization Act of 1946; Legislative Reorganization Act of 1970.
3. Richard F. Fenno, Jr., *The Power of the Purse* (Boston: Little, Brown, 1966), p. 647.
4. Ibid., pp. 635–641.
5. Ibid.
6. Ibid.

7. Donald Riegle, *O Congress* (Garden City, N.Y.: Doubleday, 1972), p. 100.
8. Warren Weaver, Jr., *Both Your Houses—The Truth About Congress* (New York: Praeger, 1973), p. 135.
9. Fenno, *The Power of the Purse,* p. 663.

Index